# French Romanticism

Parallax Re-visions of Culture and Society

Stephen G. Nichols, Gerald Prince, and Wendy Steiner
*Series Editors*

# French Romanticism

Intertextual and Interdisciplinary
Readings

*Frank Paul Bowman*

The Johns Hopkins University Press
Baltimore and London

The Johns Hopkins University Press
701 West 40th Street, Baltimore, Maryland 21211
The Johns Hopkins Press Ltd., London

The paper used in this publication meets the minimum requirements of American
National Standard for Information Sciences—Permanence of Paper for Printed
Library Materials, ANSI Z39.48-1984

*Library of Congress Cataloging-in-Publication Data*

Bowman, Frank Paul.
    French Romanticism : intertextual and interdisciplinary readings / Frank
Paul Bowman.
        p.    cm.—(Parallax: re-visions of culture and society)
    "ANSI Z39.48–1984"—T. p. verso.
    Bibliography: p.
    Includes index.
    ISBN 0–8018–3884–3 (alk. paper)
    1. French literature—19th century—History and criticism.
2. Romanticism—France. 3. France—Intellectual life—19th century.
4. Literature and society—France—History—19th century. I. Title.
II. Series:  Parallax (Baltimore, Md.)
PQ287.B78   1990
840.9'145—dc20
                                          89–15422
                                            CIP

# ❧ Contents

Etenim omnes artes quae ad humanitatem pertinent habent quoddam commune vinculum, et quasi cognatione quadam inter se continentur.

For all arts which pertain to culture have a certain link in common and so to speak are held together by a kind of kinship.

—Cicero, *Pro Archia poeta*

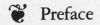 Preface

The epigraph of this volume derives from a statement made by
Cicero when he defended the Greek poet Archias's claims to Roman
citizenship in 62 B.C., suggesting a justification and methodology
for humanistic studies, which Petrarch rediscovered with enthusiasm in 1333 (and which I had to learn by heart in secondary school
in 1943). The essays in this volume, translations or revisions of
work previously published in French, all illustrate in one way or
another the possibilities and problems of the approach suggested by
Cicero's statement, that is, what today is called "intertextuality" or
"interdisciplinarity" in literary studies.

They also all discuss, in one way or another, the debate about
religion in France during roughly the first half of the nineteenth
century, but do so by dealing with texts, from various disciplines,
which are not often examined together: novels, poems, and plays as
well as religious literature, and political, philosophical, historical,
and even scientific (medical) texts. I came to these texts because of
my interest, several decades old, in producing a synthetic study of
the figure of Christ in French Romanticism. That study, published
as *Le Christ des barricades* (Paris: Editions du Cerf, 1987), was written for a fairly large public and is somewhat more "traditional" in
its presentation at least than the essays presented here. That project,
it soon became apparent, had to explain a diachronic change. The
image of Jesus in the literature of the Revolution of 1789 is far
different, in quantity and quality, from that of 1848. In the first
Revolution, the evocations of Jesus are rare, often anticlerical, often
comic. In 1848, Jesus is widely evoked, and often presented as the
advocate of a new utopian order, of communism, and even as a
figure who justifies revolutionary violence. Manifestly, that change

was of political, as well as of theological and literary, importance, and could not be satisfactorily described by limiting oneself to poems about Jesus, or, for that matter, to political pamphlets. Indeed, I soon suspected that the all too frequent comparisons between the poet and Jesus (both soothsayer scapegoats) had significance in this development of an essentially political image. Whence these readings, which have taken me well beyond the canon as traditionally defined, to evoke their pertinence for one current critical debate, and have also brought me face to face with the problem of how to articulate texts stemming from different discourses—an ongoing problem in humanistic studies.

I have undertaken these studies despite the fact that as an undergraduate I was nurtured by Brooks and Warren ("the plain text and Dr. Johnson" was the battle cry, but what a world Dr. Johnson does open up . . .), and despite the fact that many of these essays appeared during a period when going outside the text, or dealing with historical problems while also writing about literature, was not a very fashionable activity in some circles. I owe a debt of gratitude to the "Humanities" requirement of my alma mater, Reed, which, still then stalwartly *Geistesgeschichtlich* in its structure, rather contradicted what my brilliant and excellent teachers of literature were telling me. Then at Yale, though the New Criticism held sway, Herni Peyre taught Romanticism as an interdisciplinary phenomenon. Erich Auerbach also demonstrated that textual analysis could be combined with a concern with history. Auerbach inadvertently introduced me to the writings of Ernst Robert Curtius, whom he considered his archenemy (so we students of Auerbach, of course, read Curtius assiduously). I sometimes think I have spent much of my scholarly life trying to juggle Auerbach and Curtius together; Curtius made clear that I had to take into account how topoi survive and yet change through history, and several essays in this volume are primarily concerned, on the methodological level, with that problem. I also owe much to the fact that I spent a year at the Ecole Normale Supérieure, rue d'Ulm, when Michel Foucault, Jacques Le Goff, Louis Marin, and Emmanuel Le Roy La Durie were there. In 1950 our heroes were Gaston Bachelard, Vladimir Jankélévitch, Marcel Mauss. Not only were literature, philosophy, and politics lumped together as a common object of discourse, as Cicero had suggested they should be, but three other provocative ideas were blossoming in that hothouse: that language was not transparent but to some degree formative of thought; that all cultural phenomena had to be analyzed from a radical, anthropological stance; that the subject was an object of suspicion. One further encounter should be mentioned, back in New Haven, with Louis Massignon, who cannily grasped what I was concerned with and should be about, and who sent me his writing on Notre Dame de La Salette and on the cult of Marie Antoinette. Massignon not only informed my definition of what the "religious" was but also provided a model of where I should situate my readings, that I not only had to take into account the religious dimension of Romantic discourse but also had to read well beyond the canon—read even the "madmen." I owe much both to his methodology and to his ecumenical spirit.

I could go on with my intellectual autobiography, describing my debt to Will Moore who taught me not to oversimplify, to Basil Guy and Simone Balayé and Marc Fumaroli who, by sharing in it, shored up my *libido sciendi* during those lean years when learning was too often considered the opposite of brilliance, to Léon Cellier who moved Illuminism into the canon of studies on French Romanticism and was directly responsible for setting me at the task of studying the Romantic Christ, to Jacques Seebacher and Claude Duchet who made me come to appreciate the Marxist approach to problems such as these; to my colleague Lucienne Frappier-Mazur, who has done her best to keep me intellectually alive.

Of course, many problems remain, and I am far from satisfied with what I have done (even if I have enjoyed doing it), and I have grave questions about how I have done it, but it seems better to discuss those in the conclusion of this volume.

❦ The first chapter, on the comparison of Jesus and Socrates, was also the first of these articles to appear, in the *Revue des sciences humaines* in 1966; it was reprinted in my *Christ romantique* (Geneva, 1973), and traces how a venerable apologetic topos is renewed, then questioned, then put to new uses as a proof that the suffering of the poet or prophet guarantees the validity of his message. Chapter 2, on another topos, "Christ put an end to slavery," first appeared in *Le Christ romantique;* here, the topos not only is used—and questioned—for apologetic purposes (the civilizing influence of Christianity) but enters into the abolitionist debate and then becomes subject to scholarly scrutiny, and finally gets killed off. Chapter 3, on Napoleon as a Christ figure, first appeared in *Europe* in 1969 and was reprinted in *Le Christ romantique*. The chapter concerns not only the origins of the Napoleonic legend but also the much debated Romantic messianism. All three of these chapters deal with literature, politics, religion, and history, but also quite centrally with what forms imitation takes in Romanticism, particularly how topoi, dislodged, so to speak, from the rhetorical tradition which helped fix their meaning, become subject to permutations. Chapter 4, on the pastiches of Lamennais's *Words of a Beliver*, was originally delivered as a paper at a 1982 Lamennais colloquium in Paris and then printed in the *Cahiers mennaisiens* in 1984; it deals with the imitation not of a topos but of a text, and with the very fundamental issue of religious justifications for violence. These four chapters share a common concern with how texts get rewritten in terms of an ongoing polemic.

The second section is concerned with thematics as it moves among various discourses, here including the medical as well as the literary, historical, and political. Chapter 5, on the circulation of the Precious Blood, appeared in *Romantisme* in 1981, Chapter 7, on nineteenth-century treatments of the seventeenth-century diabolic possessions at Loudun, was written for the Festschrift, *Du visible á l'invisible*, published in 1988, for Max Milner, that great expert on the devil in Romanticism.

The essays in the third section are more synthetic. They attempt to define what I believe are two fundamental Romantic modes of thinking, which again operate not only in literature in the strict sense but also in philosophy and theology and historical studies. I first discussed the theory of harmonies in an article in *Romantisme* in 1973, in an issue devoted to that problem which I edited; I treated the question more extensively in my *Christ romantique*, and here in Chapter 7 have chosen to revise that text somewhat. My earlier perspective now seems to me too limited; it describes the discourse on harmony primarily in theological terms, with a few excurses into political theory. Properly, the chapter should deal more centrally with theories of language and more thoroughly with poetic practice—for instance, show how Lamartine in his *Méditations* had already used metaphors of nature in a very transcendent way. But to treat the problem properly, one would have to write another book on Romanticism; I only hope that this manifestly limited perspective of a "péché de jeunesse" will lead others to broaden it. The

chapter on "symbol and desymbolization" was originally given at
the Nineteenth-Century French Studies colloquium at Harvard in
1983 and appeared in *Romantisme* in 1985. Much more needs to be
done on this important problem. I try to capture modes of thought
and discourse prevalent in the Romantic age but which today have
disappeared or at least taken quite different forms.

The final section is an effort at proving the pudding by reading
particular texts in the light of the approaches and methodologies
elaborated in the other studies. Chapter 9, on the "Mémorables"
passage in Gérard de Nerval's *Aurélia*, was originally delivered at
the Nineteenth-Century French Studies colloquium at Vanderbilt in
1985 and published in *French Forum* in 1986; in it I try to show how
a text that many have considered incomprehensible or the product of
madness can be rewardingly read if it is situated in its intertextual—both generic and political—context. Chapter 10, on Flaubert's *Temptation of St. Anthony*, was given in Paris at the Flaubert
colloquium organized by the Société d'histoire littéraire de la France
in 1980 and then published in the *Revue d'histoire littéraire de la
France* in 1981. It pleasantly coincided with a study that Jacques
Neefs presented at the same colloquium, in demonstrating that
Flaubert's text was a highly satirical work, and much involved in a
contemporary polemic about comparative religion and the nature of
mythology. The reading of texts in the light of their intertextuality
is for me a major classroom activity, and I hope these essays will
suggest possible new ways of reading and explicating.

❦ I have published many other articles that reflect some of the
concerns discussed here. Some are hopelessly erudite, some practice
the "systemic" analysis of a given problem in a given author. A
number of them center on the Coppet group (Mme de Staël, L.
Simonde de Sismondi, B. Constant) which I consider of particular
interest so far as it presents a transition from Enlightenment to
Romanticism. The problem of what happens to utopian thought in
the Romantic age is clearly present in many of these essays, and I
have published about it extensively; my article "Utopie, imagination, espérance: Northrop Frye, Ernst Bloch, Judith Schlanger," in
*Littérature* 21 (1976), makes explicit some of the presuppositions
operative in the essays of this volume. Another main concern of
mine (which has also produced a number of articles) has been the
tension between the desire for self-expression and topoi, language,

the literary tradition, the religious definitions of the self. But I do not think that on this somewhat more fundamental problem I could presently offer the kind of synthetic statement I here attempt.

❦ In some instances, one chapter echoes or recapitulates what is discussed in another. The problem of religious syncretism and the quarrel about Alexandria, for example, appear in Chapters 7, 8, and 10, but in each of the focus and context is different.

In the notes, the place of publication is indicated only for cities other than Paris.

All translations are my own. The word *Romanticism* is not used in the strict sense to refer to a group of writers with a common credo—or several credos—combating classicists or realists in the 1820s or 1840s, but as a shorthand term for French thought between 1789 and 1848, often polemical and controversial within itself. I try to suggest in the conclusion why I prefer this broad usage (common in France) to the more restricted one still preferred by such excellent English scholars as D. G. Charlton. *Traditionalist* is used, not in the contemporary sense of someone who is loyal to the pre-Vatican II Church, but in the nineteenth-century sense of a belief that the truths of Christianity are contained in a universally revealed, even if often corrupted tradition. I have generally used *logos* to translate *Verbe* as in "the Word was made flesh" of the Last Gospel; the importance of this notion in these studies made it seem wise to demark it by using a transliteration of the Greek.

Acknowledgment is gratefully made for permission to publish these translated and revised versions of texts originally published in French to Alain Dufour and the Editions Droz for Chapters 1, 2, 3, and 7; to *Romantisme* for Chapters 5 and 8; to the *Revue d'histoire littéraire de la France* for Chapter 10, to Louis Le Guillou and the *Cahiers mennaisiens* for Chapter 4, to Stéphane Michaud and the Librairie José Corti for Chapter 6; to *French Forum* for Chapter 9.

My colleague Stephen Nichols is to be blamed for prodding me into translating these essays and diuscussing, in the conclusion, some of my ideological and methodological concerns.

# ❦ I

## Topoi and Echoes:
## Literature, Politics, Religion,
## Erudition, and Imitation

# 1 ❦ The Comparison of Jesus and Socrates

"Go on, in the name of Jesus, in the name of Socrates," says Trenmor to Sténio in George Sand's *Lélia* (Garnier ed., 1833, p. 283), urging him to face that great trial every genius is predestined to undergo. The juxtaposition of the names of Jesus and Socrates, far from being rare, is a commonplace of French Romantic literature. The three times Mme de Staël mentions Socrates in *On Germany*, she also mentions Jesus (Hachette ed., 1810, 4:117, 383; 5:122). This comparison, as Léonce de Grandmaison has shown, goes back in the apologetic tradition to the second century, A.D., and indeed has a Latin name, the *confirmatio christianorum per Socratica*, but Mme de Staël indicates what was the Romantics' immediate source—the parallel that Rousseau drew between Socrates and Jesus in his "Profession of faith of the Savoyard Vicar" of *Emile*.[1] George Sand may, however, have been echoing her friend Pierre Leroux, who was convinced that Christianity was a combination of Platonism and Stoicism, and that Christ and Socrates offered the same moral message: man is the son of God and should love his neighbor. His detractors often accused Leroux of having stolen that theory from Hegel. Balzac cites Jesus and Socrates together on a number of occasions, even in the "Avant-Propos" to the *Human Comedy*, usually in order to suggest that the good, just man will suffer, as Jesus and Socrates suffered; this was one of the major meanings the Romantics gave to the topos. In this Balzac may have been indebted to J. G. E. Œgger, a former vicar of Notre Dame Cathedral turned Swedenborgian, who proposed Jesus and Socrates as images of the necessary suffering of the just in his *Manuel de religion et de morale* (1827, p. 162) and again in *Le Vrai Messie* (1829, p. 225). Any study of the sources of so widespread a theme is bound to be both almost impossible and of little interest; on the other hand, an analysis of its forms, permutations, and ramifications can reveal some significant characteristics of the Romantic imagination.

One can deal fairly rapidly with the uses made of the theme in apologetics, for they are rather monotonously repetitive. Many apologists claim that Rousseau's parallel, which asserts that if the life and death of Socrates were those of a man, then the life and death of Jesus prove that he was divine, demonstrates that Rousseau was a good Christian and offers today's skeptic a good argument in favor of the faith. Genoude, a priest who was a good friend of Lamartine and a prolific writer, tells how, after reading Voltaire, he took up Rousseau's volume. "I finally got to that so amazing passage about Jesus; I have read it at least a hundred times, and I can still see in my mind's eye the spot where I first read it, in the woods of Brémol." He then quotes the whole passage and concludes: "This text . . . had a decisive influence on my whole life. I said to myself that, since Rousseau spoke in that way about Jesus, despite Voltaire's sarcasms, the Christian religion at least merited serious study" (*La Divinité de Jésus-Christ,* 1842, pp. 359–61). If Rousseau had converted him, Rousseau could convert others. Two decades later Mathieu Orsini, who represents the flowery, Marian tradition of spirituality, also ended his *Réfutation de Renan* (1863) with the "striking" quotation from Jean-Jacques, and Rousseau's text was similarly used by Dupin the elder to conclude his refutation of Joseph Salvador's thesis that the trial of Jesus had been perfectly legal in its procedures (*Jésus devant Caïphe et Pilate,* 1828). Other Catholics maintained that Rousseau on his deathbed was fully converted to Christianity—a nice counterpart to the myth of his suicide.[2] Few are the Catholics who reject this recourse to Rousseau: Gaston Tesseyre, the director of the Saint-Sulpice seminary who considered Rousseau an enemy more dangerous than Voltaire, and Félicité de Lamennais and Joseph de Maistre, whom I discuss later. The others all make joyous use of the Savoyard Vicar's parallel as an excellent piece of apologetic artillery. The famed Dominican J. B. H. Lacordaire cites it in his *Conférences* at Notre Dame, and the humble curé d'Ars does likewise, even adding an adverb: "If the death of Socrates was that of a sage, the death of Jesus was evidently that of a God."[3]

Often the apologists suppress all the rest of Rousseau's lengthy parallel, and even eliminate "life" from the key phrase—"If the life and death of Socrates . . . " becomes simply "If the death of Socrates. . . . "

Not surprisingly, the apologists often add other proofs of Christ's superiority and divinity in order to explicate Rousseau's text. Genoude observes that Socrates talked a great deal, but changed nothing, whereas Jesus changed the whole nature of the world (*La Divinité*, p. 1). This thesis, which reflects Chateaubriand's influential "proof" of Christianity by its civilizing effects, is widespread and is even found in P. J. Proudhon; Christ is superior to Socrates not only by his death but also because of the way he changed the world (*De la création de l'ordre dans l'humanité*, Rivière ed., 1849, 5:55–56). Lamennais underlines how superior Jesus' disciples were to those of Socrates (*Sur la foi* in *Œuvres*, 1839, 2:105). Bishop Frayssinous notes that Socrates' death, unlike that of Jesus, was unaccompanied by miraculous events (*Défense du christianisme*, 1825, 1:411). According to Bautain, perhaps the most genial French theologian of the period, Jesus cannot be put in the same class as Socrates, Confucius, Zoraster; they only knew how to teach, whereas Jesus could cure.[4]

According to some, Jesus' death was more heroic than that of Socrates, even if (or because) Edward Gibbon had said the contrary.[5] Two other arguments, which seem quite astounding today, are in fact rather typical of Romantic apologetic techniques. J.-F. Du Clot, in his lengthy *La Sainte Bible vengée des attaques de l'incrédulité* (1835), maintains that since Rousseau, a deist, praises Jesus with so much enthusiasm, the less excessive praises of Jesus offered by Josephus are surely authentic (3:225). And Frayssinous, along with many others, profits from the parallel to add that the historical existence of Jesus is much better attested, easier to prove, than that of Socrates—and yet, who ever questioned the historical existence of the Greek philosopher? The Romantics unhesitantly take a topos customarily used to demonstrate one point and apply it to the demonstration of some other point, provided an appropriate rhetorical effect is created.

Another proof of Jesus' superiority over Socrates reflects Romantic hesitations about the excellence of reason or logic. Socrates was a philosopher, who only communicated with intellectuals, whereas Jesus spoke to ordinary human beings, to the "poor in spirit."

Alphonse-Louis Constant developed this in great detail in a leftist context (*Le Livre de larmes, ou le Christ consolateur,* 1845, p. 121–22) as did Frayssinous on the right (*Défense,* 1:190). And also Napoleon, at least according to Robert Beauterne, who, in his 1840 *Conversations religieuses de Napoléon* (and whose Napoleonic authenticity has been questioned), attributes to the emperor in exile the opinion that "you have to be a metaphysician, study for years, in order to understand the philosophy of Socrates or Plato, but simple good sense, an open heart, right reason are all one needs to understand Christianity" (p. 130). The divine and the irrational join forces in combating the vain subtleties of philosophy. P. S. Ballanche, as so often a precursor, in *Du sentiment considéré dans ses rapports avec la littérature et les arts* (1801, p. 233) quotes the text as an example of the power of the "cry of the sentiment" in Rousseau—that sentiment which made Jean-Jacques a "naturally Christian soul," as Tertullian would have put it. But, alas, Rousseau was unable to resist the "murmur of reason" which led him to declare that the Gospel was unacceptable. One wonders whether Ballanche is arguing in favor of irrationalism or in favor of Christianity.

Another apologetic use of the topos helps understand Romantic exoticism. The similarities between Jesus and Socrates are not surprising for, thanks to universal revelation, Socrates had a partial apprehension of the Truth which Jesus knew in its totality. Charles Bonnetty's *Annales de philosophie chrétienne* spends pages documenting the traditions that embody this universal revelation (whence its name traditionalism) and Bonnetty often evokes Socrates as a figure of Jesus (e.g., 5 [1832]: 250–51). This theory helps in reading the various poems of the period which present Socrates as prefiguring, even in a vision, Jesus' life, teaching, and death; Maria Consolata has catalogued some of them.[6] It is also representative of an important historical change. During the eighteenth century, comparisons between Socrates and Jesus serve primarily to deprive Jesus of his unique nature as God incarnate, just as the parthenogenesis of various oriental deities is seen as raising questions about the virgin birth of Jesus. For Romantic traditionalism, any flood myth, from no matter what culture, affirms the truth of the Bible; any virgin birth, no matter of what strange oriental God, is a prefiguring, a partial representation of the truth of Jesus' virgin birth, and insofar as Socrates resembles Jesus, he proves that Jesus was indeed divine. This notion of a universal revelation, traditionalism, was propounded by Lamennais and also by Louis de Bonald and Maistre, though Bonald situates it more particularly in the linguistic and social structures of humankind. But Bonald, who despised Rousseau the political thinker, was not enthusiastic about the *confirmatio*—yet another proof that the Romantics were not always aware that, before Rousseau's *Emile*, the topos had a venerable history going back to the early Church Fathers. In his *Théorie du pouvoir* (1796, in *Œuvres*, 1840, 2:14) Bonald does cite the comparison, but only as an illustration of the often absurd nature of political life where crime is recompensed and virtue (i.e., Louis XVI) punished.

For many other authors, traditionalism allowed some fancy embroideries on the *comfirmatio*. If most Romantic evocations of the topos are limited to a comparison of the two deaths, others are very extended. Amédée Dupuget's *Démon de Socrate* (1829) identifies the daimon with the divine of F. Fénelon, considers Socrates a martyr to faith and virtue, and calls him "the chosen one of God among the Gentiles, and a precursor of that Christ of whom he was also a disciple" (p. xii); he quotes in support of his theories Justin's *Second Apology*. Dupuget was perhaps quite learned, but he also read Plato in M. Ficino's Renaissance version, so open to the *prisca theologica,* which may explain in part his interpretation.[7] He concludes that all those who knew the logos—Heraclitus as well as Socrates—were Christians, for to know the logos is to know Jesus, the logos made flesh. Dupuget raises an important question: How can the temporal transcendency, which is implicit in the theories of universal revelation as it is in cyclical theories of history, be reconciled with Romantic historicism? The two theories lead to some strange quests for parallels, as in Jacques de Norvins's poem *L'Immortalité de l'âme, ou les Quatre âges religieux* (1822). Socrates is at the center of the third age, Jesus of the fourth. But in this last age Norvins associates the triumphal entry of Palm Sunday with the theories of Tempe and Delos: two theories, a note explains, "preceded almost immediately, the one the agony of the son of Sophroniscus, the other the agony of the Son of Man; however, with this difference; the theory of Delos postponed the death of Socrates, that of Jerusalem hastened Christ's crucifixion." Norvins enriches the parallel between Socrates and Jesus, including not only their message and their death, but even minor details of their lives, and does so by seeing in Socrates a figure of Jesus in a kind of medieval, typological way. Indeed, the

Romantic uses of the *confirmatio* often reflect that kind of free, imprecise figural thinking which is so evident, for instance, in Jules Michelet's writings. As I shall shortly show, Socrates-and-Jesus served as a figural representation of a great many Romantic heroes. Finally, Norvins is quite Romantic in exploiting a theme one might expect to find more often: Jesus is superior to Socrates because he is more touching, more moving, more pathetic.[8]

In the poetry of the period, the most common themes of the topos claim that Socrates was a precursor and prophet of Jesus, or that both Socrates and Jesus are figures of the just man who speaks the truth and suffers for having done so, in short a figure of the Romantic hero. There are, however, some rich variations on the topos, similar to that of Norvins. Edouard Alletz, in his epic *La Nouvelle Messiade* (1830), describes Joseph of Arimathea as a Platonist, a disciple of Socrates. Just before converting to Christianity, Joseph undertakes a comparative study of the two doctrines and concludes that Christianity is superior, again primarily because it "speaks to the heart" (p. 105). Later on in the epic, Jesus himself evokes the parallel, in a vision of the future when "the wisdom of Plato will seem pale compared to that of the average Christian" (p. 495). But Alletz also makes use of "Socrates the prophet of Jesus" in order to praise the Greek philosopher and to predict his future glory in heaven:

> For your inspired eyes, his supreme existence
> Was already manifest here below, even in his absence;
> Now you finally behold the Christ of whom your virtue dreamed
> And know the name of the God for whom you died! (P. 171)

Alletz hardly holds a candle to F. Klopstock, his model; in the German's poem, Socrates appears in a dream to the spouse of Pontius Pilate and informs her that Jesus is God. As does the historical novel, the Romantic religious epic tends to present together as many famous figures as possible.

Alongside such embroiderings, but less frequent, one finds efforts to give the parallel a historical basis. The most amusing is surely that of J. B. Mosneron de Launay, *Vie du législateur des chrétiens, sans lacunes et sans miracles,* published in 1803, shortly after Venturini's rather similar life of Jesus in German.[9] According to Mosneron, if Jesus' teachings evoke those of Socrates, it is because he studied in Greece (after first learning medicine in Egypt and political science in Rome), and there learned everything the Socratic school had to offer. Mosneron, a Free Mason, is symptomatic of the quest for naturalistic explanations for the events of the life of Christ.

The most frequent form that the topos takes during the period presents Jesus and Socrates as the glorious victims of an unjust society. As Victor Hugo put it with admirable brevity, in one alexandrine: "Souffrons comme Jésus, souffrons comme Socrate" ("Let us suffer like Jesus, let us suffer like Socrates"; *Châtiments*, 1853, Edition Nationale, 2:431). Maria Consolata (*Christ*, pp. 143–44) quotes ten other examples from Hugo alone where the names of Jesus and Socrates are associated in order to picture how the just man is persecuted, and other Romantic poets, all a bit paranoid, also use it frequently. Cataloguing and quoting all the instances would be over-fastidious. What is of interest is that the theme is applied not only to the poet but also to the leftist political leader, and becomes a commonplace of socialist thought. In *De l'égalité* (1848) Pierre Leroux exclaims, "Oh Jesus, how great you still are, coming after Socrates, who preceded you on the *via dolorosa* and who, like you, died for the salvation of mankind" (p. 126). In *De l'humanité* (1840) he compares Regulus, Socrates, and Jesus. Each participated in the logos, and each was a symbol of divine sacrifice, a sacrifice that all disciples of the logos (which Leroux defines as the doctrine of equality) must be prepared to make. Alphonse Esquiros, with his usual hyperbolic and absolute conviction, associates Socrates and Jesus with the masses: "The masses are the spirit which enlightens, the masses are Socrates! The masses are the spirit which inspires, the masses are Jesus Christ! The masses are the spirit which sacrifices, the masses are Joan of Arc!" (*De la vie future*, 1850, p. 122). Socrates and Jesus here are transformed into figures of the masses as *vox dei*, the logos made flesh in the People-Christ. In his *Le Vrai Christianisme* (1846) Etienne Cabet concludes that since Socrates was a communist, he was necessarily a Christian (p. 628)! In 1848 the periodical *L'Evangile chrétien* (pp. 38–39) explains that Jesus and Socrates were put to death because they preached a moral virtue that threatened the economic and religious powers of their days. And *L'Artiste* on 1 July of that same revolutionary year published a text by Arsène Houssaye comparing Jesus and not Socrates but Plato, claiming that Jesus was superior as a revolutionary:

Plato was a sublime contemplator who lived in the infinite, who fled the visible world in order to renew his soul at the invisible wellsprings of beauty. As for his *Republic*, he had no faith in it.

Jesus was a revolutionary who had within himself the idea of God; who wanted to live and die so that that idea might prevail. Jesus was not just a dreamer, he was a man of action. He did not write, he spoke. His style is rich in images; he knew how to evoke the breaking waves, to call up the tempest, to move the masses to revolt; he was fraternal with the weak, the poor; he struck the rock so that the living water of love gushed forth for all those who thirsted. . . .

Plato did not want evil to be conquered by revolt; he thought that the revelation of the truth could be completely pacific. He was not one to go into the streets to fight. Jesus, who knew men better, who had suffered their sorrows and shed their tears, preached instead the sudden awakening. He visited towns and countryside, making passionate appeals. When he died on the cross, it was with a holy enthusiasm that he beheld his blood dripping onto the earth; for he knew that each drop, religiously carried forth by the sandals of his apostles, would go and seed revolution throughout the world.

Finally, the messianic eccentric Mapah Ganneau has the victims of Waterloo exclaim: "Yes! vanquished!—like Socrates by hemlock! Yes! vanquished!—like Christ on Golgotha!" (*Waterloo,* 1843). Waterloo was not only the Good Friday of France but also the day when the chosen nation, because it shared in Socrates' excellence, in his knowledge of the truth, also had to share in his suffering. The comparison, again, should not be judged incredible; the cult of the Sacred Heart of Marat, for instance, also drew parallels between Marat and Jesus, Socrates, and . . . Jean-Jacques Rousseau, the tormented suicide victim of society. [10]

Political uses of the topos were not restricted to the left; the disciples of the mystical Royalist prophet P.-M. Vintras used it to compare the way the police treated him with the sufferings of Jesus and Socrates. "Was not Our Divine Savior crucified by the doctors of his day, accused of all possible iniquity, of all possible filth? Socrates, the very wisdom of Greece, had to drink hemlock! How many martyrs of their faith, alas, and of their beliefs, have been shamefully and cruelly whipped!" (Bérard de Pontlieu, *Défense de Pierre-Michel Vintras,* 1842, p. 25). It has been suggested that Good Friday constituted the whole of the liturgical year for Romantics, poets, thinkers, or politicians; but often, as the martyr was nailed to the cross, he was also given Socrates' cup of hemlock to drink. Once more, Rousseau is the precursor. He organized his parallel of the two in such a way that it became centered not on their wisdom or goodness, but on their suffering and death. In the following half-century, in almost every occurrence of the *confirmatio*, mention is made of crucifix and hemlock, which was not true of the topos in the early Church or during the Renaissance. And the Romantics give new figural meanings to the topos—not only is Socrates a figure of Jesus, but the two are figures of the modern poet, or of the political leftist.

A few authors criticize or reject the topos, but they tend to be somewhat eccentric. Sylvain Maréchal, a valiant atheist, suggests that Rousseau must have been delirious when he compared Socrates, so wise, with Jesus, "a circus clown, or rather a miserable madman" (*Pour et contre la Bible*, 1801, p. 373); Socrates never claimed that he brought not peace, but a sword. But that is the only "leftist" criticism of the topos I know. Joseph Salvador, who in the late 1830s offered a Jewish reading of the life of Jesus, at the end of his second volume on *Jésus-Christ et sa doctrine* (1838) (the book's thesis is that Jesus was only a Jewish teacher of wisdom who alas suffered delusions of grandeur and thought he was the Messiah) rejects the parallel for rather good reasons. There is little in common between the learned, ironic, skeptical philosopher of Athens and the enthusiastic, working-class figure of Jesus. Socrates' death was the natural consequence of his criticisms of society; Jesus' was the inevitable outcome of his messianic pretentions. Rousseau's famed passage is at the most only a poetic way of suggesting excellence (pp. 203–6). On the right, Joseph de Maistre rejects the topos; he considers Plato a superficial bore as a philosopher, and the death of Socrates demonstrates the kind of moral corruption that prevailed in Athens before its conversion to Christianity. He also attacks Gibbon's interpretation of the topos. Gibbon suggests that Socrates was superior to Jesus because he at least did not complain or indulge in self-pity while he was dying; according to Maistre, Gibbon was forced to write that kind of obscenity in order to earn his living as an author in a Protestant country (England). But even Maistre accepts in part the *confirmatio* when, discussing traditionalism, he admits that Plato's ideas about God and theology are not without interest since they bear an "oriental stamp" (See *Œuvres complètes*, Lyon, 1921,

2:487–90; 3:375; 4:70–72). Lamennais, in his early *Essai sur l'indifférence,* criticizes Rousseau for not drawing the logical conclusion from his parallel—that Jesus was God—but Lamennais also sees in Socrates a figure of Christ. "A holy fraternity of love and hope unites all the generations of the just in the Savior of mankind" (*Essai sur l'indifférence,* 1817, in *Œuvres,* Brussels, 1839, 1:427). The bishop of Tulle did protest in his pastoral letter of 1843 that "Our Lord Jesus Christ is mixed up with Greeks, with Romans, even with a fistful of contemporaries; people feel they have done their bit for him when they have given him his share of praise, as a member of some kind of elite group"—but the bishop's fear that via the *confirmatio* Jesus was being assimilated to simple mortals does not seem to have many echoes—except for the *Revue ecclésiastique* (5:353), a Jansenist publication of 1842 violently opposed to traditionalism.

Seventeenth- and eighteenth-century anticlerical or antireligious literature is full of parallels between Jesus and Mohammed, Confucius, or Socrates, or between Socrates and Confucius, and so on. In the Romantic period, the only one of these comparisons that retains real currency is that between Jesus and Socrates, even if the others do appear occasionally. The analogy with Mohammed is sometimes sketched—for instance by Frayssinous, but his thesis, a part of his attack against Dupuis, is that Mohammed at least admitted the historical existence of Jesus (*Défense,* 1:137). This change can be explained in part by the fact that people read Rousseau, but not very many read François Bernier or La Mothe le Vayer.[11] More notable is that in the eighteenth century the purpose of these parallels was generally one of diminishing Jesus; the comparison was made in order to praise Socrates. In the nineteenth century this was only exceptionally the case (e.g. Sylvain Maréchal, Salvador); usually the parallel was used to praise Jesus, or, more important, to give new meaning to the Gospel message. In the eighteenth century, the parallel discredited one person, praised the other; the Romantics tended to praise both. This should not be simply interpreted as yet another symptom of the "religious revival," for, if some Catholics do resort to the *confirmatio,* many do not, and some criticize it. On the other hand, the topos crops up frequently in such dubious Christians as Balzac, George Sand, Victor Hugo, not to mention Alphonse Esquiros and A.-L. Constant, and it is also employed by enemies of the Church and indeed of religion such as Cabet, Pierre

Leroux, and even Proudhon. The frequency of the topos is better explained by a characteristic of Romanticism that historians have rather neglected: the Romantic tendency to use *figurae* in their thinking and in their writing.[12] The problem is made clear when one contrasts some texts of that age (say, the Jesus of A. Vigny's "Mount of Olives" or the rather shocking parallel that Félix de Vandenesse draws between himself and Jesus at the conclusion of Balzac's *The Lily of the Valley*, 1836) with modern texts such as N. Kazantzakis' *He Who Must Die*, 1960.

The twentieth century accepts parallels with Jesus in literature, provided they are either fairly extended and totally implicit, as with Kazantzakis, or explicit, but partial and in a somewhat comic vein, as when Marcel Jouhandeau's Monsieur Godot compares his conjugal tribulations with the Stations of the Cross.[13] Otherwise, the *confirmatio christianorum per Socratica,* or by anyone else, has quite disappeared from sermons, poems, stories, apologetic literature. The Romantics did not share our hesitations; for them, the Jesus of history and the Socrates of history were ideal figures of human fate, who gave meaning to life, to the life of each human being, and particularly to the tragic aspects of life. People as different as Vigny and Vintras discovered in the vicissitudes of their personal fates a significant destiny, because that fate, like the fate of Socrates, of Joan of Arc, of Regulus, echoed the fate of Jesus, or Prometheus, or even Don Juan. The context of the Jesus-Socrates figure, though it centered on the theme of the suffering of the righteous victim, varied considerably, and it is difficult to say what elements the Romantics considered necessary in order to validate the figure. (Norvins on Socrates and Jesus, in this respect, is no more disquieting than Edgar Quinet on Ahasverus, or Adam Mickiewicz on Poland as the figure of Christ.) Once the two terms of the comparison are defined, the figure can acquire rich meaning, a meaning already made clear by Rousseau in his parallel of Jesus and Socrates: he who says the truth suffers for having done so. And an awareness that this is so, as Trenmor says, makes Sténio's fate significant, should allow Sténio to accept that fate with joy. Whence, for any righteous victim, the renewed confirming power of the topos.

## 2 ❧ "Christ put an end to slavery"

For the entry "Christianity" in Gustave Flaubert's bitterly satirical *Dictionary of Received Ideas,* the definition is "put an end to slavery." A study of the sources of Flaubert's virulent attack on the trite (his stated goal was to put an end to all conversation!) might well seem a *reductio ad absurdum* of scholarly research. However, the permutations of this theme, widespread in the first half of the nineteenth century but rarely if ever heard—from the pulpit or elsewhere—today, illustrate how religious, political, historical, and literary discourses mingle and even conflict during the Romantic age. The theme was the subject of much controversy and was used for varied and at times contradictory purposes, but those uses suggest how these discourses related to one another. I am only concerned with examples from France, in the period 1789–1848, and I do not pretend to know all of them. The venerable apologetic topos received a new lease on life during that half-century, not only because of the Romantic religious revival and the rise of "Gospel socialism" but also for historical reasons.[1] If Christ had put an end to slavery, slavery nonetheless still existed—even though it was much questioned and attacked—in the French colonies (it had been abolished by the Revolution but was reinstated by Napoleon), in the United States, even in Catholic Poland in the form of serfdom. So the theme was frequently cited in the campaigns that led to the suppression of the slave trade in 1831, and finally of slavery itself in 1848.[2] But the evocations usually take somewhat mitigated forms—for instance, "The slave, on hearing Christ, thinks he sees his chains fall off."[3] The pure form was rather too obviously contradicted by history, and it is the variations that reveal certain traits of the Romantic mentality—and of Romantic rhetoric.

The comparison of Jesus and Socrates, we have seen, was an echo of Rousseau; here, on the contrary, the Romantics refute Rousseau—particularly his declaration in the *Social Contract* that "true Christians are made for slavery."[4] The first refutation, and perhaps the most resounding, came from Chateaubriand in his *Génie du christianisme* (1802). At the end of the chapter that describes Christianity's beneficial influence on politics and government, he proclaims: "Let us add, as the crowning contribution among so many, one which should be inscribed in gold letters in the annals of philosophy: THE ABOLITION OF SLAVERY." Perhaps wisely, Chateaubriand does not elaborate on the theme. He affirms that "the very nature of the Gospels is highly favorable to liberty," but does not offer any serious historical evidence in support of this conclusion.[5] Nonetheless, the theme often appears in various imitations and reflections of Chateaubriand's "positive apologetics"—Christianity is a civilizing force, contributing to progress, founding hospitals and schools, improving the condition of the poor and oppressed—including women—and freeing the slaves. It is automatically included in any list of Christ's deeds of social charity:

He frees the slave, he sustains the indigent
And turns sweet hope into a virtue;
He teaches the law of the love of neighbor,
Preaches charity, makes faith divine.
(Alfred Meilheurat, *Poésies religieuses*, 1846, p. 17)

Or, "Sacred sparks of the Gospel's fire, / Virtues hitherto ignored burst forth; / Woman receives her due, the slave breaks his chains" (Edouard Alletz, *Esquisses poétiques*, 1841, p. 241).

The juxtaposition of the woman and the slave, perhaps to be explained by the influence of the Saint-Simonian movement, occurs elsewhere, for instance in Hippolyte Violeau's "To a Young Unbeliever":

Nineteen whole centuries recount his glory;
Behold! Paganism crushed by the cross;
Woman, our sister, recovers her rights;
The masses shake off their ancient slavery,
And progress visits the savage's hut.
(*Nouveaux Loisirs poétiques*, 1845, p. 33)

The tone, at times, is quite bombastic: "Conquering giant, slavery insulted the world; weak, unknown, unarmed, the Son of Man attacked, conquered, destroyed it."[6] The theme reappears regularly, even monotonously, in popular Christian apologetic texts. For instance, in Mme Collin's story for young ladies, "Christian Rome or Holy Orders" (in *Les Grâces chrétiennes*, vol. 1, 1842), a servant breaks a precious vase; in great fright, he offers to give his children in slavery but the major domo assures him (with some regret) that this is a Christian household and so, at the most, he runs the risk of being fired if he continues breaking things. Examples are found in major as well as minor authors. In Lamartine's "Hymne au Christ" we read: "You appear! . . . / The master learns what justice is, / The slave, what is liberty!"[7] Victor Hugo quotes the key texts from Paul, "Christ frees us" and "Where the Spirit of the Lord reigns, there reigns liberty," at the beginning of his poem "De la liberté."[8] One could cite many other examples; the recurrence of the theme popularized by Chateaubriand in 1802 in its pure, simple form during the 1830s and 1840s is noteworthy.

The two other major defenders of Christianity at the beginning of the century, Joseph de Maistre and Lamennais, use the theme in a more complex way. Maistre proposes a close association between religious orthodoxy and political or personal freedom and emphasizes the gradual nature of the liberation from slavery.[9] Rather than to Jesus, it is to the popes that "humanity is indebted for the extinction of slavery, which they have fought against without ceasing, and which they will infallibly abolish, but without disturbance, disruption, or danger, wherever the Papacy is allowed to exercise its authority" (2:337). According to Maistre, Rousseau was wrong in proposing that man was created free and is now everywhere in chains; on the contrary, man is born in chains, for, without the aid of revealed religion, man is "too evil to be free" (2:339). Slavery was a necessary institution until Christianity had sufficiently converted the human soul to allow for slavery's gradual destruction. The decisive moment came with pope Alexander III's declaration in 1167 that every Christian should be free from slavery. Only the divine force of Christianity can triumph over "the natural bitterness of the human will and allow men to live together without seeking to harm one another" (2:343). Whence the links between religious orthodoxy and liberty: "Wherever the dominant religion is not Catholicism, slavery is legal; whenever Catholicism loses strength, a nation becomes, to the same extent, less capable of knowing any general freedom" (2:342). As an example, Maistre cites Russia, where serfdom still exists because of the absence of the *filioque* in the creed.[10] Maistre, like others, combines his discussion of freedom from slavery with a discussion of how Christianity improved the condition of women.[11] As we shall see, the antiabolitionists made much use of this association of religious orthodoxy and liberty, proclaiming throughout the 1840s that the slaves were not yet "Catholic" enough to be freed.

Lamennais's analysis is perhaps even more typical, for, if he accepts Maistre's gradualism, he soon turns it into an appeal for political action so that the freeing of the slaves begun by Christ will now come to full fruition. In his *Essay on Indifference in Matters of Religion* (1817), his attitude is quite close to Maistre's. Rousseau understood nothing about history:

> If he wanted to talk about Christianity, why did he not at least consult the Gospel, that perfect law of liberty, as one of the apostles calls it? There he could have read those words which can only engulf with admiration anyone who understands their full sense: The truth shall make you free! Christ has freed us! Wherever is the spirit of God, there is liberty!

When Jesus appeared, man was everywhere in chains; but the Savior preached the good news of salvation, that all power comes from God. And when power is identified with divine authority, power inspires respect and love, so that one can obey without ceasing to be free. In fact, one is free because one obeys.[12] Thus, in this first stage of his thought, Lamennais maintains that Christ put an end to slavery only in the sense that he gave power a new, theocratic basis:

> The essence of slavery is the subjection of the will of one man to that of another; and whoever obeys another man is his slave. . . . So it is also with nations, and the theory of the sovereignty of the people is nothing more nor less than the theory of their slavery. Which is why slavery was necessary in the pagan nations of classical antiquity, and especially in pagan republics.

Christianity both enhances power, and makes it acceptable; obedience becomes noble, for "the rule of God has replaced the domination of men" (1:446). Lamennais soon redefined this theocratic analysis of the theme of the end of slavery to conclude that liberty was to be realized in the future of history—indeed, in the near future. In *De la liberté religieuse* (1831), he repeats that Christ made men the servants of God and hence no longer the slaves of other men, but he no longer derives therefrom a justification for obedience to established authority; quite the contrary, that authority is seen as a residue of pre-Christian slavery. The most intelligent and concise explanation of this evolution of his thought was provided by his disciple Philippe Gerbet in his *Introduction à la philosophie de l'histoire* (1832). History is the history of progress toward freedom, manifest first in the messianic expectations of the Jews and other peoples, then in the gradual realization of Christ's message of freedom in fraternity:

> Christianity introduced into the world the idea of universal association, of organizing the human race along the lines of the family. It gave the world much more than the idea of doing so, it gave it the faith that this could be done. So, from its very origins, the maxims of Christianity attacked in a radical way slavery, caste divisions, nationalism. (P. 216)

Gerbet makes explicit the identification of political and spiritual liberty that is implicit in Chateaubriand, Maistre, and Lamennais. The sin of pride, of egotism, created slavery; the sacrificial love of one's neighbor in unity brings to fruition the message of salvation, which will create a new social order—and this progress toward liberty gradually unfolds in the history of humanity.

Before analyzing the political consequences of this interpretation of the topos, it should be noted that, until about 1830, Catholic apologists usually repeat the theses of Chateaubriand and Maistre; after that, Catholic authors tend to split into two groups: those who accept the social significance that Gerbet attributed to the theme, and those who reject it because of the uses made thereof by Lamennais and the socialists. The pre-1830s group includes even such notorious conservatives as Mgr Frayssinous, who, in the chapter of his *Défense du christianisme* (1825) on "Jesus Christ considered as the benefactor of the human race," while refusing to read into the Gospels any specific political program, maintains that Christianity provides the essential principles for any just society, and cites as proof the way the early Church civilized the barbarians and . . . freed the slaves. The Church could only do this because Christianity endows authority with a sacred origin, a religious sanction, where duty rather than fear induces obedience; so, concludes Frayssinous, the road to liberty leads to the reunion of altar and throne (p. 382).

Théodore Combalot says much the same thing; if he asserts that grace alone can make us free, he explains that it is a matter of freedom from the slavery to material goods, to sensual pleasures, to error and evil, giving us the one "true liberty," that of union with the Godhead. However, even he admits that this spiritual liberty brought about the end of polygamy and slavery and produced occidental civilization; he then borrows from Maistre the thesis that man is more free today in Catholic countries than in Protestant ones, in Protestant than in Moslem, and so on (Eléments de philosophie catholique, 1833).

In the 1840s, some Catholics still tried to reconcile Christianity and social reform movements by citing Chateaubriand's theses. Mgr Affre, archbishop of Paris, in his Introduction philosophique à l'étude du christianisme (1845), cited the end of slavery as central in his list of Christianity's beneficial effects on civilization. "Here is the decisive observation: tyranny, slavery, the abuse of paternal or marital power were, and history proves it, successfully reformed by a religion which condemns them in the name of God, and they could not be reformed by a philosophy which proclaims the rights of man in the name of man alone" (p. 159). Pierre Giraud, archbishop of Cambrai, who was more aware and articulate about the problems of the Industrial Revolution than any other French prelate at the time, used the theme in his Pastoral Instruction for Lent, 1845, "On the Laws of Labor," to make the transition between his thesis (work is necessary, and since Adam's fall necessarily disagreeable) and his antithesis (Christianity can take away some of the pains and austerity of labor, because of its message of fraternity which "puts an end to slavery").[13] For Giraud, again, that change was gradual, progressive; more and more Catholic authors, especially in the debates about abolitionism, would underscore the gradual way in which humankind, through a Christian influence on history, is freed from slavery. According to some, who shared Maistre's conviction that there is an organic relation between religious orthodoxy and political freedom, the slaves can only be freed after they have been completely converted to Christianity. Hardy, the director of the Seminary du Saint Esprit where clergy were trained for work in the colonies, maintained that Jesus had said, not "Go and break the chains of the slaves," but "Go and teach"; if Christianity gradually triumphs over slavery, it is only because of the religious and moral instruction it offers.[14] This point of view was common in the 1845 debates about slavery. For instance, Dubouchage asserted: "I believe Christianity holds slavery in horror, I desire its abolition, but I assert that Christianity must prepare with great care the path toward that abolition." Conclusion: one can best put an end to slavery by sending more priests to the colonies.[15]

During the July Monarchy, the apologetic theme of the end of slavery becomes a subject of controversy because of the uses made of it by certain leftist writers. Already in 1819 Alexis Dumesnil evoked the topos to justify his rather utopian political hopes, in a somewhat incoherent text, *La Manifestation de l'esprit de vérité*. Jesus proclaimed all men brothers—whence the commandment to abandon father and family and follow Christ. In other words, Jesus demanded the abolition of slavery and particularly of that form of economic slavery which private property creates. Dumesnil was a precursor; it was the disciples of Saint-Simon who integrated the topos into a meditation on the nature of history and a program of social reform. Eugène Rodrigues, in his *Lettres sur la religion et la politique* (1829), took up Saint-Simon's (or was it Auguste Comte's?) distinction between military and spiritual society.[16] The two were radically separated for the first time under the influence of Catholic monotheism, and the spiritual society explicitly condemned slavery both in theory and in practice. This liberation was Christianity's great contribution to history, but Christianity could only create a spiritual equality, and for that reason its historical mission is now completed, ended. Christ founded "a spiritual society of men based on human fraternity":

> During the second epoch—the age of Christianity—the paradise of the pagans came into being on this earth; for the Christians abolished slavery, all men were called to the divine banquet, civil bread and wine are replaced by the two species of the eucharistic feast, and the most complete equality reigns—within the temple. (Rodrigues, p. 60)

But only within the temple; now it was up to the Saint-Simonians to reorganize lay society so that this fraternal equality would be material as well as spiritual. This theory did not prevent the movement from using the topos for propaganda purposes, and over the door of their utopian community at Ménilmontant they placed the inscription, "God who sent his Christ in order to put an end to the slave trade of men, now sends him again to put an end to the slave trade of women."[17]

The Saint-Simonians gave the topos a new meaning; following their example, many writers would derive from "Christ put an end to slavery" a meditation on the nature and meaning of history and a call to political action. Romantic "Gospel socialism" generally combines a philosophy of history and an appeal to religious values. Both Victor Considérant and Pierre Leroux, for instance, stress that the unification of the world by the Roman Empire and then the Germanic invasions were necessary preliminaries to the freeing of the slaves; radical changes in social structure must always precede any significant developments on humankind's path toward fraternity and community. Christianity's gradual abolition of slavery thus offers an excellent example of the interplay of spiritual and material factors in the creation of progress. Pioneers of Catholic socialism, such as Joseph Buchez and P. C. Roux, also often have recourse to the topos; the preface of their edition of the Gospels for the working classes (1837), explains that baptism "freed children, the marriage sacrament freed womankind, the participation in all the sacraments freed the slaves" (p. xxxi)—Buchez often describes the Eucharist as a banquet of fraternity. He also emphasizes the progressive nature of this liberation; Christ gave mankind spiritual liberty, and a potential for political and material liberty. The year 1789 brought political liberty, and now the struggle for material or economic liberty had begun. This idea was widespread among leftist writers.[18]

Probably the most fecund—and perhaps excessive—use of the topos is made by the "second" Lamennais, after his break with Rome, who turns the old apologetic argument into a call for revolutionary activity. Already in 1834 *The Words of a Believer* identifies political liberty and obedience to the divine will, and defines truth as that love of God and neighbor which will abolish slavery and create liberty. All this is expressed in very apocalyptic language: "Yet three days, and the sacrilegious seal will be broken, liberty will begin." In *De l'esclavage moderne* (1839), he notes that if the Gospel abolished the principle of slavery, the fact of slavery continues to exist everywhere—in serfdom, in the downtrodden status of the working classes. The commandment "ut omnes unum sint" ("may all be one") still goes unheeded. Henceforth, "the end of slavery" in Lamennais's texts is associated with dreams of internationalism, of communalism, of mystical unity.

Some extreme leftist writers offer curious variations on the theme. Alphonse Esquiros, in his "Philosophy of Christianity," not only declares that Christ "humbles the forehead which is exalted, and raises the slave who succumbs in his chains," he also compares the flogged slave to Christ flogged during his Passion: "When you hear the whistle of the lash on the backs of the slaves, flee! flee! For it is Christ who is being flogged!"[19] Mickiewicz, with his intense awareness of the problem of serfdom in Poland, remained convinced that Christ had initiated humanity's moral progress. "The masters freed their slaves, and saw in them their brothers; and the kings, annointed in the name of God, honored the law of God which was above them, and justice returned to the earth."[20] Chilon, an eccentric prophet who thought that Jesus was really Joshua, nonetheless maintains that Jesus' essential message was a message of freedom, and moreover that the freeing of the slaves involved a new, egalitarian distribution of landed property.[21] The topos crops up even in leftist authors such as Reghellini who deny the divinity of Christ. According to Reghellini, Jesus was an invention of radical zealots who exploited him as an emblem of the doctrines of Liberty, Equality, Fraternity already present in rabbinical writings—including, of course, the end of slavery; indeed, "the death of Christ is an allegory of the fate of slavery" (*Examen du mosaïsme et du christianisme*, 1834, 2:161, 213).

These leftist variations also show up frequently in imaginative literature, particularly in Balzac. The traveling salesman Gaudissart, who had read Saint-Simon and Leroux, proclaims that "the exploitation of man by man should have stopped the day when Christ—I say Christ, not Jesus Christ {a Saint-Simonian way of distinguishing between the Word and the Jesus of history} came to proclaim that all men were equal in the eyes of God" (*L'illustre Gaudissart*, Pléïade ed., 1958, 4:39). Michel Chrestien, somewhat more intelligent, says much the same thing: Jesus was "the divine legislator of Equality" (*Illusions perdues*, Pléïade ed., 1958, 4:654). One of Ballanche's disciples, Justin Maurice, writes: "The crown of thorns wounds alike the foreheads of slaves and kings."[22] The topos occurs frequently among the "worker poets" of the 1840s, who often identify the slave and the laborer and attribute contemporary political significance to their liberation. "He must have been divine, he who / Breaking the shackles of a thousand fallacious tyrants, / Shouted with a loud voice to the enslaved nations, / 'Free men, arise! Your Father is in heaven.' "[23] Only rarely does one come across an original use of the topos. In François Cristal's *La Passion de*

*Jésus-Christ* (1833), Valérie Pilate, Pontius's wife, a member of the Gracchus family and a "Park Avenue pink," wants to save Jesus, not because of any dream she had had but because he is "a reformer. . . . Who, shuddering at the evils which cover the universe / Would like to destroy the shackles of the oppressed."

Needless to say, the topos is also widespread in abolitionist poetry, which, however, usually specifies that the task of freeing the slaves, if Jesus ordered and began it, must still be brought to fruition. Ange-Benjamin Marie du Mesnil's *L'Esclavage* (1823) is typical. It is true that, thanks to Jesus,

> Truth triumphs, and from the altars
> God proclaims all feeble mortals equal;
> He created us all for the same purpose . . .
> Wherever his word spreads his sweet empire,
> Man recovers his rights, humanity breathes once more (P. 16)

But Christianity has been betrayed and perverted, slavery still exists, and Charity, guided by Faith, comes forth to complain:

> Did not God create out of the same dust
> The different peoples whom his light doth warm?
> And to save them all, idolaters, Gentiles,
> Did he not let his Son die on the cross?
> The Africans are then his children, your brothers!
> Christians, put an end to their long miseries (P. 27)

What Marie du Mesnil, in the 1820s, said about Africans in the 1840s was applied to the poor of France, to the proletariat, and the theme of the end of slavery was transformed, as we have seen, into an appeal for social and economic reform, and even for revolution.

These political uses of the topos, particularly those of the apostate Lamennais, inevitably provoked a Catholic reaction. This reaction, frequently quoting "My Kingdom is not of this world" or "Render unto Caesar the things that are Caesar's," limits liberty in the Christian sense to the purely spiritual realm and thus attacks the very basis of Chateaubriand's apologetics, his thesis that Christianity was true, good, and beautiful because it had contributed to the excellence of life here below. The reaction merits attention, for it prefigures how much Catholic thought during the following century would take essentially conservative positions in reaction to the theses of the Gospel socialists and most particularly of Lamennais.

Louis Bautain, in his quite intelligent *Réponse d'un chrétien aux Paroles d'un croyant* (1834), goes so far as to assert that man's political liberty is a matter of no importance for the Christian. Man can be free in the Christian sense even if he is in chains. Bishop Guillon, who was the confessor of Louis-Philippe's wife, maintains that the Church never taught that the slaves should revolt, should break their chains; rather, the Church said: "Brothers of God, who Himself did not hesitate to take on the form of a slave to ransom us all from the slavery of sin, remain submissive toward your masters, even when they mistreat you."[24] Pierre Boyer goes much further, saying that the Church has always defined liberty as freedom from the passions of pride, ambition, avarice, lust, the appetites of the senses: "As for political and civil liberty, they are of no concern to the law of God" (*Examen de la doctrine de M. de La Mennais,* 1834, p. 305). According to du Plessis de Grenédan, Christianity did not put an end to slavery because slavery is a perfectly acceptable form of salary, or a punishment for sin or misconduct, or a consequence of war—and there, it is clearly more moral to enslave your enemies than to kill them. "The Christian religion has never condemned slavery; it has never told the masters to free their slaves; on the contrary, it has taught the slaves to obey their masters" (*Examen des Paroles d'un croyant,* 1840, p. 62). Fr. Rigord, a priest from Martinique, goes even beyond that in his *Observations sur quelques opinions relatives à l'esclavage* (Port Royal, Martinque, 1846). Neither the Bible nor the Church Fathers ever express any objection to slavery; on the contrary, they teach obedience. The slave trade is an excellent way of liberating the Blacks from paganism and submitting them to the influence of Christianity. Finally, religion "is only secondarily concerned with man's material condition; it matters little whether man is free or bowed down under the yoke of slavery; indeed, religion rather says 'Happy are those who suffer, happy are those who weep, for they shall be consoled.' " The most curious text is perhaps Alfred Rivet's poem *Les Voix coloniales* (1840) where a Martinique proprietor, fearing that England may impose abolition, compares the slave owner to the crucified Christ, the English to Caiphas. Eventually, everyone in nineteenth-century France gets compared to Jesus.

Refutations of the topos are not limited to Catholic reactionaries; they are also produced by liberals and even leftist writers. But they are rather rare prior to 1830. E. Senancour is elegantly ironic in his

*Observations critiques sur le Génie du christianisme* (1815):

> Did Christianity really abolish slavery? It tolerates it, when the slaves are not Christian, or when they have a black skin; and moreover Christian serfs are slaves in the present sense of the term. Christianity has perhaps diminished slavery, but it has not destroyed it. If Christianity were to disappear, as Mr. Chateaubriand formerly predicted that it would, would we then reinstitute slavery in Europe, that slavery Europeans have practiced in their colonies while they've been zealous Christians? "On earth, Christianity has abolished slavery." Mr. Chateaubriand repeats this proposition often, but the Black in America, stretched out under the Christian's whip, will be a bit difficult to convince. (P. 228)

Charles Nodier, in his curious "M. de la Mettrie ou les superstitions," uses a lightly ironic tone; Christ did suppress slavery, but "it was no mean task, for everytime one tells slaves that they are equal to their masters, they immediately want to turn their masters into slaves; but Jesus presented his lessons with such a sweet, conciliatory ethics."[25]

It is only after Lamennais's break with the Church that the topos is subjected to violent attacks by leftist writers. Harro Harring, in his pamphlet *Les Paroles d'un homme, dédiées au Croyant de Lamennais,* exclaims: "The black slave, who by meditation discovers the truth, is treated as a rebel, whipped, shot to death, by his Christian master, if he decides he wants to become a *man*—these are the fruits of Jesus Christ's doctrine of equality among all men."[26] The Belgian Louis de Potter, here as elsewhere, is dogmatically opposed to Christianity. If Christianity had wanted to give the slave the same rights before God as his master, indeed the natural and necessary consequence would have been the abolition of slavery, but "that was not at all the case. The slaves were given the hope of going to heaven with their masters, but only after having lived through a number of years of real hell here below, in order to contribute to the physical well-being of those masters" (*Histoire philosophique, politique, critique du christianisme,* 1836, 1:129). Through the centuries, the Church has always defended slavery, and only the spread of enlightenment can make it disappear.

The noted abolitionist Victor Schoelcher provides a nice example of a scholarly "demythification" of the topos. His study of slavery in the colonies led him to conclude that Catholicism, far from preparing the slaves for freedom, is in fact one of the most powerful supports of slavery. The priests, completely controlled by the slave owners, teach the slaves lessons of superstition and obedience. The Church is not destroying slavery; rather, slavery is corrupting the Church.[27] According to Schoelcher, the theory that the slave must be totally converted to Christianity before he can be freed is only a way of veiling one's opposition to abolition. His criticisms of the colonial clergy probably had a sound basis in fact; even the comte de Montalembert admitted, in the 1845 debates, that the clergy "has not shown the apostolic zeal, the insuperable courage, the austere independence," which the situation demanded. It is no surprise if the Blacks refuse to listen to the missionary, for they see in him "an accomplice of the master, more or less disguised as the case may be." Montalembert then draws a rather bitter comparison between the French priests and the Protestant missionaries in the English colonies. However, a good Catholic, he does not condemn the Church, but demands a greater degree of freedom for the episcopacy (*Exposé*, p. 261).

The most virulent rejection of the topos that I know of is provided by Victor Hannotin in his *Doctrine philosophique et religieuse* of 1842. Though his political point of view is quite the opposite, he shares Maistre's theory that "popular sovereignty is contrary to the Christian faith." Documents and texts in hand, he shows how Christianity has served the cause of slavery, citing the Bible, Cardinal Fleury, Gibbon, and de Potter, noting for instance a decree of the Council of Hieria in A.D. 753 which allowed selling off separately couples of married slaves. The case is not uncommon; conservative Catholics and anticlerical leftists join hands in refusing to give the topos any political meaning.

One way of solving some of these contradictions would be to maintain that Christianity had at one time put an end to slavery, but that slavery had afterward reappeared, hence the present need of a new form of manumission. Indeed, such is the thesis of Alexis de Tocqueville. If "twelve centuries ago, Christianity destroyed slavery in this world," since then slavery has returned and today

> emancipation is the product of a French idea. . . . It is we the French who, in spreading throughout the universe the notion of the equality of all men in the eyes of the law, just as Christianity created the notion of the equality of all men in the eye of God, I say it is we the French who are the true authors of the abolition of slavery.[28]

The variations on the topos are endless and their echoes tiresomely repetitive.

Probably by now the reader fully shares Flaubert's cynical impatience, but there remains a problem to be studied. Hannotin was only a popularizer, but his show of scholarly erudition is symptomatic of how much the topos, precisely because of the controversies it provoked, became increasingly the subject of erudite historical research, of works that illustrate that *libido sciendi* which is one of the most important traits of French Romanticism. One can cite as exemplary the volumes of Bonnetty's *Annales de philosophie chrétienne,* a periodical whose goal was to increase the intellectual and cultural level of the clergy by offering extensive documentation of the "positive" proofs of the faith advanced by Chateaubriand, Bonald, and Lamennais. The 1830 prospectus proclaims that, among many other matters, the journal will study the history of jurisprudence to show how laws have benefited from the influence of Christianity. The first issue contains an article entitled "The Influence of Christianity on Present-day Civilization," which once again claims that Christ substituted obedience to God for submission to men, which led to the freeing of the slaves. Details on Gregory the Great and manumission, and on the Theodosian Code, are cited as supporting documentation, and Maistre is quoted with approbation: when religion disappears, slavery reappears. "The less religion represses evil instincts, the more the laws of society have to perform that repression" (*Annales,* 1:14–25). In 1831, an article "On the Slave" (2:23–24) recalls how widespread slavery was in classical antiquity. If Christianity had abolished it immediately, society would have been destroyed. But Jesus' message of freedom provided humankind with a new dignity: there is only one master, God, and all humans are equal. The author then traces the history of papal attitudes toward slavery. Another article asserts that today, as compared to the eighteenth century, everyone accepts that Christianity has exercised a civilizing influence, putting an end to slavery, protecting and encouraging the sciences. In 1835, a long article (10:429–33; 12:188–200) lists historical examples of manumissions inspired by Christianity: Paulinus, Queen Bathilda, several bishops of the early Church, the Crusades which emancipated the serfs; the conclusion praises Catholic efforts to ameliorate the conditions of slavery in the Americas. Another article (12:344) cites the writings of John Chrysostom, Lactantius et al. against slavery. The topos becomes one of the major arguments employed to convince intellectuals that Christianity exerts a beneficent social influence; historical studies show why Christ could not immediately put an end to slavery and how, through the course of history, the Church puts into practice this aspect of the Gospel message.

Bonnetty was not alone. In 1831 J. L. Bertin published a lengthy historical justification of the topos, *De la liberté considérée dans ses rapports avec le christianisme.* Liberty, of divine origin, is revealed in Christianity; all society can do is limit, to a lesser or greater extent, its exercise. Bertin draws a parallel between pagan Rome, whose population was two-thirds enslaved, and primitive Christianity, and then proposes a causal relation between the spread of Christianity and the increase in emancipations. Once Christianity became the state religion of Rome, gradual emancipation became possible, but unfortunately the barbarian invasions for a while put an end to manumissions and this aspect of Christianity's civilizing influence only began to be operative again with Charlemagne. Bertin asks, Why is religion today associated with oppression? Uniquely, he claims, because Christianity indeed oppresses the passions, proclaims not only the rights of man but also man's duties. And he concludes, as Romantic apologists so often do, "A little philosophy turns one away from religion, but a great deal of philosophy brings one back" (p. 31).

One might say that this statement is contradicted by another study of the same problem which appeared that very year, Emile Lerminier's *La Philosophie du droit.* Quite learned, Lerminier reads Christianity primarily as an effort to provide the Mosaic code with appropriate institutions. Christianity met with success in Rome as a new philosophical opinion, in part because the doctrine of the immortality of the soul not only purified the individual (Stoicism had done that just as well) but also consoled the unfortunate by promising future recompenses to the victims of the injustices of this world. Better still, Christianity taught that all men are brothers, equals in the eyes of their Creator, and thus introduced a new principle of "sociability" which has yet to bear all its fruits. The history of jurisprudence is the history of the gradual application of this principle of sociability, which included "the virtual abolition of all forms of inequality which are contrary to the nature of things," and so denied the legitimacy of slavery, an institution fundamental to pagan society. The principle continues to produce a series of social revolutions throughout history (2:72). Lerminier attributes this gradualism not so much to Jesus as to the prudence of Paul, though Paul, in teaching that all power comes from God, knew that one day this idea would become a powerful force for social reform. Lerminier studies Augustine, Gregory VII, Luther, Juan de Mariana, and others, to show how this "principle of sociability" has, through the course of history, received some, but not yet all of its applications. If Christianity would now seek regeneration at its philosophical sources, it could once more become a force for progress and its social potential be fully realized.[29]

Edouard Laboulaye, in his *Histoire du droit de propriété foncière en occident* of 1839, is even more scholarly. At the most, Christianity only "weakened slavery"; the early Councils perhaps tried to better the conditions of the slaves, but did not attack the institution of slavery. Refuting Bertin, Laboulaye shows how, rather than Christianity, it was the Germanic invasions that made possible the transition from slavery to serfdom by giving the slaves the right to have families and personal possessions. After his book, one might think not much remained of Chateaubriand's thesis, but the Church answered back in 1841 with the publication of Louis-Charles Thérou's lengthy *Le Christianisme et l'esclavage*, which also contains Simon de la Treiche's translation of Johann Möhler's *Historical Treatise on the Problem of Christianity and Slavery*. Möhler, like Thérou, considers slavery an inevitable result of original sin; humanity's ransom from that sin was thus a necessary prelude to our redemption from slavery. So both link the two slaveries, interior and spiritual, exterior and political. Thérou even combines them in his description of the Crucifixion:

> Pursuing to its last extremity the curse of slavery, Christ immolates in his own body, the image of sin, that body of slavery born of sin, and, so that his thought might be clear to all, he dies by undergoing the punishment reserved for slaves. His death, and by his death our redemption, was the highest and most energetic proclamation of universal emancipation. (P. 15)

The regeneration of moral man prepares the way for the regeneration of political man, and Thérou quotes Chateaubriand, "from the right of access to the heavenly city comes the consolation of the right of access to the earthly city" (p. 16). Because of this link between spiritual and material, Christianity prudently effected the abolition of slavery gradually. Möhler traces this gradual abolition up to the fifth century. Thérou from that date on, with an avowed indebtedness to Maistre's theories. Thérou emphasizes the links between religious orthodoxy and attitude toward slavery, suggests that the slaves are treated better in Catholic South America than in Protestant North America, and so forth.[30] This gradualism would seem to presuppose that the Kingdom of God is eventually to come about, at least to a certain degree, here below, but Thérou never states this explicitly.

A similar progressive Catholic theory of history is proposed, with even more learning, by the famous legal scholar Raymond Troplong in his *De l'influence du christianisme sur le droit civil des Romains* (1843). He also claims that the influence of Christianity contributed to the improvement of Roman law, but nonetheless Roman law is inferior to modern law, "born in the shade of Christianity, and better imbued with its spirit" (p. 4). In his lengthy chapter on slavery, he studies, among other matters, how the right to punish was gradually transferred from the slave owners to the magistrates, and provides documentation to prove that manumissions steadily increased. But it was only during the Middle Ages, when Christianity had deeply penetrated all aspects of society, that the great emancipation took place (p. 162).

Granier de Cassagnac is not one of the more pleasant figures of early nineteenth-century France, but at least his *Histoire des classes ouvrières et de la bourgeoisie* (1838) is refreshingly different. Granier is an advocate of slavery, and the author of a defense of whipping as a way of disciplining the slaves (other forms of punishment, such as imprisonment or the cudgel which may fracture their legs or arms, prevent them from working, whereas the goal of the punishment is to make them work harder). According to Granier, the unjustified, unmerited, precocious manumission of slaves has created the proletariat and all the miseries it now knows; the situation of the freeman is much worse than that of the slave who at least enjoys the paternal protection of his master. In 1844, in *Le Christianisme et l'esclavage,* he claims that Christianity in no way calls for the abolition of slavery; slavery will only disappear the day when all human beings will be completely, totally, and universally free from sin, and that is not going to happen tomorrow—a logical enough consequence to draw from Maistre's theory. He also provides historical documentation for his thesis, to conclude that the Church "has never taught the slaves that frenetic love of freedom which leads them to practice revolt, pillage, massacres; on the contrary, the Church has always preached submission to the slaves, ordered them to obey" (p. 89), and he quotes Paul's instructions to Onesimus. At the very most, the Church approves those who, in order to civilize the Blacks and convert them to the true faith, buy them from their idol-worshipping African masters and transport them to the Americas, "while subjecting them to a discipline which is in accordance with what their nature requires" (p. 88). But even Granier perceives, as he justifies slavery, an organic link between the spiritual and political states.

Granier's texts produced quite a polemic. Gougenot des Mousseaux attacked him in detail in *Des prolétaires, nécessité et moyens d'améliorer leur sort* (1846). Gougenot is yet another gradualist; Christianity, he asserts, has always taken care not to free ignorant or brutal slaves precociously. The freed slave find his only sure guide in religion; by destroying the despotism of the passions, Christianity has helped humanity rise above misery and it has planted the germs of social prosperity. Gougenot also has some original ideas; in Rome, early Christianity founded a kind of provisional egalitarian society, which was needed to correct the scandalous inequalities of pagan civilization, then came the barbarian invasions, which created the proletarian problem.

And so the quarrel goes on, more and more centered on the hows and whens of gradual freeing of the slaves, with more and more precise historical documentation for one thesis or another. In 1847 Henri Wallon published *De l'esclavage dans les colonies pour servir d'introduction à l'histoire de l'esclavage dans l'antiquité;* he attempted to trace the progress of civilization as it has been related to both the propagation of Christianity and the freeing of the slaves. For instance, civilization first flourished in urban and not rural environments because the people of the towns were free, whereas the peasant was a serf. In 1848, the association between Christianity and the end of slavery, including the betterment of the condition of the working classes, was found everywhere, in newspapers, pamphlets, the sermons of the "red priests," and in one more scholarly study, Fr. Vielbanc's *De l'enseignement catholique sur l'abolition de l'esclavage.* Another gradualist, he maintains that after spiritual liberty comes the physical liberty of the person, then the liberty to change caste or class, and finally total liberty, the reign of Gospel Liberty, Equality, Fraternity. Historical studies of the topos produce, per-

haps necessarily, a gradualist theory: Christianity gradually put an
end to slavery, or more correctly *is* putting an end to slavery, and
the meaning of the word *slavery* is broadened to include political,
social, even economic inequality.

All of which helps understand why the topos of the end of slavery
so often plays an essential role in those philosophies of history that
Romantic Catholics construct in the late 1830s and the 1840s. For
Bordas-Demoulin and his disciples Augustin Sénac and François
Huet, the destruction of slavery is the sign of the presence of the
divine incarnate in history and the symbolic representation of all
social progress.[31] For Fr. Frère-Colonna, the Incarnation created a
new alliance between God and mortals and among mortals, and by
that fact also a new hierarchy in the universal catholic community of
human beings, and the disappearance of slavery is a manifestation
of this new alliance (*L'Homme connu par la révélation*, 1833, pp. 336–
42). Blanc Saint-Bonnet's Trinitarian and eschatological theory of
history moves from the age of the Father, of Force and slavery, via
the Incarnation to that of the Son, of Justice and competition; now
comes the Joachimist third age, of the Holy Ghost, of Charity and
communion (Preface to *De l'unité*, 1841). In short, these controversies about the topos "Christ put an end to slavery," on the one
hand, produced serious, erudite studies in the history of law, of
institutions, and the like; on the other hand, they produced conjec-
tural philosophies of history. The same author often practiced both.

The topos served a variety of purposes, and these are often contradictory. Christ put an end to slavery, so there is a close, organic
relation between the material and spiritual states. Such is the conclusion of rightist authors (Granier) but also of leftists (Buchez); it
is also rejected on the right (Rigord) and on the left (de Potter). The
thesis that Christianity is hostile to popular sovereignty is defended
by Maistre, a Catholic conservative, and by Hannotin, a revolutionary atheist. Reghellini, while he denies the divinity of Jesus, claims
that he did abolish slavery. Esquiros compares the slave to the crucified Christ, Rivet the slave owner to the same Christ. Such is the
fate of many a topos during the Romantic age. Their meaning, their
context, is no longer set by a rhetorical tradition. So the topos
appears in multiple forms, and is burdened with contradictory,
even antithetical meanings. This suggests that it is probably wise to
analyze Romanticism, not in thematic terms, nor as a movement
based on a common set of beliefs and convictions, but rather in

terms of a series of exacerbated, even polar oppositions, such as pessimism and the belief in progress; subjectivity and the quest for positivist, objective truth; irrationalism and the cult of logic and of organized schemata.

Chateaubriand's *Genius of Christianity* seems to have been a sort of Pandora's box. Chateaubriand, while justifying Christianity in terms of its contributions to civilization, provoked a questioning of the history of the Church and, what is more important, raised questions about the nature of the Kingdom; was it located here below, in the future, or was it purely transcendent? The confusion of spiritual and political liberty, of the slavery of the soul and slavery of the body, so widespread and so little questioned that only extremists on the far right or far left reject it, is characteristic not only of Romantic monism which rejects the distinction between spirit and matter, but also of the ambiguities about this question of where the Kingdom is to come, on earth or in heaven. (This is another widespread topos that merits study, for the debates about when and where the Kingdom would come demonstrate quite clearly the extent to which socialism was a secularization of religious values.)

Once more, socialist thought in the first half of the nineteenth century seems in many ways a secularization of religious values, and the old apologetic topos becomes an argument in favor of the political and economic reform of contemporary society. Romantic historicism then intervenes to show that the liberation of the slaves was gradual, but, in so doing, suggests that the Kingdom comes about progressively here below, thanks to a historical process that began with the Incarnation—and which, some hoped, would be completed when the glorious utopian dreams of 1848 came true. Surely it is in part the failure of those dreams that deprived the topos of its meaning and earned it a place in Flaubert's bitter *Dictionary,* even if 1848 did finally see the abolition of slavery in all French colonies.[32] But well before 1848, the topos had been rejected or abandoned by a great many authors: Catholics, alarmed by the meanings that the left gave it, and socialists, unwilling to accept that spiritual freedom was a necessary prelude to political or economic freedom. So the debate came to be centered on the problem of the meaning of history; in the Romantic age, religious and social thought became meditations on the philosophy of history, and that history was still conceived of as, in some sense or other, teleological.

# 3   🐛   Napoleon as a Christ Figure

> Our motto should therefore be: the reform of consciousness not
> by dogmas, but by the analysis of that mystic consciousness
> which cannot understand itself, whether it be manifested in reli-
> gion or in politics. It will then be clear that for a long time the
> world has possessed the dream of something which it ought now
> to possess by consciousness so that it can possess it in reality.
> —Karl Marx

According to a tradition that is popular even in the United
States, a schizophrenic, when he does not identify himself with
Jesus, proclaims that he is the great French emperor, Napoleon,
and, placing his right hand in the famed Bonaparte position, rejects
the identity society would like to impose on him.[1] In 1840, the
year in which Napoleon's ashes were ceremoniously brought back to
Paris from Saint Helena, according to Alphonse Esquiros thirteen or
fourteen Napoleons had already been interned in the Bicêtre insane
asylum. For not only are there many legends about Napoleon, there
is also a Napoleonic myth, and that myth went so far as to propose
assimilating Napoleon and the Messiah, thus permitting a synthesis
of the two favorite identities of the schizophrenic. One wonders, is
this madness, or a simple metaphor (for who has not been compared
to Christ, especially in the first half of the nineteenth century? the
proletariat, the poet, woman, Poland, Louis XVI—the list is long),
or perhaps even a serious idea? The various forms of these identifications of Napoleon and Christ merit a study—which must also
include the identifications between Napoleon and Antichrist, for
here, as often with Romanticism, the extremes come together. This
chapter discusses the beginning and development of the parallel
from the end of the first Empire to the beginning of the second, but
the parallel did not stop there; it continued to flourish in Léon Bloy,

then Elie Faure, and, through Faure's writings, in Abel Gance's film.[2]

One could attribute its origins, at least in part, to the adulation Napoleon knew, indeed demanded, while he was still in power. The Catechism taught all French children that "God has made the Emperor the minister of His power and His image on earth"; Cardinal Maury did not hesitate to call him "the chosen one of God"; and Cardinal Caprara, after researching the Bollandist *Acta Sanctorum*, managed to come up with a St. Napoleon whose feast day was duly moved from 2 May to 15 August, the date of Bonaparte's birth.[3] It is in any case easy to understand how Napoleon quickly became a legendary figure. But he did not become a messianic figure in any important way until the 1840s, and the messianic myth of Napoleon seemingly had its origins not in the popular imagination, but in a certain occultist or Illuminist tradition; the myth was created by mystics, by philosophers and poets, aided, of course, by historical circumstances.[4] On the other hand, the contrary tradition, according to which Napoleon was not the Messiah but the Antichrist, the devil incarnate, seems to have arisen much earlier. Jean Tulard, in his *Anti-Napoléon* (1965), retraces the themes of this comparison and cites the essential texts, most of which date from 1814, 1815, finally 1821, the year of Napoleon's death.[5] By phonic analogy, Napoleon is confused with the Apollyon of the Apocalypse, first it would seem by Wendel Wurtz, one of the most productive apocalyptic spirits of the age, in his *Les Précurseurs de l'Antéchrist, l'Apollyon de l'Apocalypse ou la Révolution française prédite par saint Jean* (1816). In addition, Wendel Wurtz proves, by etymology, that Napoleon should also be identified with Magog and Tubal. Charles Nodier echoed the argument:

> It then happened that I saw a man who seemed more than a man, who had one of his feet in Africa and another in Europe. And he was called Apollyon and the Exterminator, and I recognized that he had been announced under this name in the Apocalypse of Jean. (Quoted in Viatte, *Les Sources*, 2:199)

This widespread theme reappears for example in *L'Ami de la religion et du roi* in 1814 (1:9); the periodical's authors had managed to discover in the Bollandists not a St. Napoleon but a demon named Nappoleone, vanquished by St. Zita of Lucca, who would have made a much better patron than St. Napoleon for "Buonaparte." Napoleon-Antichrist is of interest not only because the psychological procedures that turn the emperor into a god or a devil are so to speak the same (the theme of Napoleon as Messiah is also, for example, apocalyptic), but also because of the Romantic theme of the reconciliation of Satan; for some Napoleon-Lucifer, the son of Cain, would be identified with Napoleon the Messiah.

Amusingly, one of the earliest texts that helped to portray the figure of Napoleon as a Messiah pretends to demonstrate that Napoleon never existed. Jean-Baptiste Pérès's *Grand Erratum, source d'un nombre infini d'errata à noter dans l'histoire du dix-neuvième siècle, comme quoi Napoléon n'a jamais existé* (1827) is a rather clever attack against Charles Dupuis's 1795 *Origine de tous les cultes ou la religion universelle.* An advocate of the Enlightenment thesis that the parallels that exist between Christianity and the religious systems of other cultures deprive Christianity of its claim to unique value, Dupuis more explicitly demonstrates that Apollo had no historical existence, was nothing but a solar myth, and in the same way Jesus was a solar myth. The twelve apostles are the twelve signs of the zodiac, the Resurrection represents the return of the sun at springtime, Christmas is the winter solstice, and so on. In his refutation Pérès takes the techniques that Dupuis applies to Christ and applies them to Napoleon. Apollo's mother was named Leto, Napoleon's Laetitia, names that mean joy, source of light. Napoleon had four brothers (the four seasons) of whom three became kings thanks to Napoleon—just as spring rules over the flowers, summer over the harvest, autumn over the fruits, thanks to the sun. Napoleon's twelve active marshals are manifestly the twelve signs of the zodiac. The sun rises in the east and sets in the west; Napoleon came from the east (Egypt) to disappear in the ocean in the west (Saint Helena) after having ruled twelve years (the twelve hours of the day, of course).

Pérès is clever and sarcastic, playing around with etymologies and numerology, all to prove that Napoleon never existed. The implication is of course that since he did exist, so did Jesus. Pérès probably owes a good deal to the *Historic Doubts Relative to Napoleon* (London, 1819) by Richard Whately, Anglican archbishop of Dublin, who demonstrates that one can find as many miraculous and "absurd" events in the life of Napoleon as David Hume found in the Bible in his *Essay on Miracles.* The same technique reappears in 1836 with the publication at Leipzig of *Das Leben Napoleons kritisch geprüft, aus dem Englischen, Nebst einigen Nutzwendungen auf "Das*

*Leben Jesus, von Strauss"* (*A Critical Examination of the Life of Napoleon, from the English, with Some Profitable Applications to Strauss's "Life of Jesus"*), which is a reprise of Whateley's book intended to attack not so much Dupuis as David F. Strauss. Since Strauss attacked Jesus, one may attack Napoleon in the same way. Of course, neither Whately nor Pérès offers a real divinization of Napoleon; rather, Napoleon is associated with Jesus only to make a sarcastic attack on those who attack Jesus. Pérès's was a work that in principle parodied Dupuis but which was later, by some, taken quite seriously.[6] Pérès inaugurated the Napoleonic solar myth, and Maurice Rougié remarks in his *Grandeur et pitié de l'astrologie* (1940) that on 5 February, which he holds to be Napoleon's birthday, the sun rises in the axis of the Arc de Triomphe as seen from the Défense in Paris, whereas on 5 May, the day of his death, the sun sets in the axis of the Arc de Triomphe viewed from the obelisk of the place de la Concorde. Rising from the sea at the east, setting into the sea at the west, Napoleon is identified with the sun. Even Balzac's Colonel Chabert laments, "What do you want, our sun has set, these days we are cold" (p. 103).

A new controversy began with the 1840 publication of the *Conversations religieuses de Napoléon, avec des documents inédits de la plus haute importance où il révèle lui-même sa pensée intime sur le christianisme,* by Robert Antoine de Beauterne. Beauterne, the author of a number of edifying volumes, was particularly concerned with converting wellborn male adolescents to the Catholic faith, and in 1838 had published the pathetic *Mort d'un enfant impie,* a sad story of how one of his school friends had questioned Mary's virginity and received communion unworthily, and then died in the most terrible circumstances. However, Beauterne was not just an author of pious tales; a friend of the "Sanskrit baron" Eckstein, sometimes associated with Swedenborgian circles and also with the utopian "spiritual families" of François Coëssin and his disciples, he was thus in contact with a certain Illuminist tradition and also, as we shall see, indulged in writing visionary poetry. His *Conversations* was based on the witness of men who accompanied Napoleon in exile, Charles de Montholon, and, to a lesser extent, Emmanuel de Las Cases; the latter had already started the move to turn Napoleon into an apologist of the Christian faith.[7] Beauterne synthesized this portrait of Napoleon as a defender of Christianity. Thus we learn that in exile Napoleon demanded that he be given a confessor, wished to take communion, and, upon his death, wanted his coffin exposed with all due Christian ceremony. He believed in the Real Presence and gladly accepted a number of proofs of the divinity of Jesus. Some of these are commonplaces of Romantic apologetics: the exiled emperor indulges in the Socrates-Jesus comparison (see Chapter 1); Napoleon considers the Gospels a text "entirely new, nothing like it came before, nothing like it has come since" (p. 132); in discussing the Gospels he rather echoes Chateaubriand; and also finds convincing the "miraculous propagation" of Christianity. He proffers the old chestnut that Jesus was either divine or an imposter, and designates Jesus as "the master of love," a widespread Romantic term, because of his message of charity "which creates a link between heaven and earth." Other arguments are more in line with the personality of Napoleon, or at least his public image. He is impressed by the guard assigned to watch Jesus' tomb, and by the fact that Jesus, despite the absolute power he possessed over the crowds, refused all political ambition and worked only for the "spiritual betterment of individuals."

Beauterne's text finishes with a kind of prose poem that describes Napoleon's apotheosis. Satan wants to send him down to hell because of his divorce. But the Virgin intercedes for him, Napoleon restored the altars of France, and he always loved his mother, so Napoleon is admitted among the elect, and Our Lady says to him:

> Illustrious hero, who defended my cause and that of my Son, bless him for having chastised you while you were still on earth, in the life of misery! Even when you were on the throne, you rendered unto your mother what you owed her, you were a good son! Your life, short on earth, will be long in heaven. You have been purified by adversity and unhappiness. (*Conversations*, p. 300)

Beauterne thus introduces an idea which would be popular among the Napoleonic messianists, Napoleon's sufferings at Waterloo and on Saint Helena were a sort of crucifixion-expiation. The preface goes even further; there Napoleon is presented as a person of great moral worth, the creator and organizer of modern France:

> The most noble traits of divinity are manifestly written onto and reflected in this illustrious individual. He had as his mission to protect and accomplish the realization of the divine plan for this world. It was Providence which made straight for him that path which rose to such unheard of heights. (P. 12)

This passage echoes the theme of Napoleon as God's chosen one who effected the plans of Providence. Napoleon, first faithful to Christ, then becomes an instrument and even a figure of Christ. Need it be said that this transformation requires a certain indifference toward historical reality? According to Beauterne, Mme Murat alone was responsible for the imprisonment of Pope Pius VII. Nonetheless, Beauterne was read attentively, not only by young lads who, we trust, found a firm foundation for their faith, but also by three remarkable Poles who were to propagate Napoleonic messianism in its fullest forms: Hoené Wronski, André Towiansky, and the great Adam Mickiewicz.

Wronski's Napoleonic messianism should not be confused with that of Towiansky and Mickiewicz. Wronski, born in 1776, came to France before 1800 and, if he never hesitated to give highly mystical dimensions to his thought (it was on 15 August 1803 that, in a vision, he discovered the Absolute), he also owed a great deal to F. W. J. Schelling, and he admired Napoleon for a rather curious reason, part political, part philosophical; he was indebted to the *Idée napoléonienne* of Charles-Louis Napoleon (soon to become Napoleon III) as well as to Beauterne's image of a "Christian Napoleon" which Wronski accepted with enthusiasm. One morning in 1812, he recounts, he saw Napoleon and General Duroc arrive at Montmartre cemetery, and he then had another vision, as he leaned on a tomb, of the dark future of Napoleon, including the fateful Moscow campaign. This vision led him "to scrutinize the principles and the consequences of Napoleon's appearance in this world." In fact, it was only in 1840, in the second volume, "Messianic metapolitics," of his *Messianisme, union finale de la philosophie et de la religion, constituant la philosophie absolue,* that he gave a full exposition of his theories about Napoleon. He republished this text in 1853 as *Le Secret politique de Napoléon* with a preface entitled "The Decisive Question about Napoleon." The conclusion, "Declaration of the Author," urged Napoleon III to follow his advice. The 1853 version did not suppress the appeal to Louis-Philippe contained in the 1840 edition ("O monarch who unites the highest wisdom with a consummate prudence" and who has "the mission of accomplishing the glorious destinies which Providence has assigned to this great nation"). Perhaps the failure to delete that appeal was inadvertent, but Wronski, like Charles Fourier, had the mania of believing that chiefs of state were always about to bring his most beautiful dreams to fruition.

Included in Wronski's messianic thought was a complicated system of mystical mathematics or arithmosophia.[8] The end result was that, due to a fusion of religion and philosophy, a moral and intellectual aristocracy would profit from its rational awareness of the Absolute within it ("Paracletism") in order to reconstruct a hierarchical society—which nevertheless would encourage progress. Indeed, liberty and authority would be reconciled thanks to the possession of absolute knowledge. Faith in God was soon to be replaced by the knowledge of God. Conformity between religious revelation and philosophical truth would be achieved, the messianic promises would be realized, and the Kingdom of God would begin here below. The present opposition between practical reason, which considers the conversion of evil into good impossible, and speculative reason, which considers that conversion necessary, would be ended. In the historical development of this absolute philosophy, Napoleon played an essential role.

Wronski's problem in "The decisive Question about Napoleon" was how to explain the immense, unanimous admiration felt for Napoleon. This admiration could hardly have had as its object some genius with purely personal ambitions. So Napoleon must have pursued "a noble and true goal, useful to men and obedient to the designs of Providence . . . opening up for humanity a new career." (The book contains very detailed genealogical tables for Napoleon and his relatives; according to Wronski, the presence of Napoleon's blood in the royal houses of Europe is conclusive proof of his providential genius.) This "noble and true goal" toward which Napoleon directed his efforts is his "political secret" which is the "basis of the moral future of the world." Faced with the spectacle of a France where politics, philosophy, religion, and morals have been reduced to nothing by the doctrines of the Revolution and by "the existence of an invisible band of mysterious men," and yet aware that humanity had arrived at the threshold of the age of liberty, Napoleon recognized that in the interest of political order a ponderation of laws, liberty, and coercion had to be created, counterbalancing the anarchic influence of liberty by giving law a superior force, a divine quality (here I am paraphrasing Wronski); he understood that political authority is the representation of the divinely created moral laws. To make France a truly great nation, it was necessary to add to "the national sovereignty of human law" the "moral sovereignty of divine law"; this is what Napoleon accomplished when he declared himself "Emperor of the French by the grace of God and by the constitutions of the Empire." This explains the importance of the Concordat and of Napoleon's coronation, which was "a physical expression of the divine origin and human application of his sovereign authority." Wronski like Beauterne emphasizes Napoleon's "incontestable piety" (1853, p. 30). Yet there is an important difference between him and Beauterne for, according to Wronski, Napoleon also understood that it was necessary to replace simple faith by rational conviction, and, although he did not have the necessary philosophical training to create that conviction, the lonely exile of Saint Helena was at least on the right track when he underlined the practical value of religion.

What Wronski is proposing is less a new version of the divine right of kings than an original synthesis of the theory of the king's "two bodies." According to Wronski, Napoleon successfully realized this union in his own person and thus created "the rational union in a double sovereign personality." Thanks to this conception, Napoleon preserved the moral equilibrium of Europe; for instance, he rejected Talleyrand's project of allowing Austria (Catholic, the divine principle) to conquer Prussia (Protestant, the human principle).

Wronski offers three explanations for Napoleon's failure and fall from power: a regrettable "chivalrous loyalty" which weakened his power; then the "infernal plot" of an " invisible band of evil men," a conspiracy that Wronski associates with the Antichrist; finally, and above all, Napoleon lacked "the great illumination which Messianism is now providing and especially its concentration in the Absolute Union," this new moral union or association of men which will combat the "invisible band of evil men." In short, what he lacked was the theories of Wronski and his disciples. Nonetheless, says Wronski,

> We must distinguish between the REVOLUTIONARY ERA, made up of the three following phases: the Republic, the Restoration, and the "juste milieu" where the people have been led onto this dangerous path of the critical period, and the NAPOLEONIC ERA, where they were taken away from this dangerous path and led onto the salutary path of a new and decisive period in the progress of mankind. Thus we can proclaim that Napoleon was at one and the same time both a NEW SAVIOR and a LAST REFORMER of humanity. (pp. 114–15)

He merits a tomb at the Vatican, but Providence instead has given him a tomb isolated in the middle of the ocean, so that it can serve as a cynosure for the eyes of all humanity.

Although Napoleon plays a very providential role in this philosophy of history, two essential elements of Napoleonic messianism are not present here, though they are widespread elsewhere. One is the identification of the voice of Napoleon with the voice of the people and of Christ; the other, the association of Waterloo and Golgotha, the reading of Napoleon's defeat as a necessary prelude to the Resurrection of the Christ-People. It is perhaps an oversimplification to say that Wronski synthesizes in the messianic framework the two figures of the "devout Napoleon" and Napoleon as he who continued and propagated the Revolution of 1789, but his thought could stand some simplification.

❦ Jesus Christ is our defense since he is the father and source of all light which God allows to descend to this earth; and in this work he is, after God, the first agent. Afterward come the great cherubim, the holy armies of spirits. As for us, we constitute, thanks to the divine Will, the last echelon of this glorious column; above all, we are its orifice, by which the divine invisible force will be visibly manifested on earth. And you, spirit of Napoleon, by a special privilege, you are the next to the last in this holy column. To you it is given to live, to act on earth, without ceasing to be a pure spirit; to you it is given to unite yourself and bring your aid to your terrestrial instruments, so that your nation may recognize you, and, accustomed to your direction, desirous of that direction, it may accomplish the work prescribed by the Lord, as it has pleased the Lord to manifest thereby his most holy will and his dispositions. . . .

Toast to Napoleon. May the mercy of the Lord, pardon and rest, and prompt union be upon us! O spirit, dear to us, of a hero, brother, colleague, and cooperator in the holy work; o thou, enlightened master, knowing better than we the decrees of the Lord in favor of this world; thou who, after twenty years of suffering, by divine permission, in this moment sharest in our solemn assurance (and calm those concerns which consume thee, o dear shade!) that we shall do everything in our power to be docile toward thy inspirations and follow the direction to which thou art nearest, the will of God, a direction in which thou shalt lead us for the joy, rest, and salvation of thy spirit.

These two rather strange texts are from André Towiansky's *Cène* or *Banquet* (1850) and were supposedly pronounced for the first time in the presence of General Skrzynecki, the former head of the Polish insurrection, 17 January 1841, during a paraliturgical ceremony which took place at the Gros Caillou farmhouse on the battlefield of Waterloo. Towiansky had fled from Poland shortly before, and after a pilgrimage that took him to Eylau, Friedland, Leipzig, Bautzen, and Dresden, managed to arrive in Paris the very day that Napoleon's ashes did, 15 December 1840. Towiansky then went to Waterloo on "a retreat," which culminated in the revelations and ceremonies of the *Banquet*. He already knew, since 1836, that he had been called to become the one who would realize the "Work of Mercy," but the public life of the Work, if one may call it that, did not begin until 1841. He returned shortly thereafter to Paris, met Mickiewicz, and cured Mickiewicz's wife of a crisis of madness. The great exiled poet, then a professor at the Collège de France, recognized in Towiansky the prophet of the salvation of the world, and, on 27 September after a mass at Notre Dame attended by the Polish colony in exile, Towiansky announced the "Work of God," the salvation of the world by Poland, and revealed the great role that Napoleon played in all this. On 8 December, the feast of the Immaculate Conception, he had the icon of Our Lady of Ostrabrama installed at Saint Séverin, where it remains to this day, and those who lived nearby noted that the following night a strange glow marked the sky above the church. This shrine became the place where the faithful consecrated themselves to the Work.

Like many a prophet, Towiansky was subjected to persecution. In 1842 he was banished from Paris, according to him at the request of the archbishop. He first went to Avignon, still in those years a major center of Martinist Illuminism, before meeting Vintras, the advocate of the thesis that the French clockmaker Naundorf was Louis XVII (Vintras also claimed to have had a vision announcing Towiansky's arrival in France). Towiansky traveled to Rome where the pope refused to receive him; the pope also put the *Banquet* on the Index Librorum Prohibitorum. The prophet later was expelled from Lausanne, returned to Paris for the Revolution of 1848, but was arrested in June and spent some time in jail. Freed, apparently because of Edgar Quinet's intervention, Towiansky ended his days in Switzerland where he died 13 May 1878, with some of his disciples around him. Indeed, the Work continued at least until 1912, when Mme W. Szerlecka published three volumes on *Towiansky: Un saint des temps modernes,* although her work tended to deemphasize the less orthodox aspects of his thought. His ideas were analyzed in greater detail by H. Desmettre, *Towiansky et le messianisme polonais* (1947), and in the writings of Mickiewicz, who made no secret of how much he owed to Towiansky for his messianic ideas and his conception of Napoleon.

If Towiansky is manifestly a source for some of Mickiewicz's ideas, it is somewhat more difficult to determine what his sources were; indeed, he readily admitted that he could never manage to finish a book (Desmettre, p. 216). Towiansky was very familiar with the various mystical, Illuminist, particularly apocalyptic schools that flourished in the first half of the century; indeed, he seems to have preferred reading about and meditating on the life of Jesus in the version provided by the visionary Anne-Catherine Emmerich rather than in the Gospels. He surely knew the writing of Louis-Claude de Saint-Martin, the "unknown philosopher," which were widely read in Russia and in Poland, as he also knew the millenarian thought of such German Pietists as Johann Jung-Stilling and Nicolaus Kirchberger. Lamennais's *Words of a Believer* clearly marked both his style and his apocalyptic vision, but there he and Lamennais were perhaps indebted to Mickiewicz's *Polish Pilgrim.* According to Desmettre, Towiansky also owed a great deal to other Polish sources, especially for his Napoleonic messianism. Polish patriots had placed all their hopes of national restoration in the hero who had attacked Russia, and this admiration soon became a kind of cult both among Polish Free Masons and among certain Illuminist groups. Especially at Wilno, "Judeo-Christian sects were organized and consecrated to Napoleon as Messiah or as the precursor of the Messiah a cult which borrowed its rites from various esoteric liturgies."[9] From 1822 on, the rumor spread in these circles that Napoleon was not really dead, but would reappear as Savior. These elucubrations seem to have had their effect not only on Towiansky, but also on the young Mickiewicz who early began signing his name "Adam-Napoleon," and on General Skryznecki, the companion of the epiphany of Gros Caillou. The general wrote to Montalembert, on 15 December 1835:

> Try to understand Napoleon and the Christ—the force, the action, the energy of the former; the purity, the charity of the latter. The images of

these two should be in your library, facing your desk. (I. N. S., *Montalem-bert et sa correspondance inédite avec Skryznecki*, 1903)

This text already contained in a nutshell Towiansky's Napoleonic messianism. Although, like so many other Romantics, Towiansky accepted the old Montanist heresy and believed that there is a divine spark within each of us which alone allows us to understand the universe and its history; although, like Ballanche and so many others, he was a believer in palingenesis, the universal renewal, and in the purifying role of suffering; and although he located the Kingdom here below and even proposed a cycle of seven periods of liberation that must be traversed before that Kingdom comes, he was also representative of the period in his cult of action and energy, which he combined with these various mystical convictions about humanity and history. For him, the Incarnation was the process by which the logos, the will of God, entered into body and spirit so that we might understand the economy of humankind's perfection on this earth. "God created you so that your spirit could live in the body, in order that, by this life, the logos of God, until now living only in the spirit, might be lived by you on earth, as it was lived by Our Lord and Savior. . . . The sacrifice of the spirit by itself, prayer by itself, does not suffice; one must also accomplish the sacrifice of the body and of action" (Szerlecka, 2:19, 24). Thus, Towiansky announced the Work of God in the strictest sense; we should be workers, with our body and our spirit, to create the Kingdom, just as Jesus accomplished the work of sacrifice with his body as well as with his spirit. "The sacrifice of Jesus understood, accepted and reproduced, accomplished by man, saves man" (3:46). In his quarrel with Vintras, Towiansky maintained that one must be concerned with this world, here below, and not just be satisfied with visions of the world above.

Perhaps it is an oversimplification, but the religion of the French Romantics can be interpreted as a kind of tension between the two poles of Quietism and Activism, between an absolute practice of refusing the will as far as the world is concerned, and a desire to realize the divine will in this world. One could say that two Slavic authors, Mme de Krüdener and Towiansky, best represented these two tendencies. If one adds to Towiansky's Activism his thesis that our imitation of Christ is necessarily, in our premillenarian period, imperfect, and that after death we must expiate those imperfections, one easily understands his Napoleonic messianism—which simultaneously proposes a mystical cult of the emperor and unhesitantly criticizes certain aspects of his politics. But Towiansky indeed made Napoleon the object of the Romantic cult of the messianic, salvific hero and of the cult of action, and the emperor thus becomes the emissary of God, his annointed one. France had received from God the holy vocation of stimulating Christian progress in our world, but France did not heed the call, and denatured the divine will, so God, in his mercy, sent Napoleon to destroy France's lethargy, the "leprosy inherited from Louis XIV":

> The hero bearing the thought of God appeared, as great as the world because of the force of that thought which was being accomplished. . . . But soon thereafter, having turned his spirit to the things of this world, this hero lost his primitive purity, ceased to offer to God his pure intention of serving God; he began to follow the worldly way, and only that way, and so the arm of God abandoned him, his star began to pale and finally was extinguished at Waterloo; his Christian mission was interrupted. Thus this thought, this will of God, this idea Napoleon brought for France and by France for the world, was only accomplished in part. (Szerlecka, 1:31)

On Saint Helena, Napoleon recognized his sin, repented that he had not accomplished his mission, and began his penitence. After his death, God, in his mercy, had pity on him and allowed the spirit of Napoleon to take up once more its interrupted mission. In that way, Napoleon fulfilled his vocation in the other world, serving Jesus faithfully and calling us to serve him. But Napoleon's spirit was oppressed by the fact that the will of God for the French nation had not been accomplished; his spirit will remain oppressed until the day when France satisfies the desires of God. This is the idea behind the strange "Toast" that Towiansky offered to the shade of Napoleon on the battlefield of Waterloo. Napoleon, the annointed messenger of God, continues in heaven the messianic task he began, and then betrayed, during his earthly career.

❦ Towiansky's theses would only have been known among the group of Polish émigrés in Paris, were it not for the activity of Adam Mickiewicz. Mickiewicz was also an exile, but as a professor at the Collège de France in 1842–43 he gave a series of lectures on "the official Church and messianism" (reproduced in *Cours de littérature slave*, 1860, vol. 5). These lectures were attended by an enthusiastic crowd and created ripples, even waves, not only in French literary circles but also in the Chamber of Deputies. Mickiewicz maintained that the activity of the logos, Jesus, is permanent in history and continues today. Moreover, this activity takes material form, "not by lightning bolts and clouds, but by the apostles and martyrs, by men in flesh and blood" (p. 145). In this series of apostles and martyrs Napoleon plays quite a special role, which Mickiewicz defined, borrowing both from Beauterne and from Towiansky. He quoted Beauterne's theses, particularly focusing on the admiration that Napoleon supposedly felt for Jesus as a mesmerizer, as a magnetic influence, and he attributed to Napoleon the statement that "I have the gift of electrifying men, but the further away from me they get, the more they lose that force." Such was not the case for the disciples of Jesus—which proves that Jesus was more than a man. Mickiewicz associated Jesus' "electric force" and the messianic inspiration which urges us to act, to accomplish the Work that Towiansky describes (at that particular moment in history, the liberation of Poland), that blood of inspiration which makes us live and act. "To speak in a modern way, he who has received the divine spark, and has kept it in his soul, will feel develop there what Napoleon called the foyer of electricity" (p. 107). Napoleon understood, on Saint Helena, and began to realize, even before his fall and exile, the electric, messianic inspiration:

> From the depths of catholicism came Napoleon, the most complete man of the last epoch, the one who completely realized that epoch in his person, and went beyond it by his genius. . . . He is not only yours, Frenchmen; yes, he is Italian, he is Polish, he is Russian, he is the man of the globe, the most complete man. (P. 202)

This notion explained the admiration, the adulation, that the masses felt for him, that *vox dei* of workers and peasants who knew how to recognize the Messiah: "Visit the workers in their garrets, the French peasants in their cabins, and the Polish peasants in their huts. What religious objects do you find there? What emblems? What names? First you find the crucifix, which represents in résumé all the past, and then the figure of the Emperor, the symbol of force" (p. 242). The nations have suspected that Napoleon was embarked on a secret work, which neither pope nor priests understood; that he, better than they, understood the will of God, that he could help the peoples enter into the Kingdom of Power and Joy, the

Kingdom of the Gospel. Surely these praises by the author of *Pan Tadeuz* reflect an immense and long-founded admiration for Napoleon as someone who spread the Revolution throughout Europe, liberated Poland, who by his conquests united the nations.[10] Napoleon was the logos of the age. But alas, like Alexander, like Caesar, he betrayed his mission, fell into the "errors of the spirit" (p. 203). During the expiation of his exile he became aware of those errors, however. And the destiny of France remains that of continuing the work of Napoleon—of France, and of Poland, the "crucified" nation above any other nation.

> Napoleon and Waterloo! If, by the invocation of these two names it has been given to us to sense that at this moment one and the same spirit moves us, we have communed in spirit, we have celebrated one of the mysteries of the New Testament. Such a communion is a spiritual eucharist; there, for the first time these words were pronounced, the last I speak to you. (P. 300)

And Mickiewicz repeated, in conclusion, the text from Towiansky's *Banquet* quoted at the beginning of this chapter, while aides distributed to the enthusiastic audiences lithographs depicting Napoleon as the "magistrate of the logos." We have a description of the lithograph, written by Gérard de Nerval:

> Napoleon is there represented wearing the veil and the augur's crown, moving his finger along a globe of the world, tracing new divisions. The following legend is inscribed on this rather singular sheet: "Moving further toward Divine truth, ever stronger in order to make that truth real, he consumates what he began." Above the image, another text reads: "The magistrate of the logos in front of the logos."[11]

Before discussing Nerval's version of Napoleonic mysticism, another current of this messianism, this one more purely French, must be discussed.

❦ The Evadists, the Mapah Ganneau and his disciple Caillaux, were also adepts of Napoleonic messianism. Evadism, a rather strange mixture of Swedenborgianism, occultism, and the old dream of androgyny, placed in the center of its creed the belief in the hermaphroditic nature of the divinity, appropriately named Mapah. The movement also reiterated some of the themes of mystic socialism. In 1840 Caillaux published *L'Arche de la nouvelle alliance,* an exposition of their doctrine. The third Song (the text is divided into Songs) announces that the hour of the future, the hour of bread whiter than snow and of eternal peace, is at hand. It proclaims the reign of the Eve-Adam, the great crucified woman, the return to the primitive unity shattered by the Fall. Caillaux adds that the Alpha and Omega of this story of salvation is Eve who gave birth in pain and then Liberty who appeared in 1789 to crush the serpent under her feet, Liberty incarnate in the "people France." He exclaims:

> O France! O Liberty! Put on your most beautiful garments! With your disciples, empty the chalice of farewells; and make your way toward that Calvary where the liberation of the world is to be sealed! . . . What is the name of the hill you are climbing? . . . Waterloo! (P. 115)

Caillaux states that the disciple of this New Alliance, preaching fraternity to the world, must be ready to "seal with his blood the truths he proclaims," that is, to imitate Christ's sacrifice to validate the message of liberation. The Song ends with a vision both fantastic and historical, in which a ship is supported by the summits of three mountains, Golgotha, Mount Saint John at Waterloo, and Saint Helena. The central mast is topped by a five-branched cross on which a woman is dying; on each branch is one of the five parts of the world, and the head of the cross rests on Europe. Over that head a legend reads: "France: 18 June 1815: Good Friday." This tableau is followed by an image of hope, where "the same woman appeared again, but transfigured and radiant. She was removing the entry stone of a sepulchre, on which was written 'Restoration, days of the tomb, 29 July 1830, Easter.' " Finally, accompanied by her betrothed she ascends toward heaven. The figure of Napoleon, a Christ figure who incarnates France as prophetess of Liberty, nourishes this whole poetical-religious vision. Here again, the identification of Napoleon with Christ presupposes that Napoleon continued and propagated 1789; but the event that counts is Waterloo.[12]

Another Evadist text about Napoleon appeared in 1843, the poem *Waterloo: A vous beaux fils de France, morts pour l'honneur, salut et gratification! Qu'est-ce que l'Honneur? L'Honneur, c'est l'Unité!* Anonymous but published by the "Office of Evadian publications," the poem also has a lengthy subtitle:

> Good Friday. They said, the vanquished of Waterloo, yes, vanquished!— like Socrates by the hemlock! Yes, vanquished!—like Christ on Golgotha! Name of the Abysses in the depths of which is written Nothingness or Regeneration.

This subtitle may seem obscure; indeed the theses of the poem are rather complex. First, there is the idea that the abyss of suffering and death leads to regeneration. Death is not the tomb, but the cradle of a greater life; Christ underwent Golgotha and the Crucifixion before he knew the Resurrection, and in the same way France, the people of God, has been crucified. Thus "WATERLOO IS THE GOLGOTHA-PEOPLE. WATERLOO IS THE GOOD FRIDAY OF THE GREAT CHRIST-PEOPLE." At Waterloo, in the name of and by the blood of the French people, "the Christ-People died for the salvation of all People." Moreover, for the apostle of Evadism, the Napoleon-People is a Christ in the sense that it proclaimed unity:

> He who stands up for Unity and dies for Unity is the Son of God, is the people of God.
>
> There was a man by the name of Jesus, who stood up and said, "All men are Brothers," and men crucified him.
>
> There is a people by the name of France, who stood up and said, "All Peoples are Brothers," and the Peoples crucified her.

The Napoleonic wars were not wars of conquest, but an effort to create unity among men under the three seals of the mystery of the Transfiguration: Liberty, Equality, Fraternity. Finally, in this effort to create unity Napoleon plays yet another role. Beginning with the sons of Adam, humanity has been divided in two, the descendants of Abel, the men of the plow, and the descendants of Cain, the men of the sword (a widespread theme, much exploited by Hugo and Nerval). That division is now disappearing, unity is being reestablished, thanks to the two Christs, Jesus and Napoleon:

> Finally, Jesus and Napoleon: Jesus, the Abel-Christ, Napoleon, the Cain-Christ, the great beacons of the centuries, the living synthesis, the sublime forms by which History has been transformed so it can return to the Unity-Adam.

One might consider these ideas rather curious, but they do allow the synthesis of the myths of Napoleon as Christ, and Napoleon as Antichrist, of the damned race; and they reconcile Abel and Cain. In short, for the Evadists Napoleon is Christ in three ways: a son of Cain, he reconciled Cain and Abel; he created a universal fraternity among all peoples; and, at Waterloo, he knew suffering and death, the prelude to universal regeneration.

The theme that Mount Saint John was the Golgotha of France found a somewhat better expression in the writings of Alphonse Esquiros, a polygraph advocate of socialism, feminism, and the kind treatment of the insane. In 1834, in a volume entitled *Les Hirondelles,* he published a poem, "The Eagle," in which Napoleon, exiled on Saint Helena, sees an eagle fall and die on his rock and meditates on the similarities of their fates:

> In dyeing it with blood, I turned my military coat
> Into the purple robe of royalty. The English and the Cossacks
> Each stole a piece of it.
> Like the man-God nailed on Calvary,
> I saw the kings of the earth dispute
> For pieces of my coat.
> If he is the son of lightning, they said, let him dare
> Descend from the cross and drag in the dust
> The kings, the gods of humanity.
> While I, clenching my fists, foaming with rage,
> I tried, but in vain, for the storm, passing by,
> Had taken away my divinity.

In 1840, Esquiros returned to the theme in his *Evangile de la liberté,* in which, like Lamennais, Cabet, A.-L. Constant, and many others, he turned to the Gospels in order to depict a socialist, revolutionary Jesus. When he discusses the Crucifixion, he evokes the parallel between the sufferings of Christ and the defeat of revolutionary France at Waterloo:

> The royalty of Christ was, like that of France, a royalty of initiation. Humanity thus inscribes its truths and its titles in letters of blood which neither hatred nor defeat, nor the bad faith of the enemy, can thereafter destroy. After the great Passion of the crucified nation, wounded in her side by the cossack's lance, her feet bound, there remains, inscribed in red letters on the cross of Waterloo: People of France, the King of Peoples! (P. 300)

Then he introduces his lengthy poem on the Golgotha of Waterloo:

> Soon it will be thirty years that at Waterloo, the kings,
> After striking France, put her on the cross;
> Since then foreigners pass by, shaking their heads.
> Come down then, they say, you whom on a festive day
> We beheld, in towns and hamlets

Going forth in triumph in the midst of the palms!
You who put the sword in the hands of your apostles,
You who wanted to teach and free others,
Come down then from the cross! —But, with both hands nailed,
Sad, despairing about the salvation of humanity,
And about the future which disappears like a dream,
Finding only gall and vinegar on the sponge,
Sensing that the day is ending and all is finished,
France cries out, Eloi lama sabachthani!
And, Eli did not come. . . . On her solitary cross,
After a long torture (here kiss the earth),
When the veil of the temple was rent in two
She bowed her head, and, in silence, died.
A harsh cossack pierced her side with a lance;
But the others, beholding, in sad silence
The sky covered with shadows, the dead coming forth from their
    open tombs,
The earth whose surface trembled with fright,
The great sun above which hid its face
And, like a moribund, closed its eye of fire,
They said: "She was indeed the daughter of God!"
Some disciples, that night, in a corner of the kingdom,
Perfumed her body with aloe and balm
And, kissing her forehead respectfully,
Put her into a cold monument;
Mothers were there, drying their eyes.
But the kings had the tomb carefully sealed,
And the governor stationed guards about it,
Fearing the prophecy and the third day.
Christ, they say, came forth from the darkness of the tomb,
But you promised to do so, the day is now ending,
You who thirty years long fought steadfastly,
France, pierced in the side, will you resurrect?
Shall we see you one day, oh buried queen
Whom the kings guard entombed, and whom the world forgets,
Shall we see you awaken, and bursting forth from your sepulchre,
Shaking off from your shroud the dust and the insults,
Shining forth with solemn brightness,
And crushing with fright your pale sentinels
Who will all hide their faces from remorse,

Cry out: I am the Christ come from among the dead!
That day will be the day of the people's Paschal feast.
Chased like straw by the wind of our wrath,
The powers, dispersed, will go away in shreds,
The frightened prison cells will reopen their tombs,
The centurions, overwhelmed, will beat their breasts,
The old world, crumbled, will only be ruins,
And the peoples, praising God who has upheld them,
Free, clapping their hands, will say: Alleluia!

The awaited resurrection was to take place eight years later, with the Revolution of 1848, but alas did not last very long. It is noteworthy that Napoleon is never mentioned by name in this poem. For Esquiros, it is not he but France who is the Christ recrucified at Golgotha. The man-Messiah Napoleon has been integrated into a much more important myth, that of France as the Christ, the anointed nation. But, along with the Evadists, Esquiros emphasizes the motif of suffering, death, and resurrection. For Towiansky and Mickiewicz, Napoleon's messianism is revealed first by his deeds before Waterloo, and then by his expiation and his meditations on religion (as described by Beauterne) afterward; for Caillaux and Esquiros, it is rather the suffering and death at Waterloo, a prelude to a resurrection which will bring into being the utopian Kingdom, which is the seal of his messianism and justifies the comparison of Napoleon and Christ. The theme of sacrifice, the notion that out of evil, good will come, was absent in Wronski's works and only suggested by Towiansky and Mickiewicz. With Caillaux and Esquiros this theme becomes the very center of the association of Napoleon with Jesus.

The historian, however, here encounters a rather annoying chronological problem. Wronski's *Métapolitique messianique* dates from 1840; toward the end of that year Towiansky arrived in Paris for the first time. Caillaux's *Arche de la nouvelle alliance* dates from 1840, and Esquiros's rereading of the Gospels dates from that same year, the year Napoleon's ashes were brought to France. But can one talk about sources and imitations? If we suppose that in Towiansky's case there was a debt to Polish Illuminism, can we assume the same for Ganneau and his group? For Esquiros? Or are we talking about an idea, a way of thinking that was, if not widespread, at least quite common in the mystical socialist reveries of the lesser Romantics?

❦ These texts are far from the only ones to reflect the themes of Napoleon as Messiah or as the Christ. Alphonse-Louis Constant (later better known as Eliphas Lévi) should be mentioned. Constant knew Esquiros and Wronski quite well. In Constant's *Doctrines religieuses et sociales* (1841), Napoleon is identified with the Messiah:

> The revolutionary turmoil calmed down and the revolutionary idea gave birth to its Messiah. Napoleon appeared, and after chastising and frightening the kings, he chained the Pope with one hand and restored the altars with the other, and declared before the whole world that he was a Catholic. (P. 76)

Among the epics, we can mention Gaussard, a "military veteran," whose curious thirty-six-page poem *La Loi de Dieu, ou les trois grandes époques, Moïse, Jésus-Christ, Bonaparte* announces his messianic preoccupations. Gaussard, versifying the history of humanity, proclaims that when Napoleon appeared, "All cried 'Hosanna!' as in the days of the Jews, / When the Christ, the Savior, appeared among them."

Emile Debraux, in his poem "Sainte-Hélène," evokes the crown of thorns. "Ah! Could he bear for very long the chains, / He whose steps had marked the universe? / I saw his profaned head fall, / Crowned with thorns, like that of Jesus" (*Chansons complètes*, 1836, 1:61). Debraux includes a portrait of Prometheus on his rock, a parallel with Napoleon at Saint Helena that one finds in a number of other texts. In pamphlet literature, the *Résurrection de Napoléon* by J. Trullard (Dijon, 1847) is notable. The author describes a statue of Napoleon by F. Rude, and claims that Napoleon is "the Christ of the modern age, a new Messiah" (p. 16). And he proposes a number of parallels between the lives and the influences of the two. But Trullard, even if he rather recalls Mickiewicz, was a disciple of Kant (whom he translated) and he remarks that he uses the word *Messiah* "in a completely natural, entirely human sense." It is the man— Jesus or Napoleon—whose acts and deeds demonstrate an "infinite power" and who leads humanity to take "a great step forward" (p. 47). Once more, this is less a popular theme than an element in a philosophy of history.

Other texts, such as the poem "Saint Helena: Anathema and Glory" by J. Reboul, or the strange pamphlet "The Resurrection of the Emperor, or the Night of 12 December 1840," are actually anti-Napoleon. My goal here is not to compose an anthology of poetic texts on Napoleon, nor to trace the variations on the theme of Napoleon as thaumaturgist. Such texts—and there are many—often include a comparison with Jesus, for example: "Faith gave birth to miracles, and, like Christ, the Emperor healed the victims of the plague at Jaffa" (*Le Franc Maçon*, 1846, p. 100). More telling are the traces of the myth of Napoleon as Messiah among some of the important authors of the period. It is not surprising that Edgar Quinet, a good friend of Mickiewicz and the author of the best of the epic poems about Napoleon, should echo it. In his *Le Christianisme et la Révolution française* of 1845, Quinet writes:

> The only thing I saw on the Golgotha of Mount Saint John was an immense chalice filled with the tears and the blood of a great people; let us freely drink thereof, without turning aside our glance, let us empty it to its bitter dregs. For it is quite evident that that day, we were struck from above. . . . Who knows whether this death, within which we have our being, now some thirty years, was not given to us in order to renew us? Already in 1830 France rose on one knee in her sepulchre. (P. 383)

Napoleon-Christ-France suffered its Passion at Waterloo, drank the bitter cup, was put to death and went down into the tomb, but the messianic Revolution will know a resurrection.

The same theme even appears in the writings of George Sand, a very severe judge of Napoleon. In her *Lettres d'un voyageur* (1834), Sand says of him: "From my childhood on, I was fascinated, like so many others, by the force and activity of this upheaval-creating machine who has been honored with the title of 'great man,' no more nor less than Jesus." Yet this does not prevent her from attacking Napoleon immediately thereafter (p. 254). Sand associates Napoleon and Jesus again in *Le Compagnon du tour de France* (1840), where Achille says to Pierre: "You would like leaders and counselors who would combine the audacity of Napoleon and the humility of Jesus Christ. That's asking too much of human nature for any one day; and besides, if such a man came along, he would not be understood." Sand knew Mickiewicz and probably at times was influenced by him.[13] But basically Sand was as opposed to any individual messianism as she was critical of Napoleon: usually she only evoked the theme in order to refute it.

Balzac is somewhat more open, and the theme appears in the famed scene of *Le Médecin de campagne* (1833), where the old soldier offers a mythical biography of Napoleon, which contains several comparisons to Jesus. Napoleon's mother made a pact thanks to which God protected her son and her son restored religion in France. "God helped him, it's a sure thing. . . . He takes his orders from heaven. . . . That was written ahead of time for him, as it was for Jesus." The most amusing comparison is "the fact is that he was ordered to do duty in Egypt. There's another similarity with the Son of God. That isn't all." At Waterloo,

> He thought of dying; and, so that no one could look at a vanquished Napoleon, he took enough poison to kill off a regiment because, like Jesus Christ before his Passion, he thought he had been abandoned by God and by his talisman; but the poison has no effect whatever on him. Something else! he becomes immortal![14]

Balzac perhaps would have been more explicit and played up the comparison had he written the novel somewhat later. In any case, the soldier concludes, "It's not to the child of a mortal woman that God would have given the privilege of tracing his name in red as Napoleon wrote his on the face of the earth, which will never forget it."

Gérard de Nerval treats the theme in a much more complex manner; once more, Nerval shows himself to be both profoundly syncretistic and quite original in his syncretism. Jean Richer has noted and traced the weight of this theme in Nerval. What I offer here is essentially a résumé of Richer's 1964 study (*Nerval, expérience et création*, pp. 53–94). Nerval's father was a military surgeon and Nerval was brought up in the cult of Napoleon. His early poems show an interest in Napoleon; soon Nerval conceived of the emperor as a sort of new Apollo or symbol of the solar God. Then, by various arithmological calculations, and because his beloved, Sophie Dawes, died the day the emperor's ashes arrived in France; because of Gérard's meditations on his paternity; and because of an encounter with Walewski, Napoleon's illegitimate son, Nerval comes to play with the idea that he is a member of the Napoleon family, the son of Joseph, and so on. He was quite familiar with the Napoleonic messianism of Towiansky and Mickiewicz. He mentions the messianic theme three times, in *L'Artiste* in July 1844 (where he published the description of the lithograph quoted earlier), then in *La Presse* of 29 June 1845, and finally in the article "The Red Prophets," which appeared in *L'Almanach cabalistique* of 1850. Nerval's tone is rather ironic:

Indeed, we would rather fear here that we might seem to be making fun of beliefs that several very distinguished minds share; so we shall limit ourselves to calling attention to the kind of cult this sect renders to Napoleon. Humanity has certainly conceived other apotheoses which were more ridiculous. According to André Towiansky, Napoleon was the visible logos of God; but, finally refused by the obscure powers, he is now ready to come back in another form in order to complete his interrupted work. One can be fairly sure that the Chambre des Députés would say to him: "*Nescio vos,* I know you not." (*Œuvres,* Pléïade, ed. A. Béguin and J. Richer, 1974, p. 1225)

The article in *La Presse* suggests that the messianists believe that "the great man's soul, after profiting from the fact that the coffin was opened at Saint Helena, accompanied his body all the way to the Invalides and then chose the Towiansky envelope for its new home." It should be noted that in his journalism Nerval often treats somewhat ironically matters that are treated seriously in his poetic texts.

Nerval surely knew the Pérès text, not in the original edition, but probably as it was reproduced in an illustrated lithograph published in Lyon in 1840, entitled "One Day in the Reign of Napoleon or the Sun Personified," which Richer reproduces in his volume. It is probably there that Nerval found the parallel between Napoleon and Apollo and their mothers, Laetitia and Latone (both names mean "light"). Finally, in the article in *La Presse,* he mentions Mapah Ganneau and his disciple Caillaux; he does not explicitly discuss their theses about Napoleon, but he certainly knew of them, for he had read *L'Arche de la nouvelle alliance.* So, situated at the confluence of three currents of Napoleonic messianism, Nerval then developed his own theories about himself as the King of Rome, and so forth. And the theme then becomes expressed in his sonnets, including "Tête armée" and the version of "Horus" known as "A Louise d'Or . . . reine":

Napoleon calls me, the new spirit calls me,
I have donned for him the robe of Cybele,
He is my husband Hermes and my brother Osiris!
The Goddess had fled on her guilded conch shell,
The sea reflected for us her adored image,
And the skies were radiant with Iris' scarf.

In this version of the poem, Napoleon figures at one end of the Nervalian series of messiahs, and the goddess's flight is surely as much inspired by the lithograph borrowed from Pérès as it is by, say, Botticelli's painting of the birth of Venus.

The story does not end there, for the theme of Napoleon as a messiah continues well into the twentieth century. In *Ame de Napoléon* (1912), Léon Bloy takes up the motif enthusiastically, in his own mystical vein. Echoes of the apocalyptic themes of 1840 are still to be found:

> Napoleon is the face of God in the darkness. . . . Napoleon is unexplainable, and, in all probability, the most unexplainable of men, because he is, before all and above all, the prefiguration of HE who is to come and who is perhaps not far off, a prefigurer and a precursor near to us. (P. 8)

Nowhere is the parallel of Napoleon and Jesus more lengthily presented than in the remarkable *Napoléon* of Elie Faure. This book, published in 1921, inspired Abel Gance's film *Napoleon*. The book is structured on a comparison of the two figures:

> From a moral point of view, Napoleon is surely the Antichrist, as the disciples of Christ conceived of the Antichrist. And yet, in the depths of reality, he is closer to Christ, surely, than was the most powerful of his disciples, for I do not know two men, among all the men who have existed on this earth, who were further from St. Paul than Jesus and Napoleon. . . . Jesus and Napoleon acted out their dreams, instead of dreaming about their actions. . . . Alone, among all men, these two dared. Dared to the point of martyrdom. Dared to the point of death. (P. 10)

In Faure's book, one encounters once again the Evadist theme of Napoleon as he who reconciled Christ and Antichrist, and Towiansky's theme of Napoleon and Christ as the messiahs of energy and action.[15] This enduring myth survives today in the well-known Corsican anthem, composed by J. F. Costa in 1848, the "Ajaccienne":

> Awaken, o sacred city,
> In your pride and in your love;
> The Holy Family has returned,
> The exiles have come home.
> Oh! here they are, victory, victory!
> May he be feasted in his home,

The prodigal child of glory,
Napoleon, Napoleon!
Between France and Italy,
These two mothers of Ajaccio,
The one who sings and the other who prays,
It was here, the new Rome
That on the day of the Assumption
Once again God was made man,
Napoleon, Napoleon!

❦ As extreme and surprising as it may seem, it would be wrong to dismiss this Napoleonic messianism as an insignificant and meaningless eccentricity. It not only entered the popular mind, but it also represents a symptomatic case of political messianism, of that secularization of religious values and themes so pronounced and widespread in the nineteenth century. This phenomenon has been analyzed in a number of ways. J. L. Talmon's *Political Messianism: The Romantic Phase* (London, 1960) suggests that this messianism leads to a paradox in which the conviction that history possesses meaning is transformed into a cult of the *law* which is incarnate in an individual, and ends up dogmatizing nationalism, turning it into a religion. Thus messianism, if it begins as a product of the "mystical socialists" on the left, becomes, for example, via its caricature in Napoleon III, a manifestation of the fascist right, preparing the way for a cult of a Hitler or a Mussolini. We have seen how in France the idea of Napoleon as Messiah is transformed into the idea of France as the messiah of nations; Wronski's political absolutism is indeed disquieting. Talmon derives from the phenomenon an argument in favor of liberalism and diversity. Another interpretation could see the phenomenon as a justification of the thesis that one must destroy religion if one does not want the state to become a religion—or that if one destroys established religion, the state may well become a religion in its stead.

Yet another analysis is possible according to the theses proposed by Henri Desroche in *Socialisme et sociologie religieuse* (1965, esp. pp. 119–42 and 409–27). Desroche distinguishes between two sorts of religious content, one that affirms and attests established social structures and symbols, and another that contests or negates those structures and symbols. From this point of view, Napoleonic messianism could rather be read as a questioning of Louis-Philippe's regime, a rebuke of a bourgeois France which had betrayed the principles of 1789, a protestation about the plight of Poland, captive and enslaved. Above all, these texts reveal an effort to give sense to suffering, even to violence, insofar as they are centered on the comparison of Waterloo and Golgotha and on the hope of a resurrection of revolutionary values.[16] In that way, these eccentrics offer a portrait of "a world which possesses a dream."

# 4 🍎 Pastiches of Lamennais's
## *Words of a Believer*

*The Words of a Lady Believer, The Words of Another Believer, The Words of a Seer, The Words of a Misbeliever, The Believer and His Words, Some More Words of a Believer, The Words of a Man, The Words of Providence*—and there are a great many other texts which by their titles create a contract with the reader asking that they be read in dialogue with F. Lamennais's *Words of a Believer* (1834). This "second degree" literature in turn gives rise to a "third degree" literature studying it: Eugène Lerminier's catalogue of the refutations and pastiches in the *Revue des deux mondes* was published on 1 September 1834. Jules Lechavalier's article in *Revue du progrès social,* and some amusing texts by Alphonse Viollet are two more examples.[1] Quérard gathered a bibliography of this literary event, Vulliaud undertook a succinct study of the quarrel that Lamennais's little book created.[2] I am principally interested here in the pastiches and parodies of Lamennais's *Words,* rather than the refutations of a Bautain or a Lacordaire, or the appreciations of a Sainte-Beuve.

It is difficult to categorize these pastiches. Gérard Genette's *Palimpsestes* suggests how varied and complicated this literary phenomenon, in which a hypotext such as *The Words of a Believer* produces hypertexts via various forms of direct transformation, can be in contrast, say , to more simple imitation, in which a hypertext uses a generic model in adapting the hypotext.[3] Some texts that participated in the quarrel about the *Words of a Believer* also use this latter technique—for instance, La Gracerie's *Words of a Catholic Conciliator,* which transforms Lamennais in reformulating him but also clearly imitates Ballanche's *Vision d'Hébal.* I shall return to this problem of sources or confluences, for it has significant implications for literary history and for the history of political discourse.

When we look at these texts in the light of Genette's observations, certain traits become evident. If the transformations take place by several procedures (I shall try to demonstrate their variety), these are generally pastiches, and not parodies or travesties or satirical exaggerations. There is little if any change in stylistic level; such a change, by introducing a degree of vulgarity, could invite a reading as parody. When such a change does take place, it seems to have been the result of a stylistic insufficiency or incompetence on the part of the author, some of whom are anonymous and many are clearly not professional writers. The temptation to say that parody by exaggeration would be impossible when dealing with a text such as Lamennais's *Words*, whose style is already quite extreme, should be resisted. In fact, such exaggerations do exist, but they are found in the critical, polemic discourse about Lamennais's text, and not in the imitations of it. Viollet (*The Answer*, p. 4), for instance, invents this letter from Lamennais to Mlle Le Bot, the author of the *Words of a Lady Believer:*

> Dear good Miss, believe me, despite the screams of the sectarians, the concerted furors of the mystical energumens, the flat invectives of the doctors, I am incapable of committing even the smallest intemperate use of language. . . . But in my quality as Breton and Believer, I shall face the storm with the masculine energy of a man, with the profound conviction of divine aid. Soon, I like to believe, I shall prove to this world that, like inflamed lava, my name will streak the heavens in flames of fire, that it will be horrible to call the *Words of a Believer* a work of darkness when it is a work of light. And if this work has not shone for everyone with the brilliance which is its own, we shall work together to open the eyes of the blind, and to throw back at the unbelievers those sharp-edged blows which they have tried to pierce us with.

The intent of Viollet's book is not clear; he attacks Lamennais, but he also attacks such critics of Lamennais as Madrolle. On the other hand, the intent of the pastiches is always clear; they espouse, correct, or refute, for obvious and explicit reasons, Lamennais's *Words*. Thus they do not enter into Genette's category of parody; they belong to the domain of serious polemic, and not of satire (there are, of course, exceptions; Madrolle is at times sarcastic and elsewhere practices serious pastiche). This explains the absence of any comic elements, at least intended ones.

These pastiches offer a striking contrast to another hypertextual literature I have studied, the revolutionary liturgies of 1789.[4] Both literary forms consciously mix religious and political discourse, but in the revolutionary liturgies this combination aims at and produces a comic effect, a satire with many different targets. This makes it difficult to determine what the ideological stance of the text is, although there is almost always some kind of attack on religion. In these pastiches, on the other hand, the religious element—no matter what the political convictions of the author may be—is introduced as supporting and justifying the political message. In short—and this phenomenon requires explanation—Lamennais's text was hardly satirized at all; rather, others espoused and borrowed, with varying success, its content, language, style, or at least some aspects of the style, even its episodes, to say something else, or, in some cases, even to reiterate what Lamennais was saying.

I cannot describe all these texts (there are more than thirty of them), but I shall try to indicate their major points, arranging them according to the increasing degree of their formal and stylistic difference from Lamennais's text. I shall not classify them in terms of their ideological difference, for the degree of literary resemblance to the model does not correlate in any meaningful way with the degree of ideological agreement or difference between these pastiches and Lamennais's text. For example, the anonymous *Words of a Believer by Fr. F. de La Mennais When He Was a Believer* was presented, to use another of Genette's categories, as a forgery. The subtitle indicates that this text was retranslated into French from an Italian translation by a canon of Aosta. The preface explains that Lamennais, when he first wrote the text, had no "intention of composing a work of seduction and scandal." Later, he fell victim to the devils of vengeance and wrath and changed his text; but the original manuscript purportedly has been found, with its erasures, blocking outs, additions, and so on. To facilitate matters, the anonymous author used italics for the texts of the *Ur-Paroles*. The text follows Lamennais, chapter by chapter; in some cases no change is made from what Lamennais published and in others the chapters are completely redone. Most often, a positive sentence is turned into a negative, or a polar substitution of a noun or adjective is proposed, "bad" is replaced by "good," and so forth. The text is both a forgery and a tracing, but the tracing often reverses what Lamennais says.[5]

*The Words of a Believer, Reviewed, Corrected, and Augmented by a Catholic,* by J. Vrindts, uses a somewhat more subtle technique; it is perhaps the most successful of these pastiches. It imitates Lamennais's style, reproduces several of his parables and even chapters, sometimes comments on them critically, sometimes revises them to offer his own version of Lamennais's visions. The text is more a rewriting than a tracing, but remains close to the original in its style, plan, and content, while proposing a message that contradicts Lamennais.

*The Religious and Political Meditations of an Exile,* by Mgr Paul Tharin, former bishop of Strasbourg who chose exile in 1830, spends a chapter on the "fallen genius" Lamennais. He revises the scene of the seven kings, the chapters on the problem of civil and military obedience, and so on; his style keeps the verset form, but other chapters contain material not found in Lamennais, such as a hymn to the Virgin. Tharin's work is a partial pastiche as far as content goes, but it suppresses much from Lamennais and adds its own material. Many of the texts considered here are situated somewhere between Vrindts's and Tharin's techniques.

The degree of pastiche varies a great deal in the *Words of Providence* of Clarisse Vigoureux, a Fourierist; the pastiche element is considerable at the beginning of the book and in certain chapters (always short, and composed of versets), but it is in evidence elsewhere. She, like Lamennais, describes visions, writes anaphoric litanies, and liberally sprinkles the text with biblical allusions, but, especially when she expounds Fourierist doctrine, her style is much less didactic. The *Words of a Lady Believer* of Mlle Le Bot imitates Lamennais's style and form at the beginning and end of the text, but otherwise varies considerably. In other cases, the brochure claims to be a refutation, but then suddenly takes on the form of a pastiche—for example, Bouvier's *The Book, a Vision* begins with a vision that is manifestly a pastiche of Lamennais, but otherwise it only practices stylistic imitation, primarily by the excessive use of synonymy. The dream vision appears in a great many texts that initially claim to be refutations. On the other hand, Harro Harring's *Words of a Man Dedicated to the Believer of Lamennais,* despite its title, does not imitate Lamennais's style, offers no visions, and eschews Lamennais's parables. Rather, it uses the form of the *credo*, but for political purposes, to propose theses and ideas that are very close to those of Lamennais. Finally, Augustin Chaho's *Words of a Seer* does offer a kind of comic parody, in versets, in which Chaho expresses his theory about Jesus as an emblem of the sun. Yet he often attacks Lamennais: "The believer seems very convinced of the existence of the three divine persons and of the trinity of IAO; he has completely drowned his reason in the three oceans of the infinite unity." Chaho, a disciple of Nodier and advocate of the superiority of the Basque people, possessed gifts for fantasy which are rather lacking among most of Lamennais's imitators.[6]

This sketch of the gamut of imitative practices is necessarily incomplete. Other forms, for instance Vidal's *Words of a Catholic,* attempt a pastiche of Lamennais but quickly fall into what was then described as "unction," the virtue most sought after by preachers. Milon de Villiers's *Words of a Disbeliever* follows the form of quotation and refutation, but the style of the quotations from Lamennais begins to contaminate the refutation texts; one is tempted to conclude that Lamennais's style and form were extremely contagious. It is worth repeating that there is no clear relation between the polemical function of the texts and the form of imitation. If the anonymous *Words of a Thinker* accepts almost all of Lamennais's political theses and clearly tries to imitate his style, the author is less successful at imitation than Vrindts, who attacks almost everything Lamennais says while imitating both his style and his content. Disciples and enemies, on the left and on the right, Catholics, Protestants, and unbelievers all use the same techniques.

The quite distinct style of the *Words* was already analyzed, well before Yves Le Hir, by the Maidservant in the *Profession of Faith* (p. 7): "That is a very beautiful book, a holy book. . . . This gentleman is clearly a prophet; it always begins with *and, and* and then *the Son of man,* and then thunder, and then visions, and then swords, and then blood."[7] To imitate Lamennais, authors of these pastiches borrow the verset form, then the anaphoric elements, the refrains, the repetitions (especially at the beginning of each verset), and finally the synonymy of modifiers and verb complements. Biblical copula and the phrase "And I beheld" pepper the texts. Yet, and I do not know how to explain this, the verse texts written during the controversy created by the *Words*—whether it be Mercier's versification of the text, which alas I shall be obliged to quote, or the poems against Lamennais by Aloysius Huber, Victor Davin, Mme d'Arbouville, A. H. de La Haye—do not manage to accomplish a pastiche of his style. It would seem that measured verse could not, at least in 1834, express subjective and violent political conviction. Finally, as shall be seen, not everyone who wanted to write like Lamennais succeeded in doing so; some of the efforts at pastiche are rather pitiful; they end up as bombast or highly artificial. But what these texts make clear is that the *Words* was a book that had to be refuted but also imitated.

❦ A study of how these texts treat matters of ideology and political belief explains why the content of the *Words* was disputed while its style was imitated. Take the problem of nature. Lamennais's many parables using animals, bees, and so on provoked a quarrel about biology. On the one hand, the debate questioned the "Chateaubriand" tradition—the harmonies of nature show forth God—and on the other hand it questioned the old commonplaces of revolutionary and antirevolutionary discourse. The conservative refutations refuse to accept Lamennais's biological analogies, either by simply rejecting them, or else by contradicting Lamennais's statements about animals and hence his claim that liberty and equality are natural. Ponchon is sardonic: "Stop calling on brute beasts to support your system" (*The Believer and His Words*, p. 27), and Milon de Villiers rejects all these comparisons between humans and animals as false and devoid of reason. Others accept that the kingdom of nature may be bountiful, but deny that this bounty can be found in the society of men. *The Words of a Believer When He Was a Believer* notes that birds and insects do not unite to oppose the law that governs them, but rather offer a model of obedience to the laws of providence, a model men would do well to imitate. Ortolan distinguishes between human beings, who are guilty of original sin and therefore must work and suffer, and the happy natural kingdom. Enjelvas, clearly an admirer of Chateaubriand, proposes that nature, unlike unfaithful man, praises the Lord. Vigoureux shows how the animal world illustrates, not the equality Lamennais claims to find there, but the Fourierist law that attractions are proportionate to destinies. Conservative texts underline the corruption of the world of nature which belies both Lamennais's biology and his political philosophy. The *Critical Examination* details the avidity and covetousness of animals, *Some More Words* proposes that physical, moral, and intellectual inequality are of the very essence of nature, contrasting Hercules with a man bedridden with pain. Tharin in his *Meditations* echoes a venerable antiegalitarian discourse with a series of contrasts, reed/poplar, violet/rose, gazelle/lion, and sees therein a justification for the hereditary nature of political office. He concludes, "My children, be content with the station to which Divine Providence calls you by your birth"; this is followed by an evocation of the happiness of the poor and the sufferings of the rich. Vidal proposes a similar thesis with different illustrations (brooks and rivers, blades of grass and cedars); there is no equality in nature. There follows a nice anaphoric pastiche that describes the fallen state of nature:

> See how these leaves tremble in the air, swing with grace, move capriciously! Behold the image of freedom.
>
> No, that is not the image of freedom.
>
> Those leaves are the plaything of the wind, the victims of their caprice. This is an image of slavery.
>
> See how the free zebra runs in the desert, saying: This desert is mine! Behold the image of freedom.
>
> No, that is not the image of freedom.
>
> That wild animal, as he leaps, follows the impetuous movements of his nature, he cannot control them; he is driven more than he runs. This is an image of slavery. (*Words of a Catholic*, p. 63)

There are also several pat evocations of the traditional combat between birds of prey and birds of peace. Vrindts proposes that sparrows and swallows only avoid the attacks of vultures and kites by hiding in the shelter of holes provided in structures built by man, or if man chases the vulture. Milon de Villiers, on the other hand, describes how the birds cooperate to kill the vulture; but then the kites replace the vulture, causing the need for a new victorious revolutionary combat—in other words, the Revolution of 1830 must be followed by another revolution. This discourse is necessarily contradictory—Victor Hugo had not yet developed his reconciliation of the theme of universal manducation in nature and political and historical hope—but it does reveal the contradictory stance of the Romantics about the world of nature, similar to or different from that of humans, an emblem of the bounty of creation, or of the

Fall. These pastiches highlight the extent to which Lamennais's conception of nature remains in the Rousseau tradition; creation, and particularly the bees, declare the glory and bounty of God.

🐝 Often, the pastiches transform Lamennais's parables to draw a different lesson from them, more in line with the political position of the author of the pastiche. Take the parable about the rock that no man, on his own, can budge, but that all, working in association, move with the greatest of ease. Vrindts specifies that the men manage to do so because of prayer, because they follow the orders of providence and obey the man who is commanding them. Ortolan is more inventive; at first, the men working in association still cannot manage to budge the rock. One of them takes charge, organizes and directs the others, and the stone is moved. But then the workers revolt, accusing the man in charge of talking all the time and never doing anything, of exercising arbitrary authority. They stop obeying, and the stone, transformed into a kind of rock of Sisyphus, falls back into the hole.

The two chapters of Lamennais's *Words* that provoke the most rewriting are the thirteenth, "The Council of the Seven Kings," and the thirty-sixth, "Young Soldier, Where Are You Going?" Chapter 13 has a "Gothic" character as well as a political content, and Chapter 36 was the most controversial chapter of the book: few authors accept Lamennais's justification of military disobedience. Harring does, but in a very different language:

> The soldier should only be a soldier in order to defend the fatherland against the aggressions of foreign enemies. And yet he has become the policeman of the prince, in order to lead to slaughter his fellow citizens who have dared defend the sacred rights of the nation. (*The Words of a Man*, p. 34)

Mercier also agrees with Lamennais, in his versification whose wan quality is particularly apparent here:

> Young soldier, speak on, where are you wending your steps?
> To the center of those struggles
> For the cause of justice,
> The sacred rights of humankind;
> So that finally the holy cause
> Of the masses might be accomplished
> —Blessed be the sword held by your arm!
> (*The People's Harp*, p. 243)

Vigoureux, who as a Fourierist rejects violence of any sort, proposes that "the arms of a soldier can cause death, but can never create liberty" (*The Words of Providence*, ch. 9). Other texts attack Lamennais, justifying the army and passive obedience, without creating a pastiche of his text: for example, the *Critical Examination of the Work*, or the *Five Chapters*, adds that the "supposed brothers" that Lamennais says the soldier should not attack "menace public order and private property." *Some More Words* uses a double technique. First is a polemical justification of the military necessity of obedience:

> Behold the army, which, as one man, marches toward the enemy. A single will governs all its motions. A leader speaks, and his will enters the minds and is implanted in the hearts, replacing all individual wills, and the general order that results proclaims obedience, and obedience proclaims the necessity of orders. (P. 36)

Next, the author creates an imitation of Lamennais's form but with a completely different content, ethical and religious rather than military. The *Words of a Believer When He Was Still a Believer* imitates the text but "corrects" the soldier's speech: "I am going to serve the king, so that each may eat in peace the fruit of his labors, and so that the children of those who earn their bread will not be robbed by those who wish to live off the bread of others," or, still more conservative, "for the preservation of order and hierarchy on this earth, and so that the fear of prisons and punishment may open the eyes of the imprudent and put a brake on the audacity of evil doers" (p. 143). Vrindts uses a similar technique: "Young soldier, where are you going?—I know not, I am going where my officers lead me." And the soldier, something of a philosopher, lengthily justifies the necessity of obedience (*The Words of a Believer, Reviewed*, p. 152). Vidal employs a different technique, transforming the soldier into an infantryman of the late Roman Empire who practices destructive disobedience:

> "Where are you running, young soldier?"
> "I'm off to the forum, to rejoin the legion, and from there we'll go to the palace to dethrone the master of the empire."
> "What has he done, young soldier?"
> "Nothing, yesterday he doubled our pay, but that's not enough for us. After we've brought him low, we'll put the empire up for auction, and get rich by its sale." (*Words of a Catholic*, p. 125)

Milon de Villiers uses a sarcastic *reductio ad absurdum,* a fairly rare technique in these texts. Quoting Lamennais, "so that sister will no longer look in weeping at her brother who goes away never to return," he asks, "Then why are you leaving, young soldier?" La Gracerie imitates the form, but gives it a quite different, nonmilitary content. "Where are you going, axe in hand and anger in your heart?" The answer, to knock down crosses. Ponchon uses this same transference technique even more violently. "Guilty man, where are you going?" "I'm off to insult God and destroy the altars of the fatherland." "May you come to grief, haughty man!" (*The Believer,* p. 160). This goes on for six pages, with such answers as "I'm off to vomit my entrails on the earth in order to make men stink and the heart of God desolate" (p. 166).

This variety of techniques—a polemical refutation of the content, an imitation of the form in order to contradict Lamennais's message, an imitation of the form but without its content, in order to apply the style to something else—is found *mutatis mutandis* with other chapters. The characteristic trait of these imitations is not the sarcasm of parody, but a kind of violence, of exaggeration, and a polemic purpose.

❦ The scene of the seven kings is treated in a similar way, but here the pastiches can be quite imaginative. Some, like Ponchon, are content simply to say that most kings are good and have never claimed that the executioner was the essential minister of the king (*The Believer and His Words,* p. 84); Ponchon does not seem to recognize that this thesis is borrowed from Joseph de Maistre. Milon de Villiers evokes history; in trying to determine the model for Lamennais's kings, he suggests Nero and Caligula, and then offers in counterpart the atrocious activities of the revolutionaries in 1793. The *Words . . . When He Was a Believer* remains within the limits of what a pastiche can properly do; the kings continue to contemplate nefarious actions, but they are revolutionary: "Let us propagate revolt in all the nations of the earth" (p. 47). The kings also want to "break down the natural barriers which separate one people from another, facilitate communications and commerce, deprive each nation of its particular customs and uses" (p. 49); the text condemns internationalism and even cosmopolitanism. In his *Letter,* Tharin also substitutes revolutionaries for the kings. "La Mennais shows us kings drinking blood from human skulls. Is he ignorant of the fact

that it was the murderers of kings who drank blood from human
skulls, who shed that blood like water from a fountain, who constructed thrones for the masses made out of bones"—there are six
more complements to the verb. In his *Religious Meditations,* he has a
vision of seven men with the customary Gothic decor ("the shades
were palpable, and a large waterfall descended into the abyss, giving me great fright"); the golden chalice contains black blood, but
the seven men represent (1) war against God; (2) war against the
kings, for popular sovereignty; (3) liberty; (4) equality; (5) fraternity; (6) tolerance; and (7) constitution. They seal their pact with
Satan and

> immediately the skies were covered with a black cloud, similar to the veil of
> the night; and lightning flashed and thunder rolled, and I saw appear in the
> black cloud a powerful hand which seized the earth by the north pole and
> shook it effortlessly and yet with violence, as one shakes a rag in order to
> get the dust out of it. (Ch. 6)

There follow inundation, cataclysms, the conflagration of the homes
of both rich and poor, and a dance around a tree—all this is supposed to represent the Revolution of 1789. Then comes another
vision of Napoleon as exterminator. The *Counter Words* of Ortolan
uses the same technique, with a setting even more Gothic (the room
is draped in black, there is a seven-faced pyramid formed of human
bones and skulls, the chalice is full of a black powder in an intoxi-
cating liquor, etc.). The first man wants to provoke people into
revolt against their chosen kings, the second against the laws, the
third against taxes, the fourth the workers against the manufactur-
ers ("let us stop work, destroy the machines"). the seventh proposes
that one should not act too openly:

> I shall inspire the heart of a man with our spirit, and all these things will
> be united in him, and he will say them all; but he will dress them up in the
> suave colors of religion and virtue. And he will disguise the word of Satan
> as the word of God. (Ch. 6)

The version of *Still More Words* is even more immediately political.
The first demon is the seducer of Eve, the second the demon of
paganism, the third of atheism, the fourth of conquest, the fifth the
demon of liberty who proclaims that

> men with bare arms, stained with wine and blood, armed with axes and
> hammers, will open the gates of the prisons and exhaust themselves pulver-

izing humain brains. They will cut off the breast the baby suckles, and, before the mother's eyes, break the babe on the rocks, and the babe's blood will gush forth onto the mother's breast. (P. 70)

The sixth demon and his troop wear red bonnets and blue tunics, and on their chests metal plaques with their names. They attempt to create chaos by proclaiming: "To each according to his works and his talents! I even add, She who should be man's companion is now only his slave, let us give her liberty! Liberty!" (p. 70). These demons are manifestly the Saint-Simonians. The seventh demon, identified as Lamennais himself, is the "demon of prevarication" who proposes that "it is in the name of the Gospel that all authority will be destroyed, in the name of the cross that the kings will be slaughtered" (P. 71).

It is Lamennais's association of violence and the Gospel which provokes, in these texts, the most indignant reactions.

❦ The texts often accuse Lamennais of contradicting himself— this accusation is fairly easy to prove, as they contrast his early *Essay on Indifference* and the *Words of a Believer*. Lamennais used to be for Christ; now he is for Satan. Martel suggests that, like Augustine, Lamennais retracted his errors, but did so before he fell into error. Madrolle and Tharin point out how Lamennais contradicts, not his *Essay,* but the very negative review he wrote in 1819 of Alexis Dumesnil's *Manifestation de l'esprit de vérité,* a brochure that proposed a kind of revolutionary Gospel socialism. The anonymous *Dream* provides two visions that develop this theme of Lamennais's contradictions. The first vision is of a two-faced virgin who symbolizes the priest perjurer, with the *Words of a Believer* as the product of the union of the woman and the serpent, a fruit pleasant to the evil, bitter to the good. The second vision is of a basket of flowers, symbols of "poetic beauties, the flowers of eloquence which shine throughout the *Words of a Believer,"* but it is also full of snakes— "the sophistries, the false thoughts, the immoralities, which are hidden under these flowers." One finds this dichotomy in the other texts. For instance, in *The Book, a Vision* Bouvier declares, "Never in my life had I seen anything so beautiful and so horrible, so noble and so infamous, so admirable and so damned." Vidal, the anonymous author of the *Words of a Believer When He Was a Believer,* and others express their admiration for Lamennais's style quite explicitly, just as they imitate it. This distinction between a beautiful form which is approved, and a nefarious content which is condemned, both permits and justifies the practice of pastiche.

More striking is the fact that many of the texts present the *Words* of Lamennais as self-contradictory. The interlocutors in Martel's dialogue (a priest, a lawyer, a doctor) have no trouble proving that Lamennais is at times a Catholic, then a Saint-Simonian, a theocrat, and then a democrat. This is achieved through quotations from *The Words of a Believer* and Lamennais's earlier writings. *The Words . . . When He Was Still a Believer* reproduces unchanged several of Lamennais's chapters, including that one on the widow and her daughter, which is well received by almost everyone except Clarisse Vigoureux. Mlle Le Bot is disturbed by Lamennais's combination of "a sublime imagination avid for the reign of Christ" with his cult of insurrection and violence; Milon de Villiers (*The Words of a Miscreant*, p. 77) describes the *Words* as "a chaos of good and evil principles" where he is pleased to hear the precepts of reason, of philosophers, of Christ, but "a voice from on high said to me, 'Wait, listen a bit more.' Then I heard that this was but the prelude to a diatribe against all principles and against the kings of the earth." This is what Ponchon labels the "two contrary immensities" of Lamennais (*The Believer and His Words,* p. 77).

Some try to explain or resolve these contradictions. Madrolle's technique is to claim that Lamennais had not yet revealed all the horrid depths of his thought (Madrolle does it for him: "The agrarian law. Community of goods, while waiting for the community of other things, with, for the final goal of man, a community of misery" [*Secret History,* p. 29]). Bouvier, a Protestant, proposes that Lamennais is still fundamentally an advocate of a spiritual despotism which necessarily requires temporal despotism, but, no longer daring to attack liberty directly, caresses it in order to attack it. On the other hand, Victor La Gracerie, the "Catholic conciliator," is at great pains to show that Lamennais is not an advocate of violence:

Does he want to break the skepters of the kings and destroy their thrones and put the reins of empire in the hands of the masses? Yes, answer his adversaries. Is this assertion correct? Are not appearances being used to accuse someone who only calls for justice and order? Is it preaching revolt, to tell people to demand their acquired rights, to seek what means can stifle forever all germs of division and hatred, to show them the tree of the holy

mountain, to urge them to unite under its protective shadow, there to be
mutually inspired by charity and to arm themselves with prayer?

He who wishes peace has been accused of revolt. Reassured by his con-
science, he groans without anger; grief does not destroy a heart inspired by
noble and pure intentions. (*Words of a Catholic,* pp. xx—xxiii)

La Gracerie's intention is perhaps ambiguous; his pastiche of Lamennais attempts to turn the *Words* into the text La Gracerie would
like to read. Obviously, the internal contradictions that Lamennais's
contemporaries were so aware of (whereas we tend to emphasize his
appeals to violence) also justify the use of pastiche. In my opinion,
Lamennais's *Les Paroles d'un croyant,* read in the light of its recep-
tion, becomes a very ambivalent book. Bouvier and La Gracerie
offer interesting possible readings of this text, and Ballanche's reading merits particular attention.

If we think of the *Words* as a text calling for violence, it is perhaps in part because it was this violence—and the way Lamennais
associates violence with Christ—that the pastiches criticized. The
*Critical Examination* makes this clear:

> The love we feel for our neighbor . . . this sentiment which attaches us to
> the eternal being; what! love would lead us to commit acts of hatred, of
> barbarism, blood proscriptions! . . . Millions of men should *unite with
> Christ,* arms in hand, to massacre kings, princes, all the great of this earth!
> And our recompense is, we can share in their remains! . . . The principal
> idea of this work is the idea of introducing the Kingdom of Christ by blood
> and revolution. That idea belongs to the barbaric ages, to minds for whom
> Our Lord is a material God, like the golden calf of the Israelites.
> (Pp. 13–16)

Le Bot and Vigoureux express the same astonishment. Ortolan's
pastiche litany shows that liberty is the calm, and not the storm:

> Liberty! Liberty!
> You are not like a fire, which engenders flame by flame, smoke by
> smoke, which devours those near and stifles those far away.
> Liberty! Liberty!
> What are you like?
> You are like the sweet warmth which warms those numbed with cold,
> which, penetrating vein by vein, reaches the heart and makes it beat.
> Liberty! Liberty!
> You are like an ever calm sea, which receives the vessels in its midst and
> majestically leads them from shore to shore, uniting all men and all conti-

nents, bringing to one another the riches of all climates and of all minds. (Pp. 102–3)

And Ortolan devotes a whole chapter to proving that Christ did not give the incendiary's torch or the sword to the slaves. He did not tell slaves to fight, but to be submissive, to serve their masters. The *Profession of Faith* reiterates this thesis in a sarcastic interrogation:

> What must the kings not fear from the doctrine of a madman who, in the name of God himself, promises the palms of martyrdom to any people who will murder their kings and break their thrones in pieces; the doctrine of a priest who blesses, in the name of Christ, the still steaming sword of assassins who he says are reconquering liberty and creating the reign of Christ? (P. 9)

Milon de Villiers emphasizes that Christ never preached violence, adding that it was the people who crucified Jesus (*Words of a Miscreant*, p. 58). Vrindts, after lumping Lamennais with the Hussites and Adam Weishaupt, among others, accuses him of using a sacrilegious and fanatic language because "the cross on which Christ died for you bore a Christ obedient even unto death. The cross has made all martyrs obedient up to their last breath of life. The cross rejects any seditious coalition" (*Words of a Believer, Reviewed*, p. 97).

On the other hand, the "leftist" texts—with the exception of the Fourierist Vigoureux—with some nuances, accept the image of violence that Lamennais attributes to Christ. But there is another important exception: Ballanche, in his article in the *Revue européenne*, says to Lamennais,

> You have frightened those in power, whereas what was needed was to instruct them; you have excited the passions of the multitude, whereas they needed to be calmed. . . . But much will be forgiven you, because you have loved much, because your Christian bowels of mercy have been moved by the spectacle of human injustice up to the point of despair. (P. 7)

Ballanche, like La Gracerie, reads the *Words* as a "mystagogical painting whose emblems, sometimes sweet, more often terrible, should not be taken literally." Yet, it is in this respect that Lamennais's book raises a major issue in the question of the Romantic conception of Jesus. Can progress be created without violence and here what do Christ's Passion and Crucifixion signify? It should be noted that most of these pastiche texts, whatever their political stance, are marked not only by a preoccupation with violence but also by the use of violent language. Undoubtedly, the contemporary worker uprisings and their violent suppression (the *canuts* [silk workers] of Lyon, the events at Saint-Merri, the Transnonain massacres) explain this concern with violence in a very simple and immediate way; but the great contribution of Lamennais's text, in my opinion, was that it explicitly asked questions about the relationship of progress, violence, and Christianity—questions still being asked today.

On 12 July 1834, Lamennais wrote his friend Montalembert:

> After the newspaper articles, then come the pamphlets, the refutations, the parodies. I've read six or eight of them; *The Response of a Christian Etc.* by Mr. Bautain (this Bautain wants to become a bishop, but Rome is creating a great many obstacles), the *Words of an Unbeliever* and *The Words of a Seer, The Words of a Lady Believer, The Words of a Misbeliever,* and *Apostasy of M. de La Mennais* by Madrolle, etc. I send you none of all the above, for all of it is incredibly dull; but this production proves that the human fiber has been touched in all hearts.[8]

It was only two days later, before he had even finished this letter, that he learned of the papal condemnation of *Singulari Nos.* The very forms that the hypertextuality takes in this instance suggest that Lamennais was right in claiming that these varied texts proved that the human fiber had been touched to a considerable extent. How can one explain the immediate success of his little book, which broke with all generic expectations? For I do not find the models and sources that are usually cited very convincing, or very similar to Lamennais's text. Sainte-Beuve had already proposed Ballanche's *Vision d'Hébal* as a model. That philosophical epic prose poem expresses and explains, in a somewhat allusive if very complex version, the history of humanity, but it does not read at all like the *Words* of Lamennais. Certainly one can admit the influence of Ballanche's work, Quinet's epic poem about the Wandering Jew *Ahasvérus,* even Saint-Martin's *Homme de désir,* and perhaps (while Lamennais was writing his text) Mickiewicz's *Book of the Polish Pilgrim,* which is the most similar to the *Words* in many ways. One might also add the *Manifestation de l'esprit de vérité* by Alexis Dumesnil, which Lamennais had lambasted fifteen years earlier. This work offers a Christian justification for revolutionary hope, and for the sufferings of the revolutionaries, in the form of anaphoric, exclamative versets. Lamennais's book surely results from a mixture of some of these earlier texts; as one of his "pasticheurs," Ortolan, rather cleverly if sarcastically points out, Lamennais's style is an imitation of many sources: the Bible, the Koran, Volney, Arabic poetry. The ancestry of the *Words,* then, is complex; its progeny, including the pastiches, is also very rich. Jules Lechevalier, a former disciple of Ballanche who had turned Fourierist, criticized Lamennais's "neo-Gospel style" in the *Revue du progrès social* (1 [1834]:518–36). According to Lechevalier, the *Words* was not appropriate to the age because fear was no longer an effective motivating force. Yet the number and variety of pastiches suggest that Lechevalier was wrong. Furthermore, pastiches continued to be written long after the immediate publication of the text. I quote one from 1847:

> But greetings to the poet . . . who will chant, venerable bard, those rejected by civilization, and who one day will meditate on their vestiges.
>
> The division of labor has produced the degradation of work; this is why I have summarized work in the machine and the shop.
>
> The machine has only produced slaves, and the shop wage earners; this is why I have called for competition.
>
> Competition has engendered monopoly; this is why I have created the state, and imposed a withholding on capital.
>
> The state has become for the worker a new slavery, and I have said: May the workers stretch out their hands to each other from one nation to another.

The text is from Proudhon's *Système des contradictions* (1847), 2:106. Proudhon more than anyone else rejected "the thick fog of religiosity" which, according to him, "weighs these days on every head" (2:387). One need only mention A.-L. Constant, Alphonse Esquiros, even Cabet who was glad to see Lamennais "associate his apostolic voice to that of the Republican press." I have presented elsewhere a brief anthology of these imitations of Lamennais in 1848; there are many texts which could be added to it.[9] The fact that by 1834 these hypertexts espouse their hypotext predicts the success that future imitations of Lamennais were to achieve. In part, surely it is a matter of the communicative value of this politico-religious style, in which biblical inspiration and imitation provide a justification for the message, in which the text, and parts of the text, are brief but filled with repetition, synonymy, and excess.

These factors provoke meditation, appeal to the emotions, suggest a causality deeper than what logic detects or describes.

Lamennais's text is, as far as I know, a turning point in the history of political discourse. Beginning with Saint-Simon's *Nouveau christianisme*, (1825), socialist discourse had taken on religious tonalities. But Lamennais proposes a political and religious justification for violence. Such justification was absent in 1789, but quite widespread by 1848. I should like to believe that the justification originated in Lamennais's meditations on the events connected with the canuts' revolt at Lyon. As Ballanche perspicaciously remarked, "The *Words of a Believer* and the catastrophe of Lyon for me are one and the same event." Beginning with that catastrophe, things were no longer simple, violence as well as hope had to be justified, and the authors of our pastiches were quite correct to center their polemic on this aspect of the text. If the *Words* did indeed answer a need in terms of propaganda, it also reflected a new secularization of religious space; Ballanche was probably Lamennais's ideological (as well as stylistic) precursor, offering not only the verset form but also meditations on the political and historical significance of suffering. Ballanche also said, commenting on Lamennais's text, "The mystery of death must be accomplished, if the mystery of the resurrection is to take place."[10] But Ballanche never knew how to write for the people. Lamennais did. Above all, he knew how to reintegrate the working classes and their problems in a discourse that was charismatic, but turned its back on the nostalgia for 1789 or for Napoleon to examine the relations between violence, the sacred, and progress. As our pastiches show, Lamennais relocated the discourse of hope.

# II

# The Intertextual Flow of
# Romantic Discourse

# 5 ❦ "Precious Blood" in Religion, Literature, Eroticism, and Politics

La terre s'enivrait de ce sang précieux.

The earth became inebriated with this Precious Blood.

—Gérard de Nerval

During the Romantic age, the Precious Blood of Jesus, indeed religious blood in general, not only flows; blood bursts forth, streams, jets, pushes through the skin of the stigmatics, pulsates through the ventricles of the Sacred Heart. It also circulates in a different sense, perhaps historically more significant; the Precious Blood, a source of grace and salvation in Christian thought, also penetrates into erotic literature, in both poetry and fiction, and into medical literature, and, perhaps most important, into political texts. In Joseph de Maistre's words, "Faster than lightning, more active than thunder, the theandric blood penetrates our guilty entrails in order to wash away our filth,"[1] thus procuring for us, thanks to the "reversibility of the merits of the innocent ransoming the guilty," "SALVATION THROUGH BLOOD."

This theory of the efficacy of the sacrifice of Christ's blood and its repetition throughout history is, for Maistre, both a theological conviction and a political theory. The theory meant the same to others, such as H. J. Schmitt.[2] This political theory is authoritarian, but, as Bernard Sarrazin has shown, it lent itself to radical leftist and indeed prorevolutionary applications.[3] One could quote as an extreme instance of such radical uses a text from the first issue of the newspaper *Le Christ républicain* during the heyday of the Revolution of 1848:

We, poor workers, we are reds, because Christ shed his blood in order to redeem us, his blood by which we hope to become regenerated. We are red,

81

because the angel of extermination has marked our lintels with the blood of the Lamb so that on the day of Vengeance those chosen by God may be distinguished from those he condemns.[4]

The blood of the efficacious sacrifice of the innocent victim is shed by Christ, by Louis XVI the martyr king, by the suffering proletariat, even by the prostitute-victim. Of all Romantic metaphoric systems, that of religious blood, dynamic, organic, rich in allegorical applications, provided the best way to reach God, or the utopia of Justice, via pain and suffering, linking Good and Evil.

The devotional literature of the age, centered on the contemplation of the passion and the Crucifixion, of the Sacred Hearts of Jesus and Mary, of Mary *mater dolorosa,* of the Blessed Sacrament, is rich in baroque imagery where blood plays a major role.[5] I only offer a small sampling; indeed, it is difficult to establish what is specifically Romantic. Devotional literature is highly imitative, deeply marked by tradition, and texts that seem superbly exemplary of what Mario Praz termed the "Romantic Agony" turn out to be paraphrases of seventeenth-century masters such as Bossuet. Historically, what is of interest is not so much the presence of dynamic images of the Sacred Blood in devotional texts, but their reflection in other literary forms. A few examples show from what religious tradition the nonreligious uses of the metaphor derived. Fr. Paulmier's *Le Chrétien de l'Evangile par opposition au Chrétien du jour* (1841) is symptomatic of the way this devotional literature often turned its back on the problems of the world, and justified it in terms of suffering and of blood. The true Christian refuses the world, so that he can

> bear on his body the mortifications of Christ, be dead to all the desires and all the hopes of the present age. . . . To suffer, to be silent, to be prepared for all forms of scorn, to abandon himself entirely to Providence in this life and the one to come, that should be the goal of all your desires, of your every effort. . . . One is only a Christian in order to be crucified together with the Incarnate Lord. (P. 116)

The true Christian does not merely contemplate Christ's suffering and hold himself personally responsible for that suffering, he must imitate it:

> Where should we study the nature and the depth of the love we owe God? Surely it is in the bloody history of the humiliations and sufferings of the

Incarnate Lord, in the painful scenes of Christ before Caiphas, Christ at his condemnation, Christ on Calvary. (P. 180)

And Paulmier, like many another, offers a detailed, highly colorful description of those sufferings. Typical is this passage from an anonymous pamphlet published in Lyon in 1825 for the edification of the faithful, *Jésus au prétoire:*

Therefore come and behold. Behold his executioners, who pull off his bloody garments which stick to his wounds, thus handing him over to the most cruel, most ignominious suffering. . . . Behold Jesus who stretches out on the fatal tree. . . . His flesh is torn, his bones grate one against another, his veins rupture, his blood flows in great waves. Put your hand on the cross, where Jesus' hand is. . . . What, you tremble! Where is the guilty party on Calvary? Is it Jesus, or is it you? His blood boils in his veins, exudes from all parts of his body, flows in abundance to the ground. Oh mysterious sweat, which washes your soul in the blood of God made man. Behold that flesh, ploughed by the whips and flying into bits! What noise! What a tempest! What murderous hands destroy and then other equally murderous hands continue to destroy his virgin body? (Pp. 186–87)

One might conclude that realism here rather borders on sadism, but it is the kinetics of the text that is striking, the vertiginous and synesthetic viscosity of Christ's body and blood. These texts aim to create a kind of ecstatic contemplation; they urge the believer to identify with the crucified, bleeding Christ not only morally but also with the senses. The masterpiece of the genre is surely Jean-Baptiste Lasausse's *Le Chrétien brûlant d'amour peur Jésus-Christ cruifié, ou nécessité et avantages qu'on retire de la méditation des souffrances de Jésus-Christ* (1825). Sanctity can only be acquired if one plunges with love into the heart of our dying Lord as into a fiery furnace, enters into Jesus through the openings of his sacred wounds while realizing that our sins are the swords which have made those openings: "Oh my soul! Approach with confidence, imbued with thanksgiving and love, those streams of blood you see running down!" (p. 137). In these texts, it is often the precise, realistic, even repugnant detail that opens the way of penetration into the divine presence. In *La Vierge, ou l'histoire de la Mère de Dieu* (1837), Orsini, like many others, asks the faithful to contemplate the Passion by empathizing with the vision of the Blessed Virgin, to share in her grief as we consider Jesus' face, "bruised and swollen, covered with blood and filth," but also "sweet and pitying." We are asked to hear with her "the sharp raspings of the ropes on the pulleys" as the cross is erected, the noise of the hammer blows as Jesus is nailed to the cross.

I shall return to this way that the Romantics combined *douceur* and *douleur,* sweetness and sorrow, in their contemplation of tragedy. First let us consider one more example of this devotional literature, *Elévations sur les mystères de la vie de N.S.J.C.* (1834) by Fr. de Robbiano (who was also a count). He had a particular predilection for the wound in the side of Christ opened by the soldier, for there one finds "the moment of that baptism of blood, after which you have sighed more ardently than the thirsting hart, pursued by the pitiless hunter, sighs after fresh watersprings; that moment has come" (p. 264). Robbiano's imagery derives from Psalms, but the water from the side of Christ has turned into blood. Robbiano also suggests that the believer should say to himself, at the elevations during Mass, "Oh Jesus, fastened to the cross, fasten me to the cross with you!" (p. 100).

The crop is rich and red, and poets fed on it. The classical invocation of the Muse is Christianized and becomes transformed into an appeal to the Precious Blood. To cite Edouard Alletz,

> Ready to paint, Oh Lord, the demon's plot,
> I drown my tears while murmuring your name.
> But what blood, oh my God, seems to stain my lyre?
> 'T is yours; cover me with your wing, or I'll expire.[6]

The blood of Christ coats the poets' lyres. Alletz's epic like many others owes a great deal to Klopstock's *Messiad,* translated in 1769, 1794, and 1801, much read and admired.[7] Klopstock was more influential on the French Romantic religious epic than Milton, and he described the Passion in multiple gory if verbose details. Another major source of details about the Passion arose in German lands. The *Visions of Anne-Catherine Emmerich on the Life of Jesus and on his Dolorous Passion* was translated into French by Edmond de Cazalès in 1835. Emmerich's texts embroider on the Gospels through her visions, and they intensify both the realism and the horror of the biblical narrative. Alletz, one of the most appreciated of the religious poets of the day, excels in images of Christ's blood. At the Crucifixion, "His body weeps blood; all his blood becomes as tears"; "our sins" are "daggers" which pierce that body (*Nouvelle*

*Messiade*, p. 384). At the flagellation, under the whips of the lictors, "his whole body torn open disappears, covered by his adorable blood" (p. 441). Caiphas, the implacable high priest, watches the blood of Christ flow, which, "becoming less rapid in its speed, like the rains from heaven toward the end of a storm, announces that he is reaching the shores of the torments he has exhausted" (p. 469). If the movement of the blood slows down here, it recovers its acceleration at the moment of the Crucifixion. And Alletz's poem does not only describe Christ's blood: Satan and Beelzebub need a child's blood to seal their pact, at which moment a mother appears in hell—she has killed her illegitimate child, which act is described in detail. "He dies, stoned by his cruel mother / And the blood he owes her gushes back onto her" (p. 220), typical of the fate of the blood of all innocent victims. Blood is equally abundant and pervasive in the other major Catholic poet of the age, Edouard Turquety, who composed a lengthy description of "Golgotha, still red with blood"[8] and, describing the death of an atheist—a commonplace theme of this poetry—asks, "Oh Christ? Why did he not die when he was baptized, / Covered with your blood, pure as that blood itself?"[9] Here again the blood pulsates out of the body, coats and covers.

The theme that the sins of modern humanity make Christ's blood flow once more is very widespread. Here is an example from Antony Deschamps:

> Thus, weak mortals, unfortunate sinners,
> We each day reopen the wounds and renew the sorrows
> Of Him who died for the salvation of mankind.
> When we do evil, senseless as we are,
> Do we not hear him say, in his sweet voice,
> You are crucifying me a second time?
> For throughout eternity, oh Christians, this great victim
> Suffers and holds out his arms toward us from his sublime tree
> And always our sins penetrate into his heart
> And once more make the Redeemer's blood flow.[10]

Deschamps combines the coursing blood with the theme of the sweet Jesus. The richest examples are found among the Catholic disciples of Lamartine, who specialized in versifying how faith can be found by taking the path of pain and suffering—Alfred Des Essarts, Victor Lagrange, Charles Brugnot, Robert-Etienne Thuret, and Ludovic Cailleux whose *Fragments* are perhaps the most excessive. A good example is Edouard de Blossac's sonnet on the crucifix:

> Image of my Lord, on his bed of torture!
> Shameful wood where, veiled in our infamous nature
> Christ satisfied the judgment rendered
> And washed in his blood mankind's iniquity.
> Hail! My soul at last breaks forth from its sepulchre;
> Teach your creatures the lessons of Calvary,
> And throw upon the pride of my forehead in revolt
> The mantle of pardon that a God earned for me.
> Holy cross! Shelter me from the century in your shade!
> Day and night, bless my eyes with numberless tears,
> Put love on my lips, and faith in my heart!
> Teach me how a God emptied the bitter chalice,
> Lead me to accomplish my task on the bitter paths,
> Without allowing my foot to slip or avoid any pain!
> (*Heures de poésie*, 1835, p. 13)

Blossac wishes to proclaim "both my social faith and my Christian faith"; he is one of the advocates of the "social Gospel."

Echoes of this language may be found not only in Chateaubriand's *Martyrs* but also in Victor Hugo's *Odes;* Christ's blood is evoked in many Romantic poetic texts. As a last example, and as a transition, I cite Léon Noël's "Flagellation" from his *Livre de tous* (1841), which contains a poem such as this one for each mystery of the Holy Rosary:

> The Victim is handed over
> And his flesh in shreds
> Bursts off, torn to bits
> By the whips of his torturers,
> Each blow he suffers,
> Like a fatal arrow
> Creates a mortal wound
> In his Mother's breast.

Here we have flagellation, blood bursting forth, and the loving and suffering onlooker, Mary, representative of the believer who should share in the sorrow she knew at this atrocious scene.

The Precious Blood's presence in devotional literature and religious poetry is not surprising. The same cannot be said for its frequency in erotic texts—but the Romantics often confuse or fuse Eros and Agape. The subject is a fertile one, and Lamartine alone would merit a whole article, but Musset's hero Octave is all too typical:

> My passion for my mistress was a most wild one, and my whole life was marked by it in a violent and yet monastic way. I limit myself to one example. She had given me her portrait in miniature, enclosed in a medallion. I wore it on my heart, which is something many men do. But one day, in a curiosity shop, I found a monk's iron discipline, with a plaque studded with pricks at its end. I had the medallion attached to the plaque and wore it in that form. These nails, which pierced my chest at my every move, created in me such a strange sense of voluptuousness that often I pressed the medallion against my chest with my hand so that I could feel the pricks more intensely. I know that this is madness; but love leads to many kinds of madness.[11]

Religious blood here expresses the sweetness and pain of eroticism. There is an obvious echo of Pascal's jabbing the pricks of his discipline into his side whenever he found himself enjoying a conversation, but for Octave the act serves to intensify or exacerbate sexual passion. In this instance, the text is manifestly and willfully perverse and sacrilegious, but there are many others from the period which today seem much more problematic. Lacordaire, the saintly Dominican and great religious orator, provides an example. In 1866 the Dominican Bernard Chocarne published his official biography, *Le R. P. Lacordaire de l'ordre der Frères Precheurs,* where one reads:

> The time has come to penetrate further into the secrets of this religious soul, to what he considered the source of all virtues, his love for the crucified Christ. The fact is strange, but even before his conversion this preoccupation with the cross of the Son of God seems to have marked him. He yearned to suffer, as his Master had, in public; he dreamt only of whips and whipping posts. Very often, when he remembered his sins, he had the idea of asking a Savoyard boy to whip him in front of everyone, and then giving the boy some money for doing so. . . . By contemplating the wounds of the Man of Sorrow, he understood the mystery of strength in love, he saw the cure for all our miseries in humiliation and suffering, in the sufferings of the spirit and the body. . . . He chose an Order which made use of corporal punishment in order to be encouraged by the example of his brethren and obtain from them services he could hardly demand of strangers. . . . I have

often wondered how I could or whether I should reveal what we know about this side of his life. Would it be best to hide the details under the transparent cloud of figural terminology, for fear of disturbing delicate souls, or would it be better to state the details frankly, clearly and simply, whatever the risks and dangers? This latter approach seems to me more worthy of the man whose virtues we are describing. . . . He often felt very strong bursts of love for God, which he sought to satisfy in the cell of one of the novice monks. He would enter, his face still radiant with the holy joys of the altar, kneel before the novice, humbly kiss his feet, and ask him kindly to do him the service of chastising him for the love of God. He uncovered his shoulders, and . . . the novice had to give him a hearty whipping. He ended up covered with bruises, but remained a long time, his lips glued to the feet of the person who had beaten him, expressing his gratitude in the strongest possible terms. . . . On other occasions, after the discipline, he begged the young monk to sit down again at his desk, and, prone on the floor under his feet, Lacordaire stayed there for fifteen or thirty minutes, finishing his prayer in silence and with a devout delight at having the feet of his humiliator on his head. He repeated these penitential exercises frequently, and those he chose to execute them experienced considerable difficulty in accepting the assignment. . . . But they got accustomed to it bit by bit, and Lacordaire [asked] for more and more in order to be treated as he desired. They had to slap him, spit in his face, talk to him as if he were a slave. . . . When he got up, his body broken and his face in tears, his soul experienced cries of love toward God which no human language can transcribe. "Do you love me?" he would ask the person who had made him suffer, "Do you love me a little?" "Yes, Father, I love you; I think I've showed you I do." "Ah! if the world only knew how much happiness can be found in being whipped by the Person who loves you." (Pp. 392–406)

This text was republished seven times, and translated five times during the nineteenth century. It leaves today's reader astonished. Masochism? Homosexuality?[12] Fetishism? Exhibitionism? Chocarne is already worried about the reactions of ill-minded readers, and we have probably all become so ill-minded. But to what extent is our reading of the text unhistorical? Is the blood of the religious discourse here transformed into a lived experience, or does it simply serve to disguise perversion? The question can only be answered by saying that the Precious Blood, highly dynamic, is situated at confluences, that Lacordaire's conduct was surely at the time already considered ambiguous, reflecting the fundamental ambiguity between suffering in expiation, which is saintly, and a pathological sexuality. This is but one of the ambiguities produced by the circulation of the Precious Blood; probably more fundamental is the ambiguity between sweetness and suffering, already present here in the tender, joyful effusions that accompany physical pain and humiliation. Lacordaire was not alone; the hagiographic literature about the curé of Ars, Jean-Baptiste Vianney, recounts in similar detail how he conquered the flesh—his sheets were stained with blood—but he seems to have practiced his penitences in solitude.

The age underwent a change in attitude toward this and other matters of moral theology. The decisive moment came in 1832 when Cardinal Thomas Gousset published his *Justification de la théologie morale du B. Alphonse de Liguori* with its "equiprobabilistic" stance, midway between the laxness attributed to the Jesuits and the rigorism associated with the Jansenists. If, since the seventeenth century, the Jansenist positions on grace and on ecclesiology had been generally rejected, the French Church compensated by adopting an extremely rigorous moral theology (France was, for instance, the only country where actors and actresses were automatically excommunicated). Many felt that this moral theology only led either to hypocrisy or to a complete separation of the Christian from the realities of everyday life. Liguori, as propagated by Gousset, created a modernist revolution in moral theology. He was concerned with such matters as usury and sexuality, but the new moral theology also studied the problems of asceticism and penitential discipline. In these matters, Pierre Debreyne, a medical doctor and a Trappist monk, was an exceptionally qualified and competent guide. He began as an opponent of "innate" ideas and mesmerism (*Paroles d'un croyant catholique*, 1839), but became better known as the author of texts for confessors about matters in which a medical doctor could be of help, such as how to determine when the moment of death is near, or sexual matters, extensively discussed in his *Moechealogie, traité des péchés contre le 6ᵉ et 9ᵉ commandements* (1846). Of particular interest for our subject is his *Essai sur la théologie morale considérée dans ses rapports avec la physiologie et la médecine* (1842), which provides a long discussion (beginning on p. 461) on "instruments of penance, such as hairshirts, metal belts, cilices, and particularly whips." Debreyne was against physical penance in general; it endangers the health, produces pulmonary illnesses, and so on. To control the flesh, it is far better to practice fasting, abstinence, above all hard labor which tires the body. The goal of self-flagellation

> is probably admirable, since the penitent strives to imitate, although imperfectly, the horrible flagellation of Our Savior Jesus Christ. But, in everything concerning exterior matters, let us not be too attached to the surface, as the Pharisees were. . . . Rather, we should be concerned with spiritual matters, strive at the same time and even more to discipline and whip vigorously our hearts. (P. 461)

And if one insists on using the discipline, let it be administered on the back of the hands, or the forearms, or the feet, or below the knee. Debreyne is not without irony when he describes the dangers of catching cold if one undresses to receive the discipline; moreover nakedness "might also well present a certain moral danger." Above all,

> one must avoid the grave and unpardonable imprudence of taking the discipline *super clunes,* as is sometimes suggested by inexperienced and imprudent directors, or confessors or superiors. This practice, far from calming carnal passion, instead excites it, because of a physiological law of organic sympathies. (P. 465)

Libertine tradition, he notes, has known about this physiological law for a long time. There are children who love being spanked or whipped in this way; they find real pleasure therein, he notes, and when the pleasure is not complete, they discover the dreadful habit of masturbation in order to complete it. Clearly, Debreyne had read Rousseau's *Confessions* but one must conclude that the Church at the time was quite conscious of the possible links between religious discipline and sadomasochistic sexuality, between the Precious Blood and the blood of eroticism. Our modern reading of Chocarne on Lacordaire was also quite possible then. What made this interpretation possible was that the religious discourse on blood had become, to a certain extent, a medical discourse.

Nothing demonstrates this "circulation" better than the literature about the stigmata, the miraculous appearance of blood on the hands, feet, forehead, and side in imitation of the wounds of Christ at the Crucifixion. Dr. H. Imbert-Goubeyre, professor of medicine at Clermont, published an exhaustive study of the phenomenon at the end of the century, *La Stigmatisation, l'extase divine et les miracles de Lourdes* (1894). The statistics he offers are rather surprising; 113 instances of the stigmata were recorded in France in the seventeenth century, 29 in the eighteenth, and 30 in the nineteenth, although most of these occurred in the second half of the century. The first half of the 1800s represents a low point in instances of the phenomenon. Imbert-Goubeyre cites Sr. Saint Bernard de la Croix, born in 1820, who began experiencing stigmata toward 1840 (especially on Fridays) and in 1845 received permission from her superiors to ask Jesus that the miraculous outward and visible marks cease, which request was granted. Bertine Bouquillon, born in 1800, received various messages and revelations from a dead sister and then experienced the stigmata as proof of the truth of those revelations. A commission named by the bishop of Arras, La Tour d'Auvergne, decided that the phenomenon was authentically supernatural. The case of Mme Miollis, who experienced the stigmata in 1836, is discussed in detail later, as her situation generated a good deal of literature. Victoire Claire, born about 1810, who had the stigmata from 1848 to 1860, really falls outside the period we are examining here. Finally, Thérèse Putigny, born 1803, experienced very painful red swellings on the palms of her hands and the bottoms of her feet; blood also flowed abundantly from her forehead (in memory of the crown of thorns); she also possessed the saintly gift of bilocation and had visions of Jesus' life which closely resemble those Anne-Catherine Emmerich had in Germany. The other cases cited by Imbert either only involved psychological sufferings, or the individuals acquired the stigmata in the second half of the century. In short, one must conclude that cases of stigmata were rare in Romantic France—whereas in 1894, when Imbert-Goubeyre wrote, there were ten ongoing cases.

That does not mean that there was no edifying literature about the stigmata, quite the contrary, but that literature is mostly concerned with cases from other lands, particularly the Tyrol. Maria Moerl was described for the French by Charles Sainte-Foi in the *Université catholique* in 1840, then by the devout polygraph Cazalès in the same journal in 1842.[13] Maria Domenica Lazzari and Crescenzia Michlutich were described by Fr. F. Nicolas (*L'Extatique et les stigmatisées du Tyrol actuellement vivantes,* (1843). The most important foreigner gifted with the stigmata was the visionary Anne-

Catherine Emmerich, much discussed in France. In 1845, Fr. Nicolas republished his book, adding a chapter on Mme Miollis whom he visited. His preface is quite explicit about his goals:

> In this century entirely given over to materialism, to sensuality, where anything supernatural is rejected if not as false at least as dubious, one cannot demonstrate too clearly for men that God does not disdain entering into direct communication with His creation. . . . He communicates to some of us the sufferings of His Son in order to remind all Christians that if they wish to share in the glory of Christ they must share in His Passion and retrace in themselves the image of the Crucified Incarnate God.

Once more, here blood is thought of as in motion—consider, for instance, Maria Lazzari:

> The blood continued to flow down her forehead from little wounds which figure those of the crown of thorns; it spread over her neck and over the bandages placed below her head; her hands, firmly clasped, were pressed against her breast; on the back side [of one hand], the only one visible, was a wide and deep wound from whence blood spread over her arms. Her feet, which were placed one on top of the other, presented a similar wound, even wider and deeper, with moreover this quite remarkable circumstance that the blood, notwithstanding the laws of gravity, spread upward toward her toes. (Nicholas, *L'Extatique*, p. 114)

Nicholas cites doctors who examined the phenomena and had been converted.

Mme Miollis began experiencing the stigmata in 1836, including the five wounds and the crown of thorns; the blood flowed periodically, and in addition on her breast "there was a perfectly designed cross, permanent, which sweated blood." She was also the subject of medical studies. Dr. Reverdit examined her, and, quite convinced of the reality of the phenomena, described them in highly scientific language:

> The stigmatizations with diapedesis or sweating of blood took place before my eyes, without any ascertainable cause which might have explained them, be it prickings, or pressure, or anything else; they were manifest both before, during and after her monthly periods, without seeming to show any influence resulting from that habitual morbid state.[14]

A curious instance of medical discourse on the stigmata is offered by Dr. H. Lauvergne in his *On Aging and Death in all Classes of*

*Society* (1842). Lauvergne was convinced that "comparative phrenology is the torchlight of psychology"; his belief in a "stigmatic bump" on the cranium produced some rather peculiar medical discourse:

> Once, at the bedside of a half dead body, a nun, who had this noble protuberance, underwent the martyrdom of the cross; she endured, and with great delight, the stigmata of the crown of thorns on her brow, of the nails on her hands, of the piercing sword on her side. She suffered all that, and yet she remained insensitive to those physical phenomena such as vesicatories and sinapisms, which usually cause some degree of pain. Her soul knew the tortures of the Passion, which she had desired so ardently. . . . Should she be called a religious fanatic? How can one decide? But if this state is natural for those whose brain is marked by an exclusive cult of the organ of divine love, of revelation (just as we note a parallel state in men of genius who create divine works and whom we admire but with the deep conviction that, no matter how hard we try, we can never equal them), it is unjust to condemn the most sublime faculty of a brain which communicates with God, because we possess a spirit of doubt and an awareness of our own weakness. (P. 52)

Stigmatization is thus comparable to the sublime creations of genius. Debreyne himself, albeit a Trappist, was much less enthusiastic about the phenomenon. He discussed the case of a girl to whom the Blessed Virgin gave pieces of sugar and baked apples and who also experienced the stigmata on her breast and feet, with some drops of blood every Friday.[15] According to Debreyne, this could not be a miracle because there was no "final purpose worthy of God," nor was it a diabolic intervention because the Devil does not need baked apples to corrupt souls, he does so quite successfully with "the honey of shameful carnal pleasure." So it must be fraud:

> Physiologists are well aware that it is quite easy to create in the mental economy certain nervous or hemorrhagic habits. . . . One can make a circular pressure just above the spot at the moment one wants the blood to appear in order to force the blood out by the spot which offers the least resistance. . . . It would seem quite easy to produce mechanically a periodic exudation of blood. . . . This is the way I should explain stigmata in subjects whose general conduct is not manifest sanctity and so does not guarantee the authenticity of the stigmata. (*Essais*, p. 400)

The major medical discussion of the stigmata from the late 1800s is surely that of Alfred Maury, the positivist polygraph and friend of Flaubert, in his long article "Ecstatic Mystics and the Stigmatized."[16] In 1894 Imbert-Goubeyre was still writing primarily to refute Maury. In Maury's view, all religious visions are "reflections of those disorders and agitations to which the soul falls prey," and he discusses Anne-Catherine Emmerich as an exemplary victim of these nervous afflictions. He also mentions Mme Miollis and another stigmatized woman, Rose Taminier of Saignan (she later moved to Saint-Saturnin-lès-Apt), who had the stigmata on her breast. The steady flow of blood formed holy images when white cloth was pressed against it. According to Maury, she, like Mme Guyon and Marguerite-Marie Alacoque, was *"media de loco et media de picaro"*—half mad, half trickster. Stigmatization can only be "the consequence of a mental disturbance created by an exacerbation of religious contemplation or by the abuse of abstinence and asceticism in constitutions previously predisposed to the disorders of enervation." Maury accepts the possibility of a psychological influence on the physical; influenced by the imagination, blood is concentrated in the region where the visionary believes that she (or he) is struck thanks to a powerful concentration of thought on the images of the stigmata. In support of his thesis, he cites Debreyne's explanations:

> Ecstatic mysticism is a long series of moral and physical hallucinations which, in the most delicate and sensitive organisms, culminate in the stigmata and later in death. This is the most striking proof of the influence ideas and the imagination can exercise on our emotion. Acts, speech, writing can all reflect the physical troubles which accompany such ecstasy, which it nourishes and which, in turn, is nourished by it. Only in this sense can it be considered miraculous, that is, one of those marvelous products of the laws of intelligence whose secret escapes us and whose extent astounds us. (P. 232)

Maury's work illustrates how the discussion of the stigmata became more and more medical. The tendency to dismiss the whole matter as a fraud appeared from time to time, but more common were commentaries on psychological pathology, and the medical discourse also found its way into devotional texts and apologetic literature. Auguste Lecanu's *Dictionnaire des prophéties et des miracles* (1854) one of the volumes of Migne's *Nouvelle encyclopédie théologique*, has a very measured tone: "One must regret very much the ignorance of people, always well meaning and pious, who interpret as divine graces what are only natural markings resulting from certain illnesses often not of a very decent sort, or from fraudulent artifices; and fraud is a most horrid trait in a matter which should be most holy." Lecanu continues, noting that the phenomenon, though its origins may in certain individuals be completely natural, becomes sanctified and even in some sense divine "because of the use they make of it and the increase in faith, divine love, patience, and Christian resignation it produces in them." He cites Anne-Catherine Emmerich, who "can in no way be accused of fraud."[17]

The year 1854 also saw the publication of the translation, once more by "Charles Sainte-Foi," of Joseph von Goerres's major work, *La Mystique divine, naturelle et diabolique,* which discusses the stigmata in great detail (2:174–242). Goerres also offers a "scientific" or at least physiological explanation of the phenomenon. The image of Christ's wounds is

> first conceived in the soul, and then given representation on the outside surface of the body in a perceptible manner. In this instance, the image and the fleshly body are linked by the vital warmth which, acquiring an extraordinary degree of intensity, forms a sort of fire and is manifested by luminous flames which go in five directions toward the corresponding corporeal organs. The rays of this light are red, for red is the color which accompanies heat. They are white when the stigmata do not appear on the body's surface, but remain enclosed within the organism. (2:202)

Goerres sought the physical or natural bases of mystical phenomena through physiological and psychological studies. Sainte-Foi admits in his preface that he had a great deal of trouble translating this "scientific" part of the original German text, published in 1836, and has expressed "the sense of the propositions rather than the literal text" (1:7).

❦ Religious blood also circulates in another guise, particularly in devotional and spiritual texts. In addition to the blood of Jesus crucified, there are evocations of the blood of his Sacred Heart, of the Virgin Mary, of the child Jesus. These evocations help to understand the importance of the sweetness-sorrow dialectic, the relation between these two poles of that Romantic spirituality that André Rayez correctly defines as the quest of the love which seeks to suffer.[18] This love is what informs the devotions to the Sacred Heart and the Marian devotions. The child Jesus might seem an object of pure love without any element of suffering, but the Romantics turned even him into a figure of suffering. The phenomenon is worth studying, for it is similar to what one finds in the political uses of the blood of the crucified Jesus which I shall examine afterward.

Devotion to the Sacred Heart was at the time "the normal and ordinary way for the Christian to express his love of God" (Rayez, *Histoire*, p. 311). What was, before the Revolution, primarily a convent devotion, for various reasons, partly because the Vendée Royalists used the Sacred Heart as a talisman for protection against bullets, became a widespread devotion. In 1792 Louis XVI reportedly consecrated both himself and France to the Sacred Heart before his death: "It is in your adorable Heart that I wish to place the effusions of my afflicted soul." The year 1800 saw the foundation of the Congregation of the Sacred Hearts of Jesus and Mary. Later, the Benedictines of the Sacred Heart at La Pierre-qui-vire were established, and during the Bourbon Restoration the Association of the Sacred Heart was founded and the custom of First Friday devotions began (for Louis the Desired—Louis XVIII—first took power on the first Friday of April 1814, and returned to power the first Friday of July 1815). Gradually, during the course of the century, the devotion would be less and less associated with the Royalist cause, but Louis XVI's vow was finally accomplished with the construction of the Basilica of the Sacred Heart in Montmartre in 1876, a construction not without political overtones.[19]

The cult did not go unquestioned at the time. Was the Sacred Heart a physical or a symbolic object? For Fr. Grou, *L'Intérieur de Jésus et de Marie* (1815), the Sacred Heart was only a new name for a venerable devotion; the "heart" was not physiological but the center of feelings and emotions. Our imagination needs a "perceptible object" and indeed Jesus' physical heart is admirable because of its union with his divinity, but one must not stop there, one must move on to the psychological. Mother Saint-Jérôme, in her *Mois du Sacré Coeur* (1833, much reprinted), used a rather different language; she emphasized how the faithful believer must make gift of his or her own heart to the suffering Heart of Jesus so the two hearts can be united:

Oh Jesus! I consecrate my heart to you; place it within your own! It is within your Heart that I desire to breathe, by your Heart that I desire to

love; within your heart I desire to live, ignored by the world and known
only to you; it is within that Heart that I shall find the ardors of love which
will consume my own heart! (P. 11)

The faithful should dwell within the Heart of Jesus, go out from it
to do good works, and then return to it to find refuge and strength.
Those who are not pure enough to dwell in the Heart of Jesus can
enter into It via the Heart of Mary.

The devotional manual for the confraternities was *Le Salut de la
France* (1815), also often printed. The cover has an illustration of a
realistic heart, with arteries, but girded with the crown of thorns
and surmounted by a cross.[20] (In the same way, the Miraculous
Medal of the apparition of the Virgin rue du Bac in Paris in 1830
depicts two Hearts surmounted by a cross.) The political implications of the manual's text are clear; France has been punished for
her revolt against divinely instituted authority but happily the
floods of divine grace still flow from the heart of Jesus, and France
can be renewed by the adoration of that Heart. The Sacred Heart is
more important than the crown of thorns, even than the cross; these
last two are sanctified because the Savior touched them, but his
Heart is permanently united to his divinity, it is the principal center of his virtues and his power. During the 1820s, the language of
these devotional texts becomes increasingly "baroque." In 1828
Louis Barat published *La Dévotion pratique au Sacré Coeur de Jésus et
au très saint Coeur de Marie par la médiation de saint Joseph en union avec
tous les anges et tous les saints,* which offers a history of the devotion,
litanies, rosaries, prayers, meditations. The Heart is the "rallying
point" where all other devotions meet, the only object the faithful
need to know; the heart of man offers its effusions to the Heart of
Mary who unites them with her prayers and renders them acceptable to Jesus. So we should live sheltered within the Sacred Heart,
and one of the litanies ends with the prayer: "Holy Opening, receive me! Nothingness (*anéantissement*), consume me! Ocean of bene-
dictions, drown me!" This is an adaptation of the *anima christi* in
which the faithful believer penetrates into the Sacred Heart via a
contemplation of the wounds of the crucified Christ; the devotion is
thus linked to Jesus' suffering. "Holy Heart of Jesus, overwhelmed
with bitterness and plunged into an ocean of grief, oh how great is
my desire to bring some relief to your suffering!" The Heart is the
figure of Jesus' redemptive suffering; it is also the center of love, a

"fiery furnace of divine love, whose flames rise to the height of forty cubits, like those of Babylon, and then soar to the hearts of the highest seraphim, to enflame them ever more intensely" (p. 232). Images of fire are characteristic of these texts. A number of poems praise the Sacred Heart, such as this one by C.-M. Le Guillou:

> Sacred Heart, which my heart adores,
> Divine object of my hopes,
> I burn for thee as dawn begins,
> And I shall burn for thee at even.
> My soul is the thirsty hart
> Which asks of heaven a drop of water;
> I am the unsheltered vine;
> Heart of Jesus, be my elm.
> As a perfumed breeze
> Which refreshes all the valley,
> Or as a beloved dew
> Which the heavens draw from the grass,
> So, on my wilted soul, Heart of Jesus, pour your blood;
> And may my soul then renewed
> Return to its age of innocence![21]

Fire, liquid, refuge, renewal, love, suffering. I quote as a final example a text from the Trappist Baron de Géramb, from his *Aspirations aux sacrées Plaies de N.S.J.C.* (1826):

> My God, I am seized with the most intense grief as I contemplate the Sacred Wound of your adorable Heart and the blood which flows therefrom. This spectacle, oh my beloved Jesus, reminds me that I am all the more guilty because I have caused that wound by my sins; this memory fills me with sorrow and regret. Accept, oh my beloved Savior, my deep repentance and my resolution to hate above all the sin which opened that wound. I adore it most deeply, while considering it an effect of your mercy and the source of my eternal bliss; I kiss it, I press it fondly against my heart which from today on wants to love you every time it beats. (P. 17)

Wounds and fondness, regret and hope; the blood which streams from the Heart of Jesus reconciles opposite poles.

The nineteenth century was a great century of Marian devotion, but Mary was also seen as the *mater dolorosa,* the symbol of a love that accepts suffering. This symbolism is also expressed by images of blood. In her apparition at La Salette, the Virgin bore the marks of the Passion; and Jesus spoke there as a kind of god of wrath. Mary assumes the role of protectress of humanity, the intercessor— though even she speaks rather harshly, and Mary the protectress is also Mary who suffers. One can quote as typical Anne-Marie Haute-feuille's *Vie de la Sainte Vierge* (1841):

> Mary, present at Jesus' sacrifice and immolating herself with Him, partakes of his suffering. The thorns which pierce his brow are for her a crown of pain, and the same nails which attach the Son to the cross also attach the Mother. (P. xv)

Mary, mother of the crucified Jesus and the symbol of sweetness, is seen as Mary the Crucified, the Virgin of the Seven Dolors. Grou's manual, *L'Intérieur de Jésus et Marie* (1815), one of the texts of Romantic spirituality most exemplary of the theme of penetration, emphasizes that the imitation of Jesus is not enough, we must penetrate his Heart. The model is Mary; we must die with Jesus, as she did. "Mary, dying with Jesus, had no thought for anyone else" (2:346). Sweetness and suffering are thus combined in Marian devotions.

This fusion even marks the devotions to the child Jesus. I have already cited Lasausse's *Le Chrétien brûlant d'amour pour Jésus-Christ crucifié;* the text contains a meditation on the Precious Blood shed by Jesus at his circumcision. "What suffering, during this ceremony, the child-God must have known, he whose nature was so tender! What an affliction for Mary!" Yet the child Jesus chose to undergo this experience in all humility, and if he wept, it was because of the sad spectacle offered by the human race; we must join our tears to his. The blood circulates from the crucified Christ to the circumcision in other manuals, particularly those centered on the month of the child Jesus, January, where the combination of sweetness and suffering is omnipresent. The anonymous *Jésus-Christ modèle des Chrétiens* (1828), written for young people, devotes more than half its pages to the contemplation of the Passion:

> My soul, behold his sacred flesh which flies in bits under the blows of the whips, behold his adorable blood which flows in torrents, the soldiers are covered with it, and yet their fervor does not relent! Their forces are rekindled!

Collin de Plancy, having converted from anticlerical to devotional literature, published a compilation, *Le Mois de l'enfant Jésus,* in

1845. It was reprinted thirty-eight times before the end of the century. It contains litanies ("Child, who, being life itself, was nourished with milk, have mercy upon us; Child, who, being the Word, yet kept silence, have mercy upon us," etc.) and meditations on, for instance, the Precious Blood and sacred tears that Jesus shed at his circumcision, but also on Jesus fetching water and firewood for Mary, sweeping out his room, and the like. Collin de Plancy also informs us that the child Jesus, having no need to sleep, "spent his nights going over all the sufferings he was to endure because of his love for us. . . . He particularly thought about the whips and the thorns." A poem by Antony Deschamps makes a similar transfer of the crucifixion to the child Jesus:

> There is a beautiful painting, by Albano, I believe,
> The child Jesus sleeping, stretched out on his cross.
> Any man who sees it meditates and admires Jesus
> Trying out the instrument of his forthcoming martyrdom,
> For such, alas, divine Child, is your Father's will.
> Soon this wood will be all covered with your blood;
> And when your destiny here below is ripe,
> What was your cradle will become your sepulcher.
> And so you teach us, oh child Redeemer!
> To prepare our souls for the great day of misfortune,
> And, as you did in our world of dirt,
> To sleep on our cross before we are nailed thereto.[22]

This is an extreme metaphoric manifestation of a theme which is widespread at the time, that the life of Jesus held two pages, one of blood and suffering, the other of success and glory. Not only sermons but also poems are organized according to this structure—by Xavier de Ravignan, Alletz, Esquiros, Turquety, A.-L. Constant, and others. The child Jesus who suffers and bleeds offers an extreme case of this synthesis of sweetness and sorrow, as do the images of the sweet, suffering, even bleeding Virgin Mary. One of the results of this synthesis is that metaphors describing the blood of Jesus move back and forth between suffering and sweetness. Alletz, when he describes the Crucifixion in his *Nouvelle Messiade* of 1830, evokes "the blood which runs down his cheek, imitating tears" and falls drop by drop on the marble floor, "Just as a soft rain in the late season / Before rolling down to the green grass / From the crown to the branch, from the twig to the leaf, / Flows, and, falling on the grass, finds rest in the form of a pearl" (p. 444). The metaphor may strike us as inappropriate, but was seemingly acceptable at that time. Suffering led to sweetness.

❦ The most important circulation of religious blood during the period was in political literature, and there again we find a fusion of sweetness and suffering. Whatever the author's political position, the blood of the crucified Christ serves to give a meaning—usually positive and progressive in its implications—to suffering and to the cataclysmic events of history. The subject is a very rich one; I only cite a few examples to demonstrate the wide range of these evocations.[23] We have already evoked the function of the theandric blood for Joseph de Maistre; Christ as Mediator is also at the heart of the thought of Louis de Bonald—Jesus, by choosing to make his act of sacrifice, made sacrifice the central social activity, thereby substituting the relation of love for the previous relations of fear or hatred. The sacrifice on the cross constituted a general mediation, which knows its particular applications in the repeated sacrifice of the mass. The Crucifixion is the emblem of all social structure, the key to all authority—and that authority is therefore both of divine origin and an authority of love. Christ's blood was shed, and continues to be shed, in order to create a political reign of justice. Near the end of the first half of the nineteenth century, Louis Veuillot, who shares the traditionalist perspective of Maistre and Bonald, still sees in the Sacred Blood a key to all history. In *Rome et Lorette* (1841) he repeats Maistre's theories about the links between the blood sacrifice of innocent victims and the redemption of history. If every revolution in its way represents the Crucifixion and so represents a dreadful page of history where the blood flows, that blood flows

> in order to redeem mortal man, just as the very blood of God flowed to redeem our souls. This second redemption, which goes hand in hand with the immolation of the wicked and breaks, by the same suffering and on the same scaffolding, victims whose immortal life will commence in such totally different ways—this ever bleeding Calvary where the Just dies between two thieves—that is the great lesson of history. (P. 117)

The blood of Christ is also seen as symbolic of the religious and metaphysical crisis experienced by modern humanity. The texts of Nerval, Vigny, Renan, and Leconte de Lisle depicting Christ's agony and despair in the garden were largely inspired by the German Jean-Paul Richter; Claude Pichois has analyzed these themes in a masterful study.[24] These symbolic episodes are always drenched in "bloody sweat." In one typical minor text, Gustave de La Noue's *Enosh* (1834), in a long section called "Grotto of Gethsemani" an angel shows Christ all the evils and misfortunes of history, past, present, and to come, including Julian the Apostate, Luther, and the guillotine. When Jesus asks, "Is that all?" the angel answers:

> "No. The cup is bitter to your lips;
> Your eyes weep blood, your body shakes with fever,
> And your long brown hair stands up on your forehead!
> But the abyss is so deep, that all this is as nothing!" (P. 134)

Religious blood becomes an essential element in the depiction of metaphysical despair, but this despair is provoked by the problem of the nature of history, a nature which in turn finds its symbolic meaning (or meaninglessness) in the shedding of the blood on the cross. More than anyone else, Blanc Saint-Bonnet, in *De l'unité* of 1841 and *De la douleur* of 1849, developed these themes of Joseph de Maistre and others, while also integrating them with the spirituality of the Sacred Heart. The Sacred Heart of Love is the locus par excellence of the desire for social unity and for the unity between humanity and the absolute. The Heart bleeds because it is the place where mortals are separated from God, and our arterial, pulsating heart wants to escape our breast toward the Ideal. The human heart is thus an "emblem," and the Sacred Heart of Jesus is the ideal emblem of all harmonious relations and of the meaningful, teleological structure of history, at the center of which, of course, is the Crucifixion.

> In order to reveal his mission, God came down to this globe. When, taking upon himself and within his heart all the sufferings of all the ages and bearing the cross of the world, he climbs Golgotha, a voice says: Behold the man! And man will say in his turn, if this cup cannot pass from me, may Thy will be done! Henceforth the ardent Son of Being will found a real existence in the relative, by liberty, and trace, by the paths of suffering, eternal outposts toward the absolute for that being. Everything will move according to this unique being; God has found the place where his grace might descend; the living poem of his creation will march onward toward his unity. (*De la douleur*, p. 236)

Blanc Saint-Bonnet's thought represents the final evolution of Romanticism's prolonged consideration of the social and historical significance of the Precious Blood, a consideration that began not only with the "reactionary" Joseph de Maistre but also with the "unknown philosopher," the mystic Louis-Claude de Saint-Martin, and even more with Ballanche. These two authors proposed conceptions of the function of the Sacred Blood in history which were much more open to interpretations and theories of history of a progressive nature. For Saint-Martin, the Regenerator (one of his names for Christ), by his sacrifice makes possible the concrete realization of humankind's potential for glory; by loving the Reparator (another name for Christ) and by imitating and repeating his sacrifice, the "man of desire" continues the task of reparation and can even go beyond the Reparator in realizing the task of salvation. Certain socialist thinkers would find in this thesis an argument in favor of creating utopia here below. In his *Ministère de l'homme esprit* (1802), Saint-Martin retraces the history of sacrifice which culminates in the blood of the Reparator which "reestablishes man in the fullness of his relations and on the perfect path of his return to his first beginnings" (p. 236), a path followed by each "man of desire" and by the history of humanity. Here again, the metaphor of the Sacred Blood is the vehicle of this transformation. "The voluntary shedding of his blood, to which no blood on this earth could be compared, alone could effect the transposition of foreign substances which bathed in mankind's blood" (p. 275). Saint-Martin's preoccupations were of course entirely spiritual, but others would use them, particularly disciples of Fourier, to create a political theory.

According to Ballanche, we create progress by our choice in love of suffering and sacrifice, thanks to the principle of "solidarity and reversibility." Jesus, by his crucifixion, is both the Redeemer and the Initiator of mankind in this palingenesic progress. His many disciples merit a special study; I mention as typical Martial Guillemon, who tried to combine Ballanche and the idealist philosopher Maine de Biran, but who also believed in the "revolutionary power" of the Gospel text, a power he explains in terms of blood and suffering:

Humanity was constituted by the mediation of Jesus Christ. And just as it is above all from the depths of suffering that the soul rises to God and the union of souls in God takes place, just as the charity which unites men here below is love in suffering, so the Mediator had to offer the type of this love; the Mediator needed to prolong his agony at length, before the eyes of his Mother, before crying out as He died, "It is finished!"[25]

Suffering is what creates both the uniqueness and the efficacy of Christianity:

> What characterizes Christianity and distinguishes it from the primitive initiation is that it is a religion of charity, that is the religion of love in suffering. The primitive initiation was one of love and happiness; the new initiation was one of love and suffering; it took place on Calvary. (De l'intelligence, p. 235)

And this new initiation will lead to the new social word—and world—"association." The Sacred Blood figured in the mystical socialist thought of A.-L. Constant.[26] One could also cite that other mystic socialist, Alphonse Esquiros, or Mickiewicz's texts on Poland as the crucified messianic nation, or the "new Passions" that Christ experiences in order to create with his blood the universal social salvation of humanity in texts such as Alexandre Soumet's Divine épopée (1841) or Edgar Quinet's Ahasvérus (1833).

In the political discourse of the period, the Sacred Blood circulates from right to left; religious explanations and justifications for the Revolution of 1789, including the cults of the martyrdom of Louis XVI and Marie Antoinette, become justifications for violent revolution, proposing that it is through suffering and only through suffering that the sweetness of the heavenly City/utopia can be known. The Sacred Blood penetrates and nourishes the socialist discourse of 1848, and finally flows on the barricades in June, those barricades which are thought of as the new Calvary and which presaged a new resurrection of humanity. The evocations of the crucified Christ and his blood during that revolution are too numerous and widespread to be dismissed as eccentric or marginal.[27]

What is ultimately most astounding about the Precious Blood in these evocations is its dynamic viscosity. The blood flows, pulsates, gushes, drips, spreads; it is even more dynamic in the way it circulates among various domains. Traditionally a subject of devotional literature, the blood becomes a subject of medical, scientific, historical, political, poetic, and erotic texts. That circulation requires that the precious Blood be treated metaphorically, and the play between literal, physical, and symbolic meanings is complex, but clearly the symbolic uses do not suppress the physical referent. On the contrary, both functions become simultaneously more developed and more intense. The medical tone that Debreyne employs in discussing flagellation does not suppress the spiritual register that Chocarne uses in discussing Lacordaire's flagellation. One might expect that this widespread circulation of the Precious Blood might have produced some crests where the two currents would meet; but I do not know of any text that reveals a conflict stemming from the various uses of the metaphor, or that even questions the validity of the metaphor. Rather, the literal and the metaphorical are fused, just as the various registers of discourse are fused. Political uses of the Precious Blood are made by the right, but also by the left. We may have trouble appreciating and evaluating this combination of unity and diversity so characteristic of the Romantic mind, but the circulation of the Precious Blood helps to reveal how techniques of metaphorization made that combination possible. The philosopher Vladimir Jankélévitch has shown how one may resort to irony to alleviate a sense of guilt. Metaphorization probably serves a similar function, but it also makes possible the expression of a belief in progress, in the becoming of history. "The earth became inebriated with this Precious Blood," Nerval asserts, an intoxication created essentially by its dynamic circulation in literature, religion, politics, eroticism, science, linking the poles of sweetness and suffering, a pulsating circulation which however always goes from the past toward the future, showing that out of evil, good will come.

# 6 ❦ From History to Hysteria: Nineteenth-Century Discourse on Loudun

In the mid-sixteenth century, under Cardinal Richelieu, the town of Loudun was struck by an epidemic of diabolic possessions, centered on the Ursuline convent and, particularly, on the superior of that convent, Sister Jeanne des Anges. A priest of the town, Urbain Grandier, was eventually identified as the Devil's instrument and burned at the stake. These possessions were much discussed during the nineteenth century. There are six literary reconstructions in plays or novels, some studies of the affair as a religious phenomenon, and, more important, a great many historical and medical texts that discuss the possessions, some in passing, some very extensively. One might ask why there was such a considerable renewal of interest in a phenomenon that had taken place more than a hundred and fifty years before, dramatic it is true, but the chief actors were hardly major political figures. In fact, Loudun was somehow related to, or shed light on, a number of problems of considerable concern in nineteenth-century France: politics (the relations between Church and State, and also the old dispute over a Jacobine centralized power versus a Girondin regionalist federalism), and the definition and treatment of hysteria, to name but two.[1]

Almost all of these texts make considerable use of the first major study on Loudun, published by the Protestant Nicolas Aubin in 1693 (well after the events, and somewhat prejudiced). The texts often question the validity of what Aubin says, and they particularly reject his thesis (echoed by Pierre Beyle and generally by the *philos-*

*ophes* of the eighteenth century) that the whole affair was a comedy staged by the nuns. In the course of the century, a considerable number of primary documents about the affair were unearthed, published, and discussed: in 1828–29, the autobiographical texts of the Jesuit Jean Joseph Surin, one of the exorcists, came to light; then in 1838, F. Danjou (*Archives*) reprinted much material from the Bibliothèque nationale and elsewhere; and in the last third of the century, Alfred Barbier and Charles Barbier de Montault discovered and published a great many documents. Finally the autobiography of Jeanne des Anges herself was published in 1883, although it was presented as a psychological rather than a historical document.[2]

This literature far from exhausts the subject, nor is it "acceptable" in modern scientific terms. It is highly polemic, efforts at synthetic statements are rare and not very successful, attention is generally centered on one of the actors (Grandier's persecutor Laubardemont, or Grandier, or Jeanne). And among the texts, the contradictions are many and often flagrant, not only about matters of interpretation but also about the very events and even minor details of fact. How many judges were there at Grandier's trial? The number varies from twelve to fifteen, according to which nineteenth-century author one reads. Variations about the probe used to examine (some would say torture) Grandier are quite revealing about a particular author's imagination and the degree of horror he wants to create in describing the trials Grandier underwent. He was probed all over his body to find any insensitive spots whose existence would prove that he was indeed a sorcerer (a no-win situation). Supposedly four such spots were found, one on each testicle and one on either side of the anus (not until Legué's 1874 text does one discover this, and even then the locations are given in Latin). Some authors suggest that one end of the probe was rounded, the other sharply pointed; others, that the doctor replaced the probe with his thumb for the "insensitive" spots; Jay and Dumas suggest that the probe had a hidden spring with a complicated mechanism, so the doctor could withdraw the sharp point at will.

The texts even disagree about the weather when Grandier was burned at the stake. Some describe a marvelous storm with thunder, lightning, torrential rains; others, a bright sun and clear sky. The difference depends on the kind of dramatic effect they are trying to create. One legendary element of Grandier's suffering disappears during the century: the red-hot crucifix. As was customary, when he was dying he was offered a crucifix to contemplate and adore, and Grandier supposedly at that moment threw back his head, according to some because he was a diabolic sorcerer (Richelieu's version in his *Memoirs*), according to others because the priests had heated the crucifix to a red-hot state (Petitot's version in his notes to Richelieu's *Memoirs*). In Vigny's novel, the hero Cinq-Mars discovers the foul deed—rain, falling on the crucifix, turns into steam—furious, Cinq-Mars seizes it with his cloak and strikes Grandier's persecutor Laubardemont on the forehead, creating a permanent scar. In his play, Alexandre Dumas substitutes a poisonous chemical substance for the fire. In his historical study, Dumas claims that Grandier was struck with the crucifix; blood flowed from his nose at the third blow. Finally, in 1880, Legué notes that no contemporary account makes any mention of the incident, and concludes it is undoubtedly completely legendary.

Other examples of these contradictions are more disquieting. For instance, there are discrepancies about Grandier's post of spiritual director of the Ursuline nuns. Did Grandier want the position, and did the Ursulines refuse him because of his bad reputation? Or did Sister Jeanne ask him to become director, and he refused, either because he was too busy, or for some other reason (usually erotic; his mistress, jealous, would not allow it, etc.). The second hypothesis makes it possible to explain the whole affair as a result of Jeanne's jealousy, justifying the "uterine hysteria" analysis. Bonnelier and Andral solve the problem by claiming that Grandier was the spiritual director, which is historically false.

❦ The Catholic discussions are few. The traditional defense of the possessions as truly diabolical seems to have become quite impossible to maintain, and one must await Aldous Huxley and Michel de Certeau for a new interpretation that could take into account the religious elements in the affair. Two volumes of Migne's *Encyclopédie catholique* do discuss Loudun, and in quite different ways. The first discussion is in the *Dictionnaire des sciences occultes* (1846), the second in the *Dictionnaire des prophéties et miracles* (1854), but the differences between them should not be read as indicative of any historical evolution, for the volumes in Migne's series are often contradictory in their attitudes toward politics and religion. The former claims to be an adaptation of Collin de Plancy's *Dictionnaire infernal* of 1837, but the article on Loudun belies that claim. The anonymous author maintains that the possessions really took place, and draws a picture of Grandier as a jealous man much given to the sins of the flesh, and a mesmerizer. And he adds that "God permitted this suffering and perturbation" to come upon the nuns "for reasons we have no right, nor need, to understand." In the 1854 volume, its author, Canon Lecanu, concludes that the nuns were not victims of diabolic possession. They may have wanted to be so possessed, for possession was often considered the final trial on the road to sanctity, but rather the possession was the manifestation of some kind of illness, or a fright further exacerbated by the exorcists. The nuns merit pity rather than wrath. The exorcists were undoubtedly sincere; moreover, "how could they be expected to know more about mental illness and nervous afflictions than the doctors of the age, who understood what was going on no better than they did?" Lecanu writes with charity and comprehension; he suspects that political pressures were at work. This Catholic priest produced one of the most measured evaluations and analyses of Loudun of the whole century. In contrast, Fr. Leriche (1858), represents a reactionary Catholic viewpoint. He still maintains the total truth of the possessions and claims that only the Church can combat them; science is quite powerless when faced with epilepsy or catalepsy, not the mention possession. According to Leriche, there was no imposture, no malingering, it was not a matter of melancholia or of hysteria ("a quite rare illness, neither epidemic nor contagious"); the Ursulines manifested all the true marks of possession. Eudes de Mirville, writing in 1854 and 1855, defends quite similar theses.

Since Michel de Certeau's studies, the fascinating person for us in the whole affair is not so much Grandier as the Jesuit Surin, who arrived on the scene after Grandier's death to take over the exorcism of the superior, Jeanne des Anges. He decided to reduce the number of exorcisms to one session per day, in the afternoon. He spent the mornings trying to enrich her spiritual life, justifying this by a rather medical kind of reasoning: the best way to help the soul resist the Devil is to increase its sanctity. What ensued almost constituted a kind of psychoanalysis, an experience that Jeanne at first resisted violently, and which also encountered the strong opposition of the other exorcists and of Surin's Jesuit superiors. But he persisted. And his therapy was, in a way, successful; Surin transformed Jeanne into a kind of traveling miracle worker, who bore on her fingers the stigmatized names of Jesus, Mary, and Joseph. She also possessed a corset marked by a balm sent by St. Joseph, which was very useful when applied during childbirths. But, to accomplish this transformation, Surin had to undergo all the classical trials of psychoanalysis. Jeanne's hatred for him was transformed into an amorous passion, whose dangers he recognized and managed to avoid. Then came a long period when she tried to test him, and finally the phenomena of transference took place. When the devils left Jeanne, it was only to harass Surin. He spent many years obsessed with the devils (one is possessed by devils when they are inside one, obsessed when they attack one from the outside), unable to speak, convinced that he was damned, possessed with a "furious desire" to throw himself out windows or down wells. But he, like Jeanne, finally triumphed over all these trials.

What did the nineteenth century think of Surin? The record is quite disappointing. For Bertrand, Surin is only remarkable by his astounding combination of piety and credulity. Sauzé, who knew of the existence of Surin's autobiographical texts, did not bother to read them. He senses that Surin innovated in his exorcism techniques, but only discusses his use of flagellation. And he attributes the Jesuit's madness, "the most complicated cerebral affection one could possibly imagine," to his chastity, and nothing but his chastity. The exorcisms, he adds, intensified Surin's sexual desires. For Legué, Surin was simply a tried and true fanatic, a mind impregnated with the most mystical ideas and driven mad by religion. The only major exception to these negative judgments are, in France at least, two articles published in *L'Ami de la religion* in 1825, occasioned by the publication of Surin's autobiographical texts. The author speaks with admiration about Surin's work at Loudun and with sympathy about his persecutions; Picot's article of 1867, follows the same line.

Surin was better appreciated in England by Edward Pusey, one of the founding fathers of Anglo-Catholicism. After having been instrumental in restoring the religious life in the Anglican communion, Pusey sought to enrich the spiritual literature that was available for the regular clergy; also, deeply ecumenical, he made many efforts to blend Anglican and Roman spirituality. Accordingly, in 1844, he translated and wrote an introduction to Surin's *Foundations of the Spiritual Life*. Pusey's long introduction expresses great admiration for the spiritual grandeur of Surin's life and for his twenty

years of suffering which tempered his soul in the fires of purification. In Pusey's eyes, Surin offered an admirable example of the
sanctity of privation. The two, Pusey and Surin, in fact rather re-
sembled each other. The Anglican also knew a difficult life, was
persecuted by his church, subject to depression. He was able to
understand Surin's greatness.

❧ The Romantic adage, "You can do violence to history, provided you get her with child" should be transformed, when one
comes to the literary presentations of Loudun (novels, plays, short
stories) to "You can do violence to history, provided she gives birth
to a malformed fetus." The authors of these works do such violence
to history knowingly and unhesitantly. Bonnelier justifies the practice: only thus can one whip up the emotion that the Loudun affair
should produce in our day. For, more often than not, Loudun is
used for virulent anticlerical propaganda. These texts, which are all
tendentious, turn Grandier into a martyr-hero and are full of the
trappings of the Gothic novel (subterranean passages and caves,
hypnotisms, incest, various forms of magic). The only important
evolution has to do with Grandier's sexual mores. In the depictions
of the beginning of the century, he knows, but resists, the tempta-
tions of the flesh. Later on, he becomes a great lover as well as a
priest, a Casanova type, without being criticized for this—except
for Benia, who regrets that Grandier spent time philandering that
could better have been spent pursuing his career as a free thinker.

The best text is probably by Vigny, the worst by Alexander Dumas. Vigny's use of Cinq-Mars as a "naive witness" gives his description a certain realism; but introducing Cinq-Mars into the tale
obliges the novelist to make considerable changes both in Jeanne's
role in the possessions and in her later life. She is identified as
Laubardemont's daughter. After Grandier's death, she goes quite
mad, tries to assassinate Richelieu, and ends up a barmaid in a
posada on the frontier between France and Spain, where she dies
along with her brother. That brother is a superb criminal hero.
Vigny also kills off, one by one, all of Grandier's judges. In part,
these are efforts to tie up the loose ends of a complicated plot.
Vigny's book is still quite readable today and its political theses,
discussed later, at least have some seriousness about them.

Dumas is inventive about what happened before, not after, the
trial. In his drama, Grandier was first a soldier, in love with Ursule

de Sablé, and formerly the lover of Laubardemont's daughter, who is also, alas, the victim of her father's incestuous lust. Jeanne persecutes Grandier because he refused to make love to her, but he pardons her while he is burning at the stake, for, like Mary Magdalene, she has loved much. In addition, Grandier has a brother who is gifted with second sight when he is properly hypnotized—a gift that is of great use in organizing a highly complicated plot structure, facilitating changes of place. All this is not even good Dumas as playwright. And the action is slowed down by innumerable dissertations in favor of hypnotism, against the cloistered life, praising natural religion.

A special place should be given to *Urbain Grandier, ou les religieuses de Loudun, drame historique* (1836). The work, by an unknown writer, is not without merit; in many ways, it dramatizes the Loudun part of Vigny's novel. The humanist Quillet plays an important role (as in Vigny's novel, he is already a priest, which was not the case historically), as well as Fr. Joseph, Richelieu's gray eminence. As a result, the Church gets somewhat equitable treatment; it has both good and bad representatives. And there are a number of striking scenes. For instance, as in Vigny, a boy describes the tortures of Grandier from his perch high up in the assembly room, where he can see into the spot where the torture takes place; horrified, he wants to get down, but the mob, eager for gore, forces him to stay there and continue his description. At the stake, Grandier gives a very impressive speech synthesizing Eros and Agape, his loves for Madeleine de Brou and for God. Of all these literary texts, this one is closest to history. In Bonnelier's story, Laubardemont rapes the sister of Cinq-Mars and the child of that union is a Ursuline nun at Loudun, who tries to bring back to the path of virtue Laie, the nun who is in love with Grandier and accuses him out of spite. But Sister Jeanne and especially Fr. Joseph make sure that the ending is tragic, allowing Bonnelier to include an impressive depiction of how Grandier's mother goes mad.

The two literary reconstructions of Loudun from the end of the century are disappointing as well. Lennat's play is quite incredible. A certain "old man of Loudun" helps Grandier by hiding him in a marvelous subterranean chamber he had constructed for his own purposes years before. For the "old man" in his day had also been a priest, with advanced ideas about religion and moreover in love with a woman. In his subterranean chamber, he practices magic and punishes a woman who has accused Grandier of sexual misdeeds by making her copulate with a legless cripple. Thomas Benia composed both a poem and a short story, and they are equally bad. The poem praises the "revolutionary" virtues of Grandier ("This liberal priest, who suffered martyrdom, / Sounded the first death knell of a damnable regime") and also contains a number of erotic passages. The short story, which owes much to Legué's researches, only studies Grandier during the year 1617, when he was supposedly already the object of the persecutions of Richelieu and Fr. Joseph, who try to assassinate him. According to Benia, Grandier had three mistresses during that year, which makes him a libertine in both senses of the word.

Why is this literature, at least to our eyes, of such bad quality? It reveals quite crudely its propagandistic purposes. It is reductionist, treating Loudun in uniquely sexual or political terms. It does its best to turn Grandier into a martyr-hero, a role for which the historical person did not really possess the qualifications. The plot devices, the strings pulled in order to provoke the reader's emotional reactions, are too obvious. The Gothic trappings, the quest for scandal, the complicated plots, tend to exclude any psychological development. But perhaps there is a more fundamental problem: how can one re-create the events of Loudun in literature when there was little if any agreement about their meaning among historians, theologians, and psychologists?

The major historical debate about Loudun in the nineteenth century revolved around the question of Richelieu's responsibility for Grandier's persecution. Aubin had already accused the cardinal of having had Grandier burned, and this thesis is echoed by many of the medical writers on Loudun, by the novelists and playwrights, and also by a number of historians (Jay, Lesourd, Figuier, Legué, Henri Martin, Tiby, even the *Grand Dictionnaire universel* by Larousse). These authors disagree about Laubardemont's role. They explain the acts that they attribute to Richelieu in several ways: revenge for insults he had received from Grandier when he was bishop of Luçon; Grandier was the author, or coauthor of the anti-Richelieu pamphlets attributed to the "cordelière" of Loudun; or, in Henri Martin's view, Richelieu's superstitious nature led him to believe that Grandier was really possessed of the devil. Others (Barbier) refuse this thesis, depicting a Richelieu who, quite enlightened, abjured any such belief in the devil. Then, between the late

1830s and 1850s, a number of authors come to question, at times severely, this thesis about Richelieu's responsibility in the affair (Abel Hugo, Bazin, Fournel, Lecanu, Michelet), claiming that the affair was of too little importance to engage Richelieu's concern, or if indeed he thought that Grandier was the author of pamphlets against him, he could have found a number of much more expeditious ways of dealing with him. Only Vigny links Richelieu's responsibility with a political thesis (here he is indebted to Montlosier); Richelieu was the ancestor of Jacobinism, of the abuses of overly centralized power, which is what Vigny primarily criticizes in *Cinq-Mars*. Richelieu's complicity in Grandier's persecution is essential for his thesis.

There are other interpretations. For Leriche, the fact that Richelieu believed in the diabolic possessions is a proof of their historical reality! The nicest contrast is offered by Mirville and Gasparin. According to Mirville, a Catholic, Laubardemont was a true hero, a sincere, upright man, who acted on his own; Richelieu's bitterness played no role in the affair, and Mirville concludes, quoting Joseph de Maistre, "Our history is nothing more than a long series of lies and fabrications." For Gasparin, a Protestant, the affair was an infamous, bloody farce. Laubardemont was perhaps the main agent but he could not have acted without the support and at the instigation of a bitter Richelieu. And Gasparin adds that the cardinal is "a worthy specimen of the kind of regime many would have us return to." With Mirville and Gasparin, at least the political positions are clear. Elsewhere, it is difficult to explain these varying judgments about Richelieu, who according to some was superstitious, according to others enlightened but manipulating others' superstitious credulity to his own ends. For some, the cardinal was seeking revenge, for others he was quite indifferent to what was going on in Loudun.

Toward the end of the century, several new hypotheses were proposed. The earlier texts, which I have just discussed, are generally satisfied with sharply criticizing religious fanaticism. Michelet there is an exception. He borrows from Jay the parallel with two similar events, the persecution of Fr. Gauffridi and the possessions at Louviers. In all three events, the situation is the same: nuns possessed of the devil, a priest accused of sorcery, a jealous monk, the priest burned. Michelet also addresses the problem of the largely Protestant population of Loudun, but his reading is nonetheless essentially a sexual interpretation. He begins by evoking the heresy of the *alumbrados*, the doctrine that wishes "to kill off sin by having recourse to sin," seeks to quiet the demands of the flesh by satisfying them. There are no signs that any such heresy was present at Loudun. Michelet, if he is against those who burn, has nothing to say in favor of those who got burned; he refuses to indulge in the cult of Grandier as a holy martyr of free thought.

The whole problem of Loudun was revived, at the end of the century, because of the studies of Legué and the two Barbiers. Legué provides a good illustration of the virtues of erudite scholarship. His first study consists primarily of quotations and exclamations of horror, followed by a medical explanation; in our day, Satan's place is occupied by mental illness. By the time of his second work, he has become fascinated with what archival study can reveal about the affair. He begins with Grandier's arrival in Loudun, notes the complexities of social relations in the town, deeply divided between Protestants and Catholics, between those who supported Richelieu and those who remained faithful to Jean d'Armagnac, the representative of surviving feudal structures. Legué seems to have known about Barbier's discovery and analysis of the correspondence between Armagnac and Grandier before its publication, which shows the importance of Grandier's role in opposing the destruction of the keep at Loudun, which Richelieu wanted to destroy along with many others throughout France. Legué grasped that there was a link between the destruction of the fortified keep and the destruction of Grandier by Laubardemont, Richelieu's faithful servant.

❦ The most interesting literature of the century on Loudun comes, however, from doctors and especially psychiatrists. It evolves, and must be traced chronologically. Pétroz, in an 1813 article on "catalepsy," explains the "possessions" at Loudun by a theory of fluid sensitivity. The fluid, if concentrated in one channel, diminishes in others, and this produces phenomena of ecstasy, of stiffness, of cephaloplegia. The remote cause is usually some violent disappointment, some unhappiness in love. In his view, the possessed nuns of Loudun offer an exemplary instance of this nosology. Montègre's 1813 article "Convulsionaries" is primarily an attack against the "hypnosis" explanation of the Jansenist convulsions at Saint-Médard. Attacking Deleuze, Montègre claims that there is a reciprocal reaction between the physical and the psychological. He analyzes the possessed of Loudun as an instance of nervous illness or disorder; hypnotic manipulation of body "fluids" are in no way an explanation of the phenomena. Montègre was a disciple of Georges Cabanis, and he explains everything by a displacement of sensitivity. Both sorcerers and possessed are victims of this unhealthy displacement, the former alienated by their own dreams, the latter by the impressions they receive from the dreams of others. The events at Loudun show that the phenomenon often takes on an epidemic character. Montègre also attributes considerable weight to unrequited sexual desire. It is of little import whether the result is somnambulism, or ecstasy, or convulsions. These forms of displacement vary according to circumstances, to the temperament or the physiology of the person involved, although the disequilibrium always remains of the same nature.

The following year, Esquirol published his article on "demonomania," which was to become an influential text for medical practice. He described the events at Loudun as a very typical form of melancholic monomania. He considered this disorder to be characteristic of religious periods in history and religious temperaments; he believed that such events were diminishing in frequency and intensity as religious fervor waned. Esquirol underlined the epidemic nature of the phenomenon, which attacks women more than men, and often takes on erotic forms among women. The fundamental cause is human ignorance, weakness of the mind; fear or fright may bring on the crises, but the trouble stems primarily from false religious ideas. The therapy is the same as for monomania and melancholy; exorcism only makes matters worse.

Georget, writing in 1821, is more mundane: the nuns were simply putting on a show, practicing fraud. Alexandre Bertrand discusses Loudun at length in his *Traité du somnambulisme* of 1823 and in his *Du magnétisme animal* (*On the Hypnosis of the Mind*) of 1826. The *Traité* proposes that the exorcists were hypnotists, capable of producing the phenomena of direct communication of thought (this is why, for example, the nuns could speak or understand foreign languages that they had never learned). However, the success of these hypnoses can be explained by a hysterical affliction that exacerbated the imagination and which can have a contagious effect. The nuns were not guilty of fraud, but ill; the symptoms they present are commonly observed among sleepwalkers. *Du magnétisme animal* categorizes the disorders of Loudun among the forms of ecstasy, a natural phenomenon whose manifestations vary according to the religious context. Produced by moral exultation, ecstasy plays a great role in the history of religions. All the traditional characteristics of diabolic possession—and Bertrand enumerates them—are also characteristic of ecstasy (but Bertrand refuses to admit levitation; at the most, the ecstatic or possessed can jump in quite remarkable ways). Men (and especially women) are capable of experiencing ecstasy—it is not a morbid state, an illness, even though convulsive afflictions and certain circumstances can predispose individuals for the experience. Indeed, we continue to see many such ecstatic states in our time, especially thanks to hypnotism.

During the July Monarchy, this medical literature becomes even more abundant. Andral, 1836, who gets a great many of the details about Loudun wrong, joins Bertrand in identifying the phenomena as forms of ecstasy similar to those produced by artificial (that is, hypnotically induced) somnambulism. Frédéric Dubois, 1841, also follows the same lines as Bertrand. Except for levitation, these are all symptoms one can find in hypnosis-induced somnambulism. Dubois does suggest that Superior Jeanne was involved in fraud. Sauzé's 1840 doctoral thesis in medicine begins with a long historical study of the discourse on Loudun. He justifies his choice of thesis subject by the fact that not only was the affair abundantly documented, but it also has been the subject of considerable medical writing; Loudun is a worthwhile subject for scientific medical study. His diagnosis proposes that the phenomena represent a combination of catalepsy, hysteria, and demonomania; he applies this diagnosis to a number of the possessed and to their exorcists as well. To begin with Jeanne was sick, a hysteric; later, to please the mob and the exorcists, she practiced fraud. The nun Claire de Sazilly suffered catalepsy combined with erotomania, and so on. The therapy that Sauzé proposes is very simple indeed. All the trouble arose from the practice of chastity. Celibacy is unnatural; sexual satisfaction would have solved everything. All religions create these sicknesses of the imagination. Often catalepsy and hysteria are found together and therefore—the observation is important historically, even if it runs counter to Sauzé's emphasis on sexuality—hysteria does not have its locus in the uterus, which at the most contributes to its intensity, but in the brain. Thus men—and Surin is cited as an exemplary case—can be hysterics. Perhaps Loudun's greatest contribution to history was to help take hysteria out of the uterus.

Calmeil, in *De la folie* (1845), to my knowledge offers the first effort toward writing a history of madness; he spends more than fifty pages on Loudun. He shows a certain sympathy for the nuns, and rejects as improbable the thesis that they conspired together, or with the exorcists, to put on a show. His nosology is rather eclectic, sometimes describing the problem as cataleptic ecstasy with hallucinations, sometimes repeating the parallels with hypnotically induced somnambulism, but also evoking hysteria and demonopathia. One gets the sense that the terminology of mental illness had become quite vague in the mid-1800s; it did not remain so for long.

Loudun frequently receives mention and consideration in the immense controversial literature of those years about hypnosis, "turning tables," séances, and so forth. Alphonse Testu, *Le Magnétisme animal expliqué* (*Psychological Hypnosis Explained*, 1845), spends the necessary pages on Loudun, suggesting an evolution that is nearly the opposite of that of Sauzé. It all began as a fraud, but the nuns later experienced real convulsions, in part because of the nefarious effects of the exorcisms. Gasparin also follows this same schema of fraud at first, then an exacerbation of the nervous system.

Briquet represents a major turning point in 1859. Thereafter the study of Loudun would be linked with the phenomena at Morzine, where in the late 1850s a whole village underwent diabolic possession. The possessions persisted for some time despite the often harsh interventions of the clergy, the medical corps, the police, even the army. At the same time, the terminology of melancholia and demonopathology disappear, and fraud ceases to be cited as a reductionist explanation. Instead, Loudun becomes an example of a malady that was becoming more and more fashionable in medical discourse, hysteria. Briquet locates Loudun in a series of epidemics of hysteria combined with convulsions; he also raises serious doubts about the uterine origin of the sickness. If the boredom of the cloister and sexual abstinence contributed to the etiology, stomach disorders as well as convulsions were and are major marks of hysteria. Figuier in 1860 demonstrates how this new medical discourse influenced historical writing about the affair. Both the possessed and the exorcists, he claims, suffered from convulsive hysteria with a variety of complications; the affliction is also extremely contagious. Its forms extended to catalepsy and to artificial somnambulism, provoked by the exorcists. For some time, it would be impossible for any historian to write about Loudun without serving it up in a medical sauce.

Legué, who was a disciple of J. M. Charcot, contributed considerably to this medical discourse (1874, 1880, 1886). He situated Jeanne's hysteria not in the uterus, but in the gastric system. The course of the disease begins with hallucinations and proceeds to convulsions; then sensory perceptions are marked either by hyperesthesia (a sharpened sense of smell, so-called double sight, etc.), or by anesthesia. The disease then proceeds to more physiological manifestations, neuralgic symptoms in the ribcage, gastralgia, hepatalgia, together with secondary manifestations such as masturbation, exacerbated eroticism, a passionate desire to lie, to mislead, to accuse the innocent—all these symptoms are typical of hysteria, and the epidemic at Loudun went through all the forms of this morbid state. Loudun shows that hysteria has not changed over the course of the centuries: the documents from the sixteenth century describe exactly the symptoms and developments of the disease that Charcot was scientifically observing among the patients at the Salpétrière hospital. In short, Loudun proves that Charcot was right. This same principle governs the 1886 edition that Legué prepared and printed, along with Gilles de la Tourette, of Jeanne's hitherto unknown autobiography. With a preface by Charcot, it appeared in the "Bibliothèque diabolique." The purpose of the whole collection—as Charcot announces explicitly in his preface—was to prove the validity of Charcot's diagnosis of hysteria. History here proves a medical theory. The only compliment given Jeanne, if one may call it that, is that she is as good as any well-trained pathologist in offering a detailed description of all the characteristics of afflictions of the hysterical sort, providing a very complete and hence very interesting portrait of that illness. The language of her age was unable to explain what was happening to her, but, Charcot maintains, we now can explain it. Take, for instance, her "false pregnancy":

> As for the increase in the volume of her stomach which Jeanne noted, its interpretation is very simple. The paralysis of the muscular fibers of the intestine produces a hysterical tympanitis, which can be generalized throughout the abdomen or located in certain points and then is susceptible

of forming globulous tumors which stimulate in a very impressive way, for the subject who bears them, a *uterus gravidus*. (*Soeur Jeanne des Anges*, p. 81)

(If only Jeanne had understood, she would not have been tempted to cut herself open with a knife in order to baptize and then kill the fetus.) The text also offers a medical explanation for the holy names that appeared on her fingers, generally interpreted as fraudulent, even in the seventeenth century. Far from it, according to the authors: these were cutaneous hemorrhages produced by autosuggestion, which induced a deep vasomotor perturbation. Her attempt at suicide is common in many hysterics—who always stop short of the final act and carefully construct an impressive scene for suicide. Here again, Jeanne is exemplary. Surin is given similar, even harsher treatment. He was a victim of anemia, marked by all the characteristic symptoms of hysteria; his writings were "theological inanities." He and Jeanne were "two hysterics well made to understand and complement each other." A note adds that Surin, "the victim of erotic delirium, had the Superior strip down completely in order to whip and exorcise her," which is historically incorrect. Surin's innovations in exorcism are not mentioned.

We must be grateful to Legué and la Tourette for making available Jeanne's previously unknown text. It is an interesting work, on the borderline between spiritual autobiography and the autobiography of madness, but it does not hold a candle to Surin's autobiography. Jeanne was a rather superficial person, Surin lived out his adventure in full awareness and to the very depths. Yet one senses an immense gap between the lived experience recounted by Jeanne and her editors' commentaries. Both are quite self-satisfied, Jeanne about her holiness, the editors about their science which denies that holiness.

❧ I have divided this presentation of the nineteenth century's representation of Loudun into religious, historical, literary, and medical discourse, although the phenomenon requires an interplay among all these discourses. The nineteenth century managed to achieve that interplay between historical and medical discourse. Meanwhile, the literary discourse tended to stay on the sidelines, lurid and highly politicized perhaps, but little informed by what the historians and doctors were saying. Most remarkable is the relative absence of religious discourse. The authors in other fields were unable to understand that the seventeenth century used religious terminology and categories to discuss and express matters which at other times were expressed in other forms of discourse. Yet, the theories of Ludwig Feuerbach were well known in France from the late 1840s on. The discussions of Loudun at times owe a clear debt to Victor Cousin's thesis that religion must disappear, giving way to philosophy and science. Religious space does change and even, if one wishes, diminishes. Yet this does not seem to me to justify the nineteenth century's manifest incapacity, here, to comprehend religious discourse in its historical context. To explain that incapacity, one would have to undertake a historical analysis of the relations between Church, State, and University during that century. My study of Loudun reminds me of two personal experiences, one a reading experience, the other a lived one.

The reading experience came with Roger Martin du Gard's *Jean Barois* (1913). His *Thibaults* was one of my favorite novels when I was an adolescent, so I went on to read *Jean Barois*. As an American Episcopalian, I was totally incapable of understanding the bitterness toward religion manifested in the text. I now understand that anger somewhat better, but I still think that there is something rather naive about both Leriche's religious commentary on Loudun and the anticlericalism of many of the other texts. The lived experience took place at Tetuan, in Morocco, in 1985, where in the souk I was witness to a religious procession complete with a gilt-horned calf being led to sacrifice, a guru, musicians, followed by hysterics, crying, convulsing, gesticulating. The latter were being both gently beaten and protected by the members of the confraternity, and were probably on their way, observed my friend and guide Jean-Claude Berchet, to be cured. Jeanne and Surin were cured, and the nineteenth century could not take that therapy into account.

# ❦ III

# Redefining Romanticism by Interdisciplinarity

# 7  ❦  The Theory of Harmonies

The poet receives at birth the key to the symbols, the understanding of the figures; what seems to others incoherent and contradictory is for him a harmonious contrast, a distant chord on the universal lyre.

—Sainte-Beuve, *Pensées de Joseph Delorme,* 1829

The word *harmony* recurs frequently in Romantic writing, as the title of a poem or collection of poems and also in socialist texts, in theology, philosophy, even in science. It is more difficult to indicate what idea, or ideas, the word then conveyed. I leave aside here cases where no philosophical question seems at stake. For instance, when Stolberg's translator says that the Catholic religion is "a temple all of whose parts are in perfect harmony with each other," he is simply claiming that one must believe the whole faith.[1] Nor am I concerned with the common esthetic sense of the term, the agreement between parts of a work in a proportion which creates a pleasing effect—indeed, that kind of harmony is not notably characteristic of Romantic art. On the other hand, various synonyms of the word must also be studied. Bonald, who theorized greatly about harmonies and theology, rarely used the word, preferring *rapport* (relation) or analogy. It is the way of seeing which is behind these words that is of interest—a quest for consonant relations between dissimilar entities, in particular between the divine and human, or the transcendent and immanent. If indeed what the Romantics called a harmony we often now call an analogy, it is perhaps because the perception of the relation between X and Y is no longer the same. For the Romantics, the harmonious analogy reveals and makes real, materializes, the profound unity of divine creation. Because this is a unity in which we no longer very much believe, we must be satisfied with simple comparisons. In Romantic thought, establishing a relation between two things not only allows one to delineate them better by a play of contrast and identity, but it also helps one discern some common transcendent element from which the two derive. If they preferred Nicolas de Malebranche to Descartes, it was because Malebranche gave innate ideas a transcendent locus of origin. Even a Portalis, who wanted to remain faithful to neo-Lockean sensationalist philosophy and nonetheless prove the existence of God, turns to a hypothetical "interior self" through which our "moral afflictions" and "intellectual faculties" make us aware and thus sure of "our secret relations with the author of all perfection."[2] The goal of many thinkers of the first half of the century was to establish and define this link between the divine, the self, and the world, and this link is usually conceived of as a harmony.

In religious discourse, the goal was partly to renew apologetics. After the Enlightenment, the revolutionary persecutions, and the decadence of neo-Cartesian theology—not to mention such old proofs such as the claim that if Jesus was not divine, then he must have been an impostor or the miraculous propagation of Christianity (despite Gibbon, this and other equally exhausted arguments were frequently cited), it was clear that some new artillery was needed. One could offer new proofs (for instance, the civilizing virtues of Christianity) or rejuvenate old ones by extending them in some way or other. And this is where harmony enters into play. At the risk of oversimplifying a very complex issue, one could say that the notion of harmony informs three apologetic efforts.

First, the venerable theme, *coeli enarrant gloriam dei,* "the Heavens declare the glory of God," was developed through a new kind of physics of creation. This old theme was recast to view creation as an emanation of and hence as an emblem of the divine in order to suggest that "a la matière même un Verbe est attaché," to quote Gérard de Nerval, the logos is present in matter itself. Nerval's "Vers dorés" and Baudelaire's "Correspondances" are the best-known poetic statements of this theory of harmonies; they presuppose an emanationist theory of creation with a divine presence throughout the Great Chain of Being. This is exemplary of what Albert Béguin calls Romantic panentheism; it detects a harmony between the world perceived by the senses and the divine. That harmony is reflected not only by the recourse to organic metaphors, but also in that conception of an intimate relation between human beings, nature, and God that marks so much Romantic poetry. The image ceases to be decorative and rather conveys meaning.

Second, the ancient theory about prophets and *figurae* found a similar sort of extension. The Romantics, turning the comte de Volney and Charles Dupuis around to make them serve the cause of Christian apologetics, read pagan religions as imperfect but harmonious parallels with the Christian revelation. Here, the theoreticians had to invent, not a physics, but a theory of history, of some kind of universal primitive revelation contained in language, or in symbols and myths, and corrupted in some way or other. The danger to be avoided here is not pantheism, but religious syncretism—and the Romantics were not very successful.[3] If all religious forms attest the same religion, it was too easy to conclude that all these forms were then equally valid. Here, the theory of harmonies did vastly extend the corpus of what the Romantics read as "sacred texts"—even to include their own inspired writings—but it also required the development of a new kind of analogical hermeneutics.

Finally, the fusion of the logos of the Fourth Gospel with that of Plato was nothing new, and the Romantics, again, were readers of Malebranche. In this case, a metaphysics had to be invented to establish a harmony between the divine and the various forms of intelligence: ideas, mathematics, or language (which thus is identified with the logos in two different ways). Reflecting the Romantic "neoplatonist" rejection of sensualism in favor of a kind of enthusiasm that Mme de Staël had already defined as "God in us," the theory of harmonies provided a basis for the conception of the poet as inspired *vates*. The danger, here, was that one might end up with a solipsistic ontology, and many did. Indeed, the distinction among these three sorts of ideas is not always clear, for, hidden beneath all this kind of thinking, there is a more profound problem: what are the modalities between unity and diversity? At least some of these modalities offered the hope of a radiant future where all would become harmonious; and then harmony ceases to be just an apologetic argument or a formula for artistic creation to become a means of creating utopia. In the work of Hugh Doherty, Fourier and Bonald were combined. Louis de Tourreil would add on panentheism, and then harmony becomes "fusion," the means of creating the ideal City.

Let me flesh out (and perhaps complicate) this schema by citing some texts, chosen for their representativity, although at times they owe that representativity to their eccentricity.[4] The texts are selected primarily from religious discourse, but they illustrate the new esthetic and political uses of harmony and its synonyms.

### ❦ The Harmonies of Nature

The theme that nature declares the glories of God and its harmonious developments does not require extensive treatment; popularized by Chateaubriand and Lamartine, it is well known. Bishop Frayssinous's *Conférences,* published in 1825 when he was Grand Master of the University, is less well known.[5] Frayssinous devotes a section to the "existence of God proved by the order and beauties of nature." In rather enthusiastic language, he says:

> The luminous globes which, for so many centuries now, have majestically moved through space, without ever leaving their orbits, nor crashing against each other in their revolutions [and he evokes the sun, the moon, the fecund earth, the immense sea, the course of the seasons], does not all this form a concert, an ensemble of separate parts, where you cannot take any one away without ruining the universal harmony? and from that, one must elevate one's thoughts to consider the principle, the author and keeper of this admirable unity, the immortal spirit who, embracing all in his vast foreknowledge, makes all move toward his ends with as much force as wisdom. (P. 150)

If this theme remains, in its elementary forms and even in spite of its Rousseauist, "Savoyard Vicar" side, a common coin of apologetics, of preaching, and of a certain religious poetry, outside the Church the notion ramifies and turns pantheistic. The result was a cult of the presence of the divine in all forms of nature. A theory of creation, indebted to Gnosticism, as emanating from the divine logos which remains present to greater or lesser extent throughout the whole Chain of Being, provided the "physics" needed to justify this pantheism. This is a very widespread belief, reflected not only in the piercing glance of the eye of God in the blind wall of Gérard de Nerval and in Baudelaire's nature as a living temple. I take an extreme case, Madrolle, who in his *Démonstration ecclésiastique où l'on fait sortir enfin à tous les hommes la magnificence et l'infaillibilité de l'Eglise* (1838), describes harmonies in which nature becomes emblematic of the mysteries of faith. For Madrolle, what illustrates the divine becomes confused with what is a manifestation of the divine, a kind of confusion many others knew. If the polyp, cut into pieces each of which becomes an independent but complete hydra, explains the presence of God in each particle of the consecrated Host, it is not by simple analogy but, for Madrolle, because unity in multiplicity is the very essence of creation and of the Creator. This idea entails some very strange links between religious orthodoxy and the state of nature; taking up an old satiric argument of the Counter Reformation, he proposes an amusing (but for him quite serious) relation between the quality of wine and the religious faith of the wine-producing country. Wine is "rubicond, strong, generous, straightforward" in the Most Christian Kingdom of France but

> unknown or worthless, disgusting and even dangerous, on the shores of the Danube and especially of the Elba (Luther's maternal land), or of Lake Geneva (Calvin's adopted land), or the Thames, where the nectar of the gods (which formerly flowed there, before the Reformation) has been replaced by sad beer and black punches, thick, smoky, lethiferous, true caricatures of our wines, just as the superb Catholic truths are replaced in those degenerate lands by the servile errors of Calvin (from *calvo, calvor,* etc., to mislead, and even from Cain, etc.). (P. 77)

For Madrolle is also an extremely inventive etymologist. If England returned to the Catholic faith, good wine would flow once more, and the harmonies would be renewed.

For good reasons, these abusive examples of the *coeli enarrant* theme which try to link the discovery of divine harmonies to the contemplation of nature soon became the object of attacks by philosophers and theologians. Maine de Biran, who called Bonald a "clown in philosophy," caustically commented:

> To try to derive the idea of God from the contemplation of nature, of the order of exterior things, is to draw from a bad source; following that path, one finds not the living God, but the God of Spinoza; the personality of God is only understood as a type of the personality of the self which only knows itself by an immediate internal perception, by consciousness. (*Journal,* ed. Henri Gouhier, Neuchatel, 1954, 2:380)

In the same vein Isidore Goschler, a perspicacious disciple of the theologian Louis Bautain, in his *Du panthéisme* (1839) affirms strongly that the world is a "non-self forever distinct from the absolute self" (p. 141); one cannot confuse God with his creation, identify him with his work, even figuratively. Goschler is less worried about Spinoza and traditional pantheism than about the "modern pantheists" Fichte and Hegel. Indeed, pantheism as a justification of the "harmonies of nature showing the road to God" enjoyed a kind of renewal in the late 1830s and 1840s because of the propagation of the "new German philosophy" in France, but that renewal occurred largely outside the Church. Consider the case of Auguste Kératry, whose philosophy offers a good basis for developing the theory of harmonies:

> At the beginning there was only Being; but Being was intelligent. He desired to create, and suddenly he penetrated nothingness, that immense void where matter and spirit had resided in a potential state since all eternity. He lent them being, and gave them reality; he did so in combining them with each other in a thousand diverse forms. From these forms came all the individual existences which populate the universe and vary it infinitely. In our world there resulted three great groups, minerals, vegetables, and animals, mixed beings who all present an alliance of the spirit with matter, but with the difference that, in the first, the spirit is without unity and matter without organs; in the second there is a beginning, and in the third a complementarity of virtual unity and material organization. These beings live in this state as long as the laws which govern them allow; afterward, they die, and then in each of them spirit and matter become separated, not in order to return to nothingness, but to continue being by entering into new forms and combinations.[6]

These are the ideas, if not the prose, of Victor Hugo. One could cite other examples of such emanationist philosophies of creation, for that was the normal Romantic way of understanding creation. Such a philosophy not only lends itself to forms of thinking of harmony in which the created reveals the presence and the will of the Creator, but also to the great dream of the regeneration of creation, in which the harmonies of nature become the keys—or means—of transforming matter. Let us return to the faith, and we shall drink better wine.

### ❦ The Universal Figures

More important was the transposition of the old theory about prophecies, *figurae* or types, to traditions, mythological systems, the witness of other religions, thanks to the various theories about a primitive revelation. Joseph de Maistre played an important role here, and such theorizing was also an essential part of the efforts by Lamennais and his disciples to prove that the Catholic faith was what had been believed everywhere, always, by everyone. This quest for parallels proving the universal revelation produced a great many learned works in anthropology and comparative mythology and Charles Bonnetty's periodical *Les Annales de philosophie chrétienne* devoted most of its pages to publishing proofs thereof. The orientation was not limited to France; perhaps the most impressive compendium is Hermann Joseph Schmitt's *Rédemption du genre humain annoncée par les traditions et les croyances religieuses, figurée par les sacrifices de tous les peuples*, first translated in 1827 then reprinted in 1843 by Migne as Volume 13 of his *Démonstrations evángéliques*. Schmitt studied all available evidence from comparative religion in his quest for the doctrine of the reconciliation of fallen man by the intercession of a Divine Savior who sacrifices himself, and he found traces thereof everywhere, reading those traces as proof of the harmony among different religious systems. Even more picturesque are the studies of Roselly de Lorgues, much admired by Bonnetty, *Le Christ devant le siècle* (1835), and above all *La Croix dans les deux mondes* (1845). Roselly, like so many others, associated universal revelation, philological and etymological theories, and theories about numbers and arithmosophy. One quotation, concerning the sign of the cross, will suffice.

> Combined with the idea of innocence and supplication, it served to express perfection, that sanctity whose test is suffering. And the sign of the Cross expresses perfection. And as the highest social perfection is the reunion of many in the one, this sign of perfection was adopted in the language of numbers, and it signifies unity in plurality, ten, which is one and several at the same time, which has a generating power, a force of multiplication on which all our system of calculating is based. In Hebrew the number ten bore the very name of perfection and justice, "haschar," and was represented by the cross. Among the Mexicans, the highest and most perfect of their numbers was developed around a Cross. In China, the Cross also held an immense power among the hieroglyphic symbols. (P. 170)

Roselly continues with considerations about the Southern Cross, the move of civilization toward the west, the cross as a key to knowledge, and so on. One of his friends, Fr. Mathieu Orsini, provides a similar treatment for parthenogenesis in *La Vierge, histoire de la Mère de Dieu, complété par les traditions d'Orient* (1837).

Clearly, the Christianizing of myths always runs the risk of making Christianity itself mythical. For example, P. Caze, in his *Essai de philosophie religieuse sur les monuments astronomiques des anciens* (1829), proposes that all true science must be subordinated to the light of sacred theology, for the goal of reason is "to know, show, and proclaim the divine superiority of inspired and revealed truth" (p. xxiv). He tries to reconcile the Bible, the zodiac, and astronomical traditions, for he is convinced that everything is *figura:* "The language of Holy Scripture is a figurative language, destined to consecrate, under the veils of allegory, metaphor, hyperbole, the truths revealed to divinely or supernaturally inspired authors" (p. 26). From that point on, anything is possible, there are no limits to hermeneutic fantasy—Caze's study of the relations between the *pisces* of the zodiac and the fact that the disciples were fishermen will suffice as an example.

> St. Augustine teaches us that the fish is, in the spirit of Christian theology, a very natural symbol of the faith. "The tempests of this age," he says, "cannot have any effect on the true faith, no more than those of the sea on the fish." This rational interpretation, so helpful in opening up the plan of the Gospel about many matters, and especially in understanding what the profession of fisherman, attributed to so many disciples, might mean, is moreover a sure indication that in the theology of the New Testament, as in that of the Old, there is a secret concordance with the zodiac and the movements of the sun. (P. 89)

Caze is not alone in seeing *figurae* everywhere; the same period saw the "second" propagation of Swedenborgianism in France, and one of the expositors, Edouard Richer, explained, about the Bible:

> Celestial and divine matters are there figurally presented through natural representations; the existence of a science of analogies, well known during the enlightenment of antiquity, and neglected more and more ever since, teaches us how such a language is used, and the reason for the allegorical style of Scriptures becomes clear.[7]

All this could easily be turned against Christianity; Dupuis still counted a number of disciples, who used exactly the same analytical and comparative procedures as Roselly or Caze. There was, however, an important difference. Since syncretism was the fashion, the effort was not to reduce the religious, but to encompass all religious traditions, which endows the myth with profound meaning, even among adversaries of Catholicism. In 1844 Ragon de Bettignies published *La Messe et ses mystères comparés aux mystères anciens, ou complément de la science initiatique.* He analyzed all the action of the Mass in terms of the solar cult. The lavabo is a prayer to Orpheus, the Crucifixion "the emblem of the state of apparent crisis of the sun and the earth, of the painful and difficult passage of the March equinox" (p. 102), and so forth. Differing somewhat from Dupuis, although Ragon de Bettignies considers this solar cult the true religion he also sees in Christianity a valid symbolic "translation" of that religion.

With Augustin Chaho, a highly imaginative and ironic author, this translation of myths becomes quite polyvalent. A disciple of Charles Nodier who wrote extensively on the origins of the Basque language, Chaho defines Christ in his *Paroles d'un voyant* (1834) as the solar lamb, "called, according to what dialect one is speaking, Orismud, Osiris, Chourien and Christ," names which, for the seer, only constitute "expressions of seeing, of knowing, of science, of the intellectual light which the children of night call civilization" (p. ii) and which once reigned "in the garden of the south" before "the invasion of the giants of the north" (the Celts, etc.). Liberty was replaced by "slavery; light gave way to a deep night; the meridional word, the living expression of a sublime civilization, to the confused dialects of Babel" (p. ii). Chaho also believes in a primitive revelation, this logos of the south, contained in the ancient cosmogonies, of which "the Jewish Bible, the Hindu Vedas, the Zend of the Parsees', the Samarian and Christian Gospels, the Koran are only allegorical abridgments borrowed from primitive sources" (pp. xiv–xv). He dwells at length on the parallels between Buddha's life and that of Christ the Sun, reading both primarily allegorically. Thus the adoration of the Magi (who were disciples of Mithra) shows that "the magus himself willingly abandons the first cult in order to adore the eternal truth of which the physical sun is only the shadow." Moreover, "the tonsure which the priests of Christ have shaven on the backs of their heads represents the solar disk" (pp. 122–124). And the priests who refuse to admit that Christ is the sun are a "race of vipers." In 1835 Chaho published his *Philosophie des révélations adressée à M. le Prof. Lerminier,* and there shows his hand. A republican, a disciple of the Enlightenment, he demands that the believer give way to the seer, the theocrats to the democrats, superstitious faith to true light, dogma to doctrine, myth to words, symbols to definitions, mystical cults to culture of the mind.

Nonetheless, the logos—word, myth, symbol—these contain all truths. There is a universal Christ, the incarnation of Truth, but this Christ is nothing less than the civilization of the south. I quote his definition of the Trinity:

> The olympic image of an eternal old man symbolizes the life of God, who is in relation to visible, palpable, incarnate creation what the father is to his son. The beauty of a young adolescent represents the Incarnation, so prestigious in the variety of its ever fleeting and newly born forms, and in cosmogonic language, one says that the Son proceeds from the Father, is coeternal with him, God like him. The Light, that spirit of love which lightens all flesh coming into this world, is knowingly symbolized by the oceanic pigeon, the blue ringdove of the sky. (P. 173–74).

This may be the doctrine of the Enlightenment, but is hardly the language of the Enlightenment.

In short, the quest for the harmonies of universal revelation was fraught with dangers for apologists. First, there was the risk of reducing Christianity to nothing more than one of the mythological formulations of religious truth—this is Falconnet's conclusion in his intelligent article "On Rationalism and Mysticism in France."[8] He suggests that Lamennais and his disciples were admirable students of mythology, that they knew how to read myths to uncover "under the veil of allegory, the fact or mystery hidden therein, and, putting aside all the secondary elements, collect, like gold in the crucible, the primitive, universal element, Christianity" (p. 112). Then Christianity becomes "the definitive law of humanity," but only in the sense that it offers a better expression of the truth than the other myths. This was not the only danger; as Chaho's text shows, the Jesus of history tends to become lost in the universal revelation, to be replaced by Christ as a historical process, a conception that the neo-Hegelians made quite fashionable. Above all, universal revelation lent itself easily to leftist readings (Lamennais's example is telling), for finally this revelation provided a new proof of natural law rather than of Christian dogma; if dogmas and truths are universal, the moral laws derived from them must also be universal and part of a human being's very nature. Accordingly, it is the "common sense," *vox populi*, that announces religious truth far better than any revealed word.

The Catholics generally rejected these harmonies, and their arguments, often very learned, demonstrate the artificial nature of the parallels. Fr.-Ed. Chassay, in *Le Christ et l'Evangile, histoire critique des systèmes rationalistes contemporains sur les origines de la révélation chrétienne* (three volumes, 1847–49), attacking primarily Pierre Leroux, maintains that there are four persons, not three, in the Hindu Trimurtri, that Plato's logos and that of St. John are quite different, and so forth. The abuse, particularly on the left, of these mythological harmonies was such that Mgr Affre criticized syncretism quite vigorously in his *Introduction philosophique à l'étude du christianisme* (1845). The archbishop of Paris points out that the trinity of the Vedas, like that of the Saint-Simonians, only sees in god a sort of "soul or energy of the world," whereas in the Christian Trinity God is "Creator, Redeemer, and Sanctifier." Yet this did not keep Lacordaire, in his *Conférences* for 1846, from once more evoking the theme of the harmonies of universal revelation:

> The messianic idea . . . traversed the Jordan, the Euphrates, the Indus, the Mediterranean, all the oceans, and, borne by the invisible wings of providence, has penetrated among the most diverse and distant peoples, creating everywhere a uniform hope and a universal memory. (P. 559)

### ❦ Language Is the Logos

The Romantics meditated endlessly on the nature of language, sometimes giving it a contractual origin, but most were Cratylists, sometimes proposing an onomatopoetic origin (Charles Nodier); others, who interest us here, considered language as the vehicle of universal revelation, a gift of God to humans, and so believed that language in its structures repeats the structures of religious truth. Essentialists, they maintained that the sign in some sense is motivated by its divine origin. Bonald developed this interpretation particularly in terms of various Trinitarian notions, and his thinking was quite influential. If he only rarely used the word *harmony*, the idea was nonetheless central to his thought. His goal was to present "the general rapports or the harmonies of the intellectual and physical realms" to justify the institution of a theocratic society; and these harmonies explain his system:

> God / Christ / Man:   power / minister / subject:   father / mother / child:
> cause / means / effect: I / you / he, etc.[9]

But for Bonald these harmonies are located in the given of creation (institutions and language, that is, humanity's social being), whereas others claim that they are innate in each individual. According to Bonald, the harmonies are brought into realization, actualized by Christ, who is "the medium or mediator, the being who unites the universal cause with the universality of effects, and who links the Creator and the creature." Christ's role is thus identified with that of the logos, the vehicle of religious, political, and social structures. But the logos was corrupted by the Fall; then Christ, logos incarnate, restored its purity, allowing humankind once more to grasp "the harmonies of the intellectual and material world, of the world of causes and the world of effects" (p. 392).

Théodore Combalot is exemplary of the many theologians who owed a great deal to Bonald. In his *Eléments de philosophie catholique* (1833), he also unhesitatingly borrows from Eckstein, Abel Rémusat, and others, and, finding the Trinity-in-Unity everywhere, he adds a theory about the similarities of the radicals of the name of God in various languages:

> The Idea of the Universal and Absolute Being is found at the basis of all languages. . . . All the words, of all languages spoken since the beginning of time, repeat endlessly and without ceasing, the name of the absolute Being, of He who is. (P. 153)

He quotes the Vedas, Chinese sacred texts, Thales, Plato, Orphic verses, and the inscription of the temple of Saïs. H. de Valroger borrows Bonald's theses to refute Victor Cousin and Théodore Jouffroy, and to assert the divine origin and nature of language, in his *Etudes critiques sur le rationalisme contemporain* (1846). Even the Catholic socialist Joseph Buchez, in his *Traité complet de philosophie* (1838), echoes Bonald. Buchez senses that the problem of revelation and the problem of the origin of language are closely linked; he distinguishes between the language of instinct, which the theories of Etienne de Condillac can explain, and the voluntary or intellectual signs, which are neither innate nor of human invention, but are the gifts of revelation. Like Bonald, Buchez is interested less in words than in the relations among words, what we would call grammar, for that "law of relations" is "the ethics, the origin and principle of language as of all activity"; there follows a diatribe against the inadequacies of the Port-Royal Grammar, so little aware of these "rapports," and a justification for progress within revelation in terms of the evolution of linguistic structure.

These relations between language and the divine can be founded in several ways. At times, language is said to be part of the primitive revelation. According to others, language is (or should be) the exact reflection of that form of God-in-us which are our ideas. Setting aside another problem that should be explored, Malebranche's influence on Romantic thought, I shall try to evaluate the importance of the harmonies between our mind or spirit (our "ideas") and the divine.

### ❧ The Ideas Are in God

There are two possible approaches; we can start from our ideas in order to find God, or we can start from God in order to explain our ideas. In Bautain's ontology, for instance, one first accepts the Trinity by an act of faith in order to perceive afterward other forms of truth, such as the three dimensions of bodies, the three words needed to form a proposition, the three propositions needed to form a syllogism, and so on. In both approaches, an organic relation exists between the truths of faith and our ideas. One can even try to combine the two, as did the neo-Cartesian Jansenist Bordas-Demoulin:

> Each of our ideas has a corresponding idea in God and attaches us to him, that is, there are two sources for ideas, the one in us and the other in God, and the ideas that belong to us depend immediately on those that belong to God. . . . God thinks with us, and has even a greater share than we in each of our thoughts. Between our reason and his the communication is direct and constant. The divine ideas, uncreated model of ours, are the true and final measure of all things.[10]

Thus, "All substance is produced as unity and number without end, and the infinite, which is born from unity and number, united and equal, is the universal mode of existence; absolute and incomparable infinite in God, relative infinites of all orders in created beings" (p. 243). The system of Bordas and his disciples does not require any recourse to philology, or universal revelation in the tradition, in its quest for harmonies. The ideas are innate, and there is no need for tradition or language to sense the correspondences with the divine, much less of any contemplation of created nature. According to Bordas, Bonald indulged in "a puerile wordplay on the logos"; he and Lamennais are guilty of materialism.[11]

These identifications of the idea with God produce some curious apologetic gambits. For Mme de Ludre, *Etudes sur les idées et sur leur union au sein du catholicismn* (1842), ideas are born of a necessary relation, so the idea of God proves God. The more ideas one has, the more intelligent one is, and since Catholicism possesses all ideas, it is the religion of human intelligence. She goes on to suggest that the language of a given person is an obscure mirror of ideas, whereas the universal language of all human beings would be the perfect mirror of divine truth; those who have the gift of tongues, glossolalia, speak this universal catholic language which is in perfect harmony with divine ideas. Less difficult, if duller reading, is Edouard Alletz's *Les Harmonies de l'intelligence humaine* (1845). Alletz, a poet and a lay apologist, proposes to substitute for the Cartesian *cogito ergo sum* the declaration *amo ergo sum;* and, since I love, God exists. A harmony is

> an idea which, representing something immaterial, is the object of the spontaneous, unreflected, involuntary love of the soul, which is often loved by us in spite of ourselves and without our knowing it, with which our soul ceaselessly seeks union, concentrating its exclusive attention on this idea; whose possession, thus obtained by the identification of our intelligence with the idea, procures us the greatest joy we can know; which directs our spirit, long before we discover it. This idea seems incomplete if it is not conceived of as infinite, and can only exist if it has God himself for its substance. (1:59)

God is "the substance of harmonies":

> We have the idea of a perfect love, of an inexhaustible existence, of a complete truth, of a supreme intelligence, of an invincible power, of a perpetual activity, of an infinite and eternal unity, of an incorruptible justice, of an incomparable beauty, of an immense and indestructible happiness, and at the same time none of these ideas has any objective reality here below, for all love here is imperfect, all existence temporary, all intelligence limited. (1:59)

From this Alletz concludes that the need for these perfections must have been placed in our soul by our Creator, who could only perceive within himself the perfect harmonies. He is thus the infinite of love, truth, and so on, that is, "the substance of those attributes of which our soul only possesses the fleeting shades" (1:230). Three harmonies are the essential attributes of the divine substance, the ideas of existence, intelligence, and love, whence the Trinity:

> God is, thinks, loves; everything is contained in these three words. One can likewise define man as something who lives, thinks and loves. God is by himself, thinks in himself, and loves himself. Man is God, thinks by God, and loves God. Man is therefore truly a creature made in the image of his Creator. (1:59)

### ❦ The Proof by the Harmony of Ideas

Mention should be made of Fr. F. Moigno's effort to justify "interior harmonies" in his article "In What Manner Beings Are in God." The Being of creatures cannot be something added on to the Divine Being; the creature is not only similar to God, he is really in God. Being is limited in the creature and without limits in God. Thus, the Being of creatures "is only a participation, in a finite degree, in the infinite Being of God." And Moigno explains by analogies—the block of marble and the sculpture, the king and his prefects—to conclude that what he proposes is neither Spinozism nor pantheism but rather the refutation of those two doctrines.[12]

These "interior harmonies" were already discussed by Lamennais in his *Essay on Indifference:* "Everything in religion is infinite because everything is full of God. Therefore, a perfect harmony exists between religion and our faculties" (*OEuvres,* Brussels, 1839, 1:339). In that early work, however, the word *harmony* more often designates the parallel between divine essence and its manifestations. In the *Esquisse d'une philosophie* of 1841, he goes much further; the Son-Logos is the locus of all ideas and thus the source of all existence, so the divine idea inhabits all that exists:

> Since all that exists corresponds to an idea which subsists essentially and for all eternity in the Logos and is only the realization of that idea, it follows that, in everything that exists, there is something of the Logos or the intelligence. (1:170)

Moreover,

> No being can exist without the idea which gives that being form, so it follows that the Son, the Intelligence, the Logos, in which all ideas reside at the origin is the means by which the creation of beings takes place, and the mediator by which they are united to God, since, on the one hand, they

only exist, in what constitutes them in a distinctive way, by the idea, the name which determines them; and since, on the other hand, these names, these ideas, their inalterable type, are part of the Logos, they exist primitively in God and are God himself. (1:211–12)

In this schema, the harmony between the idea-God and the idea-in-us is close to pantheism; all creatures are only the idea of God become entities.

### ❦ The Harmonies of Numbers

The theory of the harmony of ideas led certain authors to propose links (often quite unexpected) between certain activities of the human mind and the truth of religion. Bonald's considerations on grammar would belong in this category if one claimed that the gift of language is innate and not, as Bonald said, social. In particular, a number of authors proposed "mathematical harmonies," which were often enriched by recourse to the old traditions of arithmosophia. Martin Etchegoyen, who was a colonel in the Artillery, published four volumes in 1839, *De l'unité, ou aperçus philosophiques sur l'identité des principes de la science mathématique, de la grammaire générale et de la religion chrétienne.* His thought is quite complex, and it seems best to quote a sample:

> For it is written that IESVS of Nazareth was crucified on the third hour; that when the sixth hour came, shadows covered the whole of the earth, and that on the ninth hour, IESVS, giving forth a great cry, died. The numbers three, six, and nine manifest, in order, in the infinite ideas, the power of the Father, that of the Son, and that of the Holy Ghost—that is, of the undivided Trinity; and since, according to the second law of mathematics, there are no forces possible outside of God, nor any movement possible unless God himself is in action, it follows that here in the agony of IESVS of Nazareth, the action of the undivided Trinity was manifested by the number in all its plenitude and so, as a result, the unique Son of the Father, made man, only perished because such was his own will. (3:229)

One might think that the problem is simplified here by the fact that the numbers occur in the biblical text, but their absence would not bother Etchegoyen. According to him, "There is nothing in the universe, beginning with God, where the number is not found"—in repetition, in adjectival verbs, and so forth. And ever since Etchegoyen perfected his method,

God has been so full of lovingkindness toward me, that I haven't even needed to know Hebrew, Greek, or Latin, to discover numerically the triple sacred name: IOVAH-IESVS-CHRISTUS which is inscribed for all eternity in the equilateral triangle. It is the first of the sacred hieroglyphs whose solution has led me to the solution of all the others. The equilateral triangle first expressed by itself the triple equality in unity. . . . Moreover, in view of this last equality, we get the following numbers: 60 plus 60 plus 60 equals 180 . . . 18 . . . 9, that is, the Eternal Logos announced three times, leading to the knowledge of the triple Holy Name. (3:230)

One can find other such mathematical proofs in Louis Machet's *La Religion constatée universellement à l'aide des sciences et de l'érudition moderne* (1833), who cites Craig's mathematical demonstration of the existence of God and rejects Laplace's refutation thereof, and then adds a number of his own arguments.[13] Or in the quite eccentric Madrolle, who in 1841 published *Dieu devant le siècle ou législation de la providence*, a book full of both mathematical and philological (he cites Nodier) demonstrations of God. His most charming work is perhaps his 1843 *Démonstration de l'evangile et explication du mal du siècle par la seule histoire universelle des nombres 13 et 666*. In this book we learn that Judas was the thirteenth of his name in the Bible, the name of Louis-Philippe contains thirteen letters, the heretical cult of Theophilanthropy was inaugurated on the thirteenth of Thermidor, and so forth.

Eccentricity, no doubt, but this eccentricity is often politically to the left. Paul-Joseph Lebourdais in his *Livre de la loi divine* (1819), written during the Bourbon Restoration, demonstrates that the three-colored flag of the Republic is the emblem of the rainbow which is in turn the emblem of the reconciliation of God and his people. (Lebourdais accepts all the miracles attributed to Jesus, including the Resurrection, but denies his divinity.) More respectable is H. de Lourdoueix's *De la vérité universelle, pour servir d'introduction à la philosophie du Verbe* (1838), replete with abstract considerations on the union of linear mathematics and logic, their application to ethics, their function as witnesses of religious truth, and also quite marked by a reading of Fourier. Lourdoueix believes that "ideas are the characters and modifications of the divine substance." Christ, by his incarnation of the logos, reestablished in man the "logical and ascending scale," allowing civilization to enter again on "the paths of reason and of truth" and hence to progress. His theory of harmony even justifies the redemption of matter, that widespread Romantic dream; "matter participates in this rehabilitation" because "the divine substance of the body of Christ, by uniting with the body of man in the eucharistic marriage" neutralizes in matter "those forms vitiated by sin" (pp. 398–405). Here the mathematical harmonies, seen as expressions of the harmonies of ideas, are linked to a belief in progress that is both social and material.

### ❦ The Harmonies of the Trinity

A kind of Trinity mania prevails in French Romanticism. Innumerable efforts seek parallels to the Trinity in the structures of language, of society, most particularly of history—by authors as varied as Charles Renouvier, Bonald, Leroux, the Saint-Simonians, and even Catholics such as Ozanam, whose example will suffice here. In his 1835 essay "On progress through Christianity" he proposes a very complex theory.[14] The three aspects of God, the True, the Good, and the Beautiful, are reflected in his traits of Intelligence, Love, and Power; in the virtues Faith, Charity, and Hope; and in the life of the Christian by Dogma, Belief, and Worship. Likewise, man, made in the image of God, possesses a triple structure which at each level involves three elements. He is Intelligence, which implies Knowledge of the self and produces Science; he is Love, desire the Good of others, has a Social life; he is Power, the "relations by means of which creatures are coordinated to work toward their purpose, and the harmony which creates beauty," which is manifested in Art (Œuvres, 8:109–15). So there are harmonies between the Trinity, human nature, and human activity; and since the Trinity is a harmonious unity, such is also at least potentially the case of human beings and society. For Ozanam, as for many others, this Trinitarianism is also historicized, and progress is defined as a realization of the Gospel and a transformation of all creation thanks to science, social life, and art, ending up with the third, Joachimist age of the Holy Ghost. This historicizing of Trinitarian thought is illustrative; the harmonies constitute not only a way of analyzing the world, but also a key for humanity's renewal.

This historicization suggests that we need to revise somewhat the analysis of Romanticism proposed by A. O. Lovejoy and Morse Peckham, according to which Romanticism substitues the organic for the mechanic, the dynamic for the static, values diversity rather than unity. On the other hand, the theory of harmonies also represents a quest for a kind of unity hidden beyond the diversity of appearances. In the religious or theological discourse on harmonies, this unity is found in the truths of the faith which reappear in mathematics, in comparative linguistics or mythology, in the phenomena of nature; the same analogical structures are traced in a great variety of phenomena. And this unity is defined as the goal of history. Two examples help clarify the mechanisms involved in this quest.

In a lengthy article of 1832, "On Religion and Philosophy in Their Opposition and Their Identity," Caroline Angibert proposed an ambitious synthesis.[15] Man possesses three faculties: sensitivity, reason, activity. The last, free and voluntary, is the product of the first two. The child knows only sensitivity, the adolescent combines sensitivity and reason, the adult tends to sacrifice sensitivity to reason. And the history of humanity, here, repeats the history of the individual. The equilibrium between sensitivity and reason, between religion and philosophy, is characteristic of the organic ages of humanity. Angibert claimed that she was faithful not only to the ideas of Saint-Simon but also of Ballanche. The organic period is a period of *harmony*, of an accord between science and faith, love and intelligence. On the other hand, unlike the Saint-Simonians, she denied that there was any need for a new religion; rather, she accepted Bonald's theories about universal revelation. "Revealed religion is the natural religion," which is always clothed in symbols appropriate for a given society or period. In Angibert's view, the "evangelical" principles of that religion should be "implanted in the social order," for history is the history of the "ascension of the people"—a law proclaimed by Christ. Angibert had read widely and sought to combine the harmonies of the Trinity, universal revelation, and the doctrine of progress to discover, in the faculties of human beings, in the periods of history and the various forms of religion, a harmonious unity coming into being thanks to an organic historical progress.

One finds rather similar theses in the curious book written by P. V. Glade, a lawyer, *Du progrès religieux*.[16] In an effort to synthesize Ballanche, Leibnitz, and Kant, he proposes a theory of history in which the unity of God and man, the unity among men, was, after the Fall, replaced by the "narrow principles of human science." A decline ensued until Christ appeared and reintroduced the double form of unity. Since then, humankind has gravitated toward the union of intelligence and ethics and union with God (in this schema, polytheism represents a refusal of the unity of God and hence of humanity, resulting in moral decadence). Jesus was the initiator of this regeneration for, by his preaching and his life, he "reunited about his divine person all the rays of light of both speculative and practical truth" (1:72). Glade concludes with a long analysis of the *Pater Noster.* "Our Father" proclaims the unity of mankind; "which art in heaven" "makes us sense the moral harmony of all the globes"; and "thy Kingdom come" is "the highest realization of order, the harmonious and sympathetic coordination of the best ensemble of moral systems" (1:290–94) For "daily bread," he provides a rather socialist interpretation. The poor will soon at last be able to eat; after eighteen centuries humanity is putting this fraternal precept into practice, entering upon the path that will lead toward the unity of humankind. Glade ends with an ecumenical dream of the intellectual, moral, and material regeneration of humanity, where people will henceforth exist in unity. The word *harmony* recurs constantly in his writings, but in an almost Fourierist sense—the evocation of the law of gravity is significant. Harmony is no longer a simple apologetic technique but a key element in the neo-Christian dream of renewing the world.

### ❦ The Harmonies of Fourier and the Harmonies of Christianity

The relations between pre-Marxist socialism and Christianity are complex. If, on the one hand, "evangelical" socialism is a secularization of religious values and proposes to locate the Kingdom of the Gospels here below, on the other hand these socialist movements manifest signs of becoming new religions, either in terms of cult-type organizations, or because they introduce religious values, emotions, institutions, and ceremonies into their socialist projects. The relation between socialism and religion is created by a sort of double movement. Significant in this respect, and symptomatic, are the numerous efforts to reconcile Fourier's theses with Catholicism; to an extent, they represent a propaganda technique, but much more is involved. Jean Touchard, in an excellent study on the Fourierist-turned-Catholic Louis Rousseau, traces an itinerary followed by a number of other adepts of Fourier who became Catholic. The reverse route was also well traveled, and both directions involved not a conversion rejection of the one for the other, but an effort to reconcile the two. I have studied these attempts at reconciliation elsewhere, examining the writing of Victor Considerant, of F. Berthault-Gras, and of Mme Vigoureux, and Charles Stoffels's curious book *Résurrection: Que votre règne d'amour arrive* (1844), a strange synthesis of Ballanche and Fourier. [17] Julien Le Rousseau, in *Notions de phrénologie*, published by the Fourierist Librairie phalanstérienne in 1847, tried to demonstrate that phrenology was a Fourierist science; he remarked that "one must follow the precepts of Christ, that star who dominates all the realms of intelligence . . . in their most general application to collective salvation, instead of just applying them to the individual self, as unintelligent Catholics suggest" (p. 21). Often—as in the case of one of Fourier's admirable feminist adepts, Zoé Gatti de Gamond, *Réalisation d'une commune sociétaire* (1840)—they try to prove that Fourierism even completes the work of freeing the slaves, the movement of fraternity begun by Christ who "created the bases of human emancipation and universal association." Fourierist doctrine is a broad and magnificent application of the Christian principles of charity and fraternity (p. 22). Fourier, unlike other socialists (i.e., the Saint-Simonians), refused to found a new religion; faith is needed to create the Kingdom, but that faith was defined by Christ, and now has acquired the plenitude of its meaning with Fourier. So there is agreement between Christianity and Fourierism, about their goals and also about the means of achieving those goals. Others go even further in their quest for a harmony between the dogmas and sacraments of Christianity and the theories of Fourier. I briefly describe three cases where the notion of harmony plays an essential role.

Victor Calland was a Fourierist who later returned to the Catholic faith and then published *De l'avenir du monde* in 1842. He defends three major theses. Unity is the conserving form of universal life and the promise of all science, which is proved by the Trinity and the universe (that is, the doctrine of harmonies). The law is the rule that conserves unity and the cause of universal movement; the proofs are charity and attraction. Justice is the sanction that conserves the law and the reason for universal equilibrium; the proofs are happiness, unhappiness. The Fall destroyed the harmony-unity of man with God and with his brothers; Christ came to restore that harmony-unity, but his work will only become complete when the institutions of harmony, partly but incompletely elaborated by Fourier, receive a religious sanction, that of the Catholic faith. Calland adds some apocalyptic prophecies: we are menaced with disasters, but out of them will come either the new, harmonious, theocratic society, or chaos and disorder. He later saw in the events of 1848 first the realization, then the failure of his hopes. His writing is heavily marked by Fourierist terminology, as well as by the dream of a material realization of unity in harmony, but his utopia has become theocratic.

Hippolyte de la Morvonnais was even hardier in his effort to combine Fourierism and Catholicism. In "How Dogmas Continue" he notes that Fourier was always against any creation of a new religion because, according to Morvonnais, the perfect religion already exists in Catholicism which agrees totally with the new scientific beliefs proposed by Fourier.[18] For example, the seven sacraments "by septenary alliances correspond to Fourier's septenary guarantees." All one need do is to shed new light on the truths of Catholicism by translating them into the Fourierist vocabulary. Thus, discussing the Crucifixion and refuting Pelletan thereon, he notes:

> If Pelletan had said that the science of harmony has as its mission and its result to generalize the full belief among Catholics, leading to mathematical intelligence, so that by ascending to one of destiny's higher forms of society, man, fallen in Adam, could even here below be regenerated in Christ, then we could have only offered him our assent. Ourselves, if today we possess that mathematical certitude, we owe it to the study of this theory. But this belief was contained in Catholicism, which teaches that, after knowing the test of the tomb like the Christ, man, Adam, humanity, should, like the Christ, come into glory. Does the harmonian science say anything different? Must we not, before reaching the state of harmony, undergo the test of the tomb? (P. 57)

The text is characteristic, for the efforts to graft socialism onto Catholicism, if they underline various parallels between the two, particularly emphasize the movement via death to resurrection, and insist that suffering is a necessary preliminary for any creation of the Kingdom. This is not the only instance where efforts to "Christianize" socialism end up justifying suffering and violence.[19]

Hugh Doherty proposes a much more developed synthesis between Christianity and Fourierism (*La Phalange*, 1845, 1:240–61 and 385–427). He tries to reconcile with Fourierism not only

Christian theology, but dogmas, rites, sacraments. Thus, on the Mass:

> The Eucharistic sacrament is the symbol of the eternal logos of truth and love, the spiritual bread and wine which should nourish the intelligence of mankind as material bread and wine nourish our bodies. After materially sacrificing his flesh and blood on the cross, Christ continually offers us the symbol of the moral or spiritual sacrifice, of social self-sacrifice which will lead us to the future harmony in heaven and on earth, to the integral or religious unity of humankind in the two spheres of life, terrestrial and celestial. (1:244)

Two levels of interpretation of the Mass result from this theory. First, "The bread and wine of the spirit are the truth which nourishes men's souls and intelligence in order to form the spiritual body and blood of the collective human race, united in God, as the material bread and wine nourish our organs and form the flesh and blood of the body of each individual" (1:245). The Eucharist is thus the "material type of the permanent influence of the logos of God"; this is why Christ, truly man and God, reigns over all the souls of our earth, and also rules over the bodies which clothe these souls. Second, not only all spiritual substance but all physical substance is under the domination of Christ. The immediate source of the body is the earth, whose main fruits are the grape and the grain, and this earth with its fruits belongs to the human race which forms a collective religious body of which the Man-God is the head. In that way, all of humanity constitutes the mystical Body of Christ.

> If then this material substance which forms the flesh and blood of men becomes the collective body of Christ, after its assimilation by the digestive organs, it must also be the property of Christ, the real substance of the collective body of humanity, before this transformation into flesh and blood. It ensues therefrom, that in symbolic, providential language, Christ could say: Verily, verily, the fluid or solid substances, bread and wine, with which you are nourished in order to form the collective body which is my body, both this bread and wine are the substance of my collective flesh and blood, since all power has been given me in heaven and on earth. So it is really the body of Christ, the matter which is subordinated to him, we assimilate when we receive the symbolic bread and wine of the sacrament, and it is really Christ's spirit that we assimilate when we receive by the intelligence the Logos of the divine revelation. (1:246)

These rather original proofs of the Real Presence, if they do not entirely avoid pantheism, at least show how analogy allowed a combination of Christian doctrine and the Fourierist mechanism in order to rehabilitate matter and create the societary union of humankind.

According to Doherty, all the Christian religion, indeed all religions, can be subjected to similar analyses; we are only at the babbling beginnings of the art of interpreting symbols. He also had a theory about the history of language, which he conceived as an organic progress. From that theory he derived a justification for the progressive interpretation of Scripture. Not only languages, but also philosophical systems possess analogies among each other, for word is thought, and both philosophy and language are linguistic bodies. He proposed a "table of equivalent terms" between Fourier and Swedenborg: what Fourier calls attraction for Swedenborg is love, what is analogy for Fourier is correspondence for Swedenborg, and so on. Doherty possessed remarkable gifts of syncretism. We shall shortly encounter another effort to reconcile Fourierism and Catholicism, by P. G. F. Lacuria, but first we must discuss the Catholic theologian of the period who most developed the theory of harmonies, Blanc Saint-Bonnet, for Lacuria was his disciple.

### ❦ *The Unity of Harmonies: Blanc Saint-Bonnet and Lacuria*

The title of Blanc's first book, *De l'unité* (1841), suggests what was his deepest preoccupation. Opposed to all forms of empiricism, he affirms that only the contemplation of the Ideal can lead to any knowledge of the truth. That Ideal had been studied by Plato, Descartes, Kant, and Lamennais, but all those philosophers erred, for, says Blanc, only the analysis of the Trinity-in-Unity, divinely revealed, allows us to grasp or know the true Ideal.

If his definition of the Trinity is orthodox, the language he uses is novel. The Father possesses all being, gives and receives existence, is power and causality, is happy. The Son engenders everything that God possesses, knows and is known, he is intelligence, wisdom, logos, by which God is happy. The Holy Ghost loves everything he engenders, he loves and is loved, he is love, the being for which God is happy. Their diversity is the proof of their felicity, as they possess one another and seek to possess one another. "The sweetness of power and the force of love create goodness, whose nature is to love, and thereby the Son is eternally engendered, in whom the Father and the Spirit find all their delight" (p. 938).

Man, created in the image of God, is necessarily a reflection of the Trinity, and here Blanc's analogical thinking really takes off. Alas, I cannot reproduce the superb design he provides (p. 960) of two equilateral triangles facing each other, where the first person, angle P (Father), opens toward the infinite; the second, angle F (Son), opens directly opposite to give an image thereof; and the two are reflected in angle E (Holy Ghost), where they are reunited. Moreover, the third person "pulls" the two others with all the weight of its love and "leads the Infinite being to overflow from its own breast" (p. 959), creating within a human being the Trinity of rationality, causality and heart. The rays of this divine triangle cross a prism, which is the locus of creation, before being projected into the human triangle. The ray of Power of the Father produces causality, the ray of Love of the Holy Ghost creates the heart, the ray of Wisdom of the Son engenders rationality. But if the heart-love reflects the Holy Ghost, it is only known by the Son-logos. The heart-love is the force that gives impetus to the quest for Unity, in humans as in the Trinity. The essence of God is reality, his nature infinity, his life felicity, but his being is love-unity. And our desire for reunion with God is love; by definition, we are beings who love, who aspire to "reenter into the essential Reality" (p. 487).

When Blanc comes to describe these matters in detail, his thought becomes more and more analogical. For example, his conception of the heart is both physiological and spiritual, and his language here is reminiscent of that of the devotions to the Sacred Heart. Since the heart is the organ of love, it represents man himself in his relations with the Absolute, it is our true person. Thus in Hebrew, the original language, the word for heart means to burn in the depths of the soul. "It is through the heart that man suffers because of his separation from the absolute Being; it is in the heart that he burns with the desire to find it again" (p. 553). The heart bleeds, for it is the place where we are separated from God; the arterial heart, in its pulsations, seeks to escape our breasts; this is the emblem (Blanc's term) of our spiritual quest. Yet the will controls the heart and directs it toward the divine: "The heart is a bark on the ocean of life; love is the wind which gives it motion; will is the rudder which steers it toward its goal" (p. 554).

Blanc offers his own and somewhat different version of Bonald's Trinitarian analysis of the family. The correspondences between the members of the family and the Trinity stem from the very origin of the family. One day as the Trinity lovingly contemplated itself, in joy, "a voice was heard saying, 'It is not good that man be alone; let us also divide him up into three persons!' and man was placed in a sleep of ecstasy. There then appeared in the distance, as a shadow of the Trinity, an iris formed of three colors—Man, Woman, Child." Blanc associates God the Father with the male, the Holy Ghost with the female, and the logos "was always concerned with the child, cultivated his simplicity and his candor" (pp. 1433–34). For the love of God is conjugal in its essence and "the joys of the Trinity and of the family are of the same nature." Blanc derives from this theory strong arguments against marriages of convenience. And he continues, proposing analogies among the Trinity, the family, and the chord in music. He also maintains a Trinitarian theory of history; he awaits the coming of the age of the Holy Ghost when humanity will be restored to unity in the heart of the Trinity.

Blanc was not, despite all this, a leftist; on the contrary, he went on to become a major theoretician of the political right. But one of his disciples, P. G. F. Lacuria, published a synthesis of Blanc and Fourier in 1847, *Les Harmonies de l'Etre exprimées par les nombres.* By means of geometrical and algebraic calculations he proves the existence of unity in diversity and also the truth of Catholicism.[20] Indeed, according to Lacuria the great need of the age is unity: intellectual, religious, political, and social.

The first chapter is a study of the Unity-Trinity, the source of all knowledge and all philosophy. Nothing is understandable except by the Trinity, and the history of humanity is a progressive development toward the comprehension of this Trinity—it was St. John, rather than Jesus, who played the role of the great initiator. The Trinity is Life, Logos, Light. The Father is Life because "life is the idea we encounter at the very depths of being, because all other ideas presuppose life, and life engenders all ideas. Life is the principle of form and of love" (1:36). The dominating characteristic of life is expansion; life tends to spread forth, but in dilating "it would only be blind and hazy immensity without that form which makes life intelligible and intelligent" (1:36). This is the function of the Son who is logos, word and form, and who engenders variety or distinction (an idea Lacuria borrows from Lamennais's *Esquisse d'une philosophie*). Life without intelligence remains confused and blind, and on the other hand intelligence without substance can neither speak nor enlighten. Thanks to the Holy Ghost, substance and intelligence are combined and everything becomes luminous. Lacuria then seeks examples of this structure of Unity-Trinity in human beings, in nature, in the economy of salvation. There ensue long discussions on fluids, colors, conic sections, and the like, ending with Chapter 8, "Concerning Substance and Personality in God," which offers a Fourierist description of the Trinity. The Father, the consciousness that God has of himself by the idea of being, is a positive consciousness; the Son, the consciousness that God has of himself by the idea of nonbeing, is a negative consciousness. The Holy Ghost is the consciousness that God has of himself by the union of the two ideas, and by this union God establishes in a harmonious unity these two irreconcilables. Thus, "Only the Father is positive, only the Son is negative. The Father of himself is positive, the Son of himself is negative, the Holy Ghost of itself is harmonic; and in finding these three names we have formulated the fundamental and universal law of being: the positive and the negative produce harmony." And there follows a magnificent series of analogies. I limit myself to one example:

> Man's physical life begins with the heart which produces a direct circulation, that of arterial blood, but that would not suffice for life, there must be a reflex circulation, which is that of venal blood; their combined action produces complete life, and, notably, the blood whose movement is direct is red, the color of the Father; the blood whose movement is reflexive is closer to blue, the color of the Son. (1:140)

Lacuria, more than any of the others mentioned here, feels a strong nostalgia for the unity which must be grasped beneath the harmonies of variety. "O triple Unity, united Trinity, when shall I be able to enter more deeply in thy breast? When may I flee all finite objects which divide my thoughts, and contemplate only thyself?" (1:184). And it is by an appeal to Fourierist structures that he hopes to reestablish, as did Blanc Saint-Bonnet, the paths toward unity via the dogmas and mysteries of the Christian faith.

### ❦ Fusion

One could propose as a symbolic conclusion to this quest for harmony a movement that was not Catholic but rather one of the new religions that flourished in the 1830s and 1840s, the "Fusion-

ism" of L. J. B. de Tourreil and Auguste Guyard. For them, everything is harmony because all is one: "All beings emanate, absorb,
and appropriate to themselves to varying degrees the substances
emanated by the beings which surround them. By emanation, all
give themselves to all; by absorption, all penetrate into all; and by
appropriation, or the combination of substances, which is an assim-
ilation, in vegetable, animal, humanity, all are united to all and in
this way establish the vast universal association" (Tourreil, *L'Explication de Dieu et de l'homme,* 1845, p. xl). It is not a matter of "Love
one another," but "Love yourself in all others," for in fact they are
physically a part of yourself. At the same time a physics, a theology,
and a sociology, Fusionism concludes with an androgyne conception
of the divinity, the cult of the *Meramourpère* ("Motherlovefather")
where even sexual division ceases in a harmonious unity, and with
the syncretism of all religions. Fusionism is also a utopianism,
which proposes a completely new, communistic, and technocratic
organization of society, which even offers a detailed vision of a most
symmetrical architecture of the ideal City, where all will be harmony, the Kingdom will be of this world, and the beatific harmonies of the spheres will be fully replicated in the harmony of human
beings on earth.

## ❦ Conclusion

These texts are difficult to read today, indeed they often seem to
be elucubrations that try to hide the factitious nature of the parallels that they propose behind a screen of jumbled words, the products of confused minds. However, I think that would be a false
condemnation of these fifty some authors—and one could quote
many more. These authors and their works are difficult to categorize. Yet the very essence of the theory of harmonies is to cross
boundaries; the quest for harmonies requires highly mobile kinds of
thinking. The harmony of myths is found in language and in numbers; the trinities of theology reappear in grammar, social structures, the circulation of blood, and history. This does not mean that
harmony is a synonym for confusion. The signification of categories
changes, and what formed a category for the Romantics is somewhat foreign to us today—words and things are grouped differently
from century to century as well as from culture to culture. Between
the Romantics and us, positivism and the Thomist revival create a

major separation. Which characteristics of categories lent themselves to the quest of harmonies are fairly evident. It is a matter of seeking for unity beyond multiplicity, an effort to discover a common essence among disparate appearances. There are several levels of appearances (language, myth, numbers, things, history) but our texts always propose that one level possesses an ideal or transcendent status. It is more difficult to say what constitutes their commonality, what allows the harmony to be certified: a number, often three, or an etymological root, or a tragic structure whose actors change name. One must distinguish between prophecy, defined as an announcement in the past of a later event; the *figura* (Moses striking the rock, a *figura* of baptism; or Socrates, a *figura* of Jesus); and harmony. If A is a *figura* of Z, for the theory of harmonies, it is for metaphysical reasons and because of the very essential nature of things. The textual juxtaposition of A and Z aims to make the reader aware of this essence. Thus the theory of harmony necessarily makes some presuppositions about the nature of things, all of them monist in character: universal revelation, language as a gift of God, creation as an emanation from God, the presence of the divine in us. In a world where God would be completely other and hidden, there could be no harmonies of the divine. The kind of relation that derives from this divine essence can be of several sorts: a relation of procession, or a dialectic one; a relation of reconciliation, or of gravitation. It is this last that seems to dominate in French Romanticism, both in Fourierism and in various innovations in Christian theology. The rather naive simplicity of the Fusionist's thesis represents the fundamental nature of this thought. All equals one, beneath appearances unity can be found again, and this unity is one of the created with the Creator; the realization of harmony will bring about the end of Satan. Elsewhere, the gambit is more complicated, and even artificial, and one can ask what credit was generally given it. Did the quest for unity via the harmonies simply reveal in some a nostalgia for the Christian faith, in others for the Golden Age? This alchemy of the logos which tends toward a transformation of history, of society, of matter, would then only be the memory of a paradise lost forever.

Nonetheless, the presuppositions of these explorations of Harmonies in theology, philosophy, and politics also informed many other aspects of Romantic thought. Homeopathic medicine was constructed on theories about harmony, hence the ease with which it was reconciled with Fourierism. Georges Cuvier's claim to reconstruct the being from its smallest part represents the organic aspect of harmonies, just as Geoffroy Saint-Hilaire's work represented its dynamic aspects. It informs Alphonse Toussenel's Fourierist studies on birds and animals, as it does J. J. Grandville's drawings of "animated flowers." And many towns in the United States were named Harmony or New Harmony. The whole of the Romantic esthetic doctrine of inspiration, if neoplatonic in origin, was recast in terms of the theory of harmonies,[21] and, even more important, the function of the image was redefined, the image serving not to illustrate and decorate, but to express the transcendent meaning inherent in the immanent, often doing so by a metaphor which becomes metamorphosis, where that metamorphosis creates the harmonious link between two realms of being. Victor Hugo excelled at such images, but they were already employed by Lamartine, Vigny, Nerval.[22] Yet the quest for harmonies, as here defined, does seem to have diminished or disappeared after the mid-1800s. Today the word *harmony* no longer possesses the deep resonances it had for the Romantics. Perhaps this chapter has suggested why.

# 8 ❦ Symbol and Desymbolizing

The meaning of the word *symbol* is already so broad and ambiguous that one hesitates to use it; do we need to add *desymbolization*, which is not in Littré's Dictionary (that excellent record of Romantic language), or in the writings of Flaubert, or in those of the philosopher Victor Cousin? It does appear, however, in a number of recent articles about Romantic literature, including Pierre-Marc de Biasi's excellent study "The Temptation of the Orient in Flaubert's *Legend of Saint Julian the Hospitaler.*"[1] Biasi's article evokes Jules Michelet who did use the word. I quote Biasi:

> The fundamental question is centered on the historical modulation of the relation between language and the notion of symbol. The general hypothesis could be stated in this way: the Orient is the cradle of symbolic language, which the Occident then adapts in order to desymbolize it into the language of law. (P. 47)

Indeed, the problem of "desymbolization" was of fundamental concern for many French Romantic thinkers, even if they did not often use the word. In analyzing Flaubert's text, Biasi proposes as an example the pair of sandals which Julian, once he has discovered that he has murdered his father, leaves behind for his wife—small detail, but why does Flaubert mention the sandals? Biasi considers the sandals of Empedocles; Moses' deposition of his sandals; citing Michelet, the sandals offered to seal cession contracts; and the deposition of sandals as a symbol of *askesis* in Plotinus. He concludes that Flaubert "constructs the discreet congruity" of this detail "by an erudite manipulation of cultural references which he associates, condenses, displaces, in order to create another kind of pertinency, the pertinency of the undecidable." It is this process that I should like to elaborate and refine. Desymbolization, a way of thinking that is widespread in theories about law, about history of religion, about hermeneutics in the second quarter of the nineteenth century, first tries to determine what the symbol signifies, and it is only after the symbol has been separated from what it signifies by a reading or interpretation that decides that signification—and that reading or interpretation is conceived of as a form or manifestation of historical progress—it is only then that the symbol acquires its "undecidable" character. This theory, it would seem, flourished particularly between 1844 and 1849.

I have discovered a source text that links the deposition of footwear and murder.

> Among the Franc-Salians, in the ritual known as *chenecruda*, related to the ceding of goods, because of the incapacity to pay the recompense for a homicide, the debtor, after performing a certain number of symbolic rites, abandoned his home, without shirt and without shoes.

This is exactly what Julian does. The quotation comes from Pierre Chassan, *Essai sur la symbolique du droit* (1847), p. 223. The essence of Chassan's thesis is that law has not always been expressed in purely verbal forms. In primitive ages, in order to understand and remember the law, people used symbols, images. And Chassan offers a taxonomy of these symbols, describes their origins and traces their transformations, proposing that in the history of law there is a struggle between two principles, on the one hand the sacerdotal and patrician, which strives to maintain the symbolic form, and on the other civil and plebeian, which strives to desymbolize. Because of the emancipation of the plebeians, law gradually moves toward a more and more verbal, abstract form, but law can never achieve total abstraction; if it did so, it would disappear. Chassan was a disciple of Ballanche, from whom he borrows his analysis of history as a struggle between patricians and plebeians, and also, as we shall see, his theory about desymbolization; but Chassan also read Hegel. His aim in part was to disprove Michelet's thesis that law in France from the very beginnings was verbal in its formulations.

The Michelet text in question is the one to which Biasi refers, *Origines du droit français cherchées dans les symboles et formules du droit universel* (1837), which owes a great deal to Jakob Grimm. Michelet accepts Vico's theory about the originally poetic formulation of law but adds that the Roman cult of abstract expression created in

French law a desymbolization that took place very early in French history. According to Michelet, if God created man in his own image, man then created images; "himself a symbol, he created symbols." Furthermore,

> The idea which is enclosed in every symbol burns with a desire to escape from the symbol and rebecome infinite. . . . Man, nature, all of existence is travailed by the infinite captured within, which seeks for revelation by generation, by action, and by art which makes and undoes its symbols. (P. lxv)

Michelet himself justifies my excursions into the areas of theology and jurisprudence as preliminary here to a commentary when he states that "the priest, the poet, the lawmaker were in primitive times the same man"; during this second quarter of the nineteenth century the problem of symbol and desymbolization was quite similar in thinking about law, theology, and literature. Before turning to theology and literature, let us note that these texts about desymbolization in law are part of a political debate, between those who maintain that law is organic, independent of political institutions and not subject to any historical influence, and those who believe in a jurisprudence that develops, grows, gradually comes into being. The theory of the "desymbolization" of law is part of the theses of this second, "progressive" school and justifies the Napoleonic Code, whereas the other school prefers a return to the organic law of the ancien régime.[2] The roots of the quarrel are complex, but it started in Germany, first, between F. Savigny and Edouard Gans, a disciple of Hegel who developed and provided historical documentation for Hegel's theories about the history of jurisprudence. His *Histoire du droit de succession en France au Moyen Age* was not translated until 1845 but his theses—and his quarrel with Savigny—were described by Lerminier in 1828. Gans spent much time in Paris, where he was a close friend of both Michelet and Ballanche.[3]

A separate study should be made about how Michelet first conceived of the idea of desymbolization and how he later came to question it. Of particular interest are the volumes of his *History of France,* but ten years before his 1837 *Origines du droit français,* in 1827, Michelet's friend and fellow historian Edgar Quinet, in his introduction to the translation of Johann Herder's *Ideas on the Philosophy of History* proposed that philosophy should break open the symbol in order to find the law hidden therein, evoking Lessing's theory on revelation as a historical, progressive process God uses for the

education of the human race, a theory that had already been quite
satisfactorily described in France by Mme de Staël in *On Germany*
(1810–14), and which was later to be of considerable influence
on the Saint-Simonians.[4] Quint's thesis is that to begin with truths
are hidden under coarse symbols; Christianity desymbolizes them
but "the law of Christ, in its turn, contains high philosophical
truths . . . which remain mysteries . . . until reason succeeds in
deducing them"; there ensues a meditation on the Passion of Jesus
as a symbol of the processes of history, one of the first such Romantic analyses I know of. Quinet's thought is quintessential, and I
shall return to it, but first mention must be made of the philosopher to whom this translation of Herder is dedicated, Victor
Cousin, who in the same year, 1827, began practicing desymbolization in religious matters at the Sorbonne. He did so by offering his
own rather personal version of Hegelianism.

In 1818, Cousin had proposed a trinity of "self/non-self/
Absolute" manifest in the Good, the True, and the Beautiful. In
1827 he substituted for that trinity a new one of finite/infinite/their
relations, and then derives from that a ternary theory of history,
where the Absolute is an active intelligence, a triplicity becoming
reorganized in unity (*Cours de l'histoire de la philosophie*, 1828). He
thus moves from Schelling to Hegel and also borrows from Hegel
his theory about the evolution of religion: first the Orient, the static
infinite, theocratic despotism; then Greece, the finite and democ-
racy; then Christianity, a synthesis of finite and infinite. This pro-
gression both is and is not Hegel—and one could say the same for
Cousin's theories about the relations between religion and philosophy. He defines the natural religious sentiment as an intuition of
God as distinct in essence from the world but where the divine
is present in this world; this natural religious sentiment finds expression in various religious systems; it creates symbols. Faith then
becomes attached to those symbols, contemplates them. Then humankind feels the need to understand the symbol, decomposes it,
and, thanks to this mental labor, the dialectic allows humanity to
progress in its awareness of the Absolute. What religion expresses in
symbolic form, philosophy translates into pure, rational truths.
Philosophy is the sister of religion, "gently elevating religion from
the twilight of the symbol to the bright daylight of pure thought"
(1:23–24). Cousin then develops his thesis that the lower classes
still need religion and that philosophy is an elitist activity; this is

Cousin's version of "religion is the opium of the masses" but he recommends the administration of the opium. In his lectures of the following year, published as the *Histoire de la philosophie du dix-huitième siècle,* Cousin provides a much more conflict-ridden portrait of this relation between religion and philosophy; religion gives birth to philosophy, but that birth is painful, and religion behaves toward philosophy as a bad stepmother. Here he adopts publicly the theses expressed by his disciple Théodore Jouffroy in his famous and much-discussed article of 1825 in *Le Globe,* "Comment les dogmes finissent."

The history of Hegelianism in the first half of the nineteenth century deserves further attention. In this quarrel, some accused Cousin of having perverted France by introducing the ideas of Hegel, others accused the same Cousin of having prevented any alliance between Hegelian and socialist thought in France. In his *Histoire de la philosophie du dix-huitième siècle,* Cousin had already rejected Hegel in two very important ways. First, Cousin substituted for the dialectic evolution of philosophy his thesis according to which each of the four philosophical systems exists throughout history, each one possessing a share of truth, but also a share of error. Then, faithful to Descartes and Maine de Biran, he conceived of the self as a voluntary power and proposed a movement from psychology to ontology; the dialectic is a human faculty, and not the principle of absolute thought. This rejection of Hegel was symptomatic of things to come in French thought; for instance, as we shall see, many French, faced with David Strauss's *Life of Jesus* (translated 1839–40), would refuse to accept what seemed to them a destruction of the personality of Jesus. When Cousin came to power during the July Monarchy, literally becoming the national dictator in matters concerning the teaching of philosophy (a year of philosophy—Cousin's philosophy—was required of all baccalaureate candidates), he would very much mute this theory of a desymbolizing movement from religion to philosophy and would do his best (quite in vain) to maintain cordial relations with the Church by proposing instead a kind of fideist separation between religion and philosophy. Only in the late 1840s, when a great polemic arose over the eclecticism of Alexandria, did a new crisis erupt when some young disciples of Cousin—Ernest Bersot, Jules Simon, Auguste Véra—having turned their backs on their master, began desymbolizing philosophy's "stepmother" religion, with passion and delight.

By then, however, Hegel's theories about the relations between religion and philosophy were well known in France, thanks to a series of more or less adequate presentations of Hegel's thought by Joseph Willm in 1835, Barchou de Penhoën in 1836, Louis Prévost in 1844, Auguste Ott in the same year, and others. Even more significant was the quarrel over Strauss's *Life of Jesus,* in which Strauss, a disciple of Hegel, desymbolized the most important symbol of Christianity, Jesus himself. Even earlier, this analysis of the relationship between religion and philosophy, between symbol and idea, had produced a new hermeneutics of religions and mythology which began to compete with Euhemerist interpretations, with those who read mythology as a figural description of the solar system or other aspects of nature, not to mention the Catholic "traditionalist" interpretation of mythology which read myths as corrupt forms of a divine primitive revelation, corrupt forms which, properly interpreted, revealed the dogmas of the Christian faith. The new hermeneutics of mythology rather read myths and religions as symbolic expressions of the philosophical, metaphysical, scientific, even political convictions of the society that produced the myths.[5] That reading in a way attributed value to the symbol, but it also proposed that truth eventually frees itself from symbolic expression and moves toward abstract expression; the mythic or religious symbol then loses its philosophical import and becomes a simple allegory, a charming bit of poetry. Historical erudition, studying the myths, nevertheless can uncover the truths that those myths originally expressed. For example, in his analyses of the political functions of religious systems, Jouffroy introduces ethnopsychology into the study of comparative religion, a precursor of the anthropological readings of theology by Ludwig Feuerbach. The major practitioner of this new hermeneutics was another disciple of Hegel, Frederick Creuzer, whose work J. D. Guigniaut began translating, supplementing, and adapting in 1825, and Creuzer and Guigniaut's *Symbolic* was to become a major source for both poets and thinkers.

However, before discussing the debate over Strauss's book, I want to mention another theory of desymbolization, that of Ballanche, for it is markedly different, in an important way, from that of Cousin. According to Ballanche, "Religion is subject to the law of progress, the law of succession; thus, it is made manifest successively. When God spoke in history, he spoke the language of the age and of the men of that point in history. The spirit contained in the letter develops, and the letter is abolished."[6] An expert in the analysis of myths as demonstrating the traditionalist revelation, myths as expressions of "Christianity before Christianity," Ballanche also believed in a progressive evolution of our awareness of religious truth thanks to "divine condescendance," where the symbol evolves; emblems and allegories are abandoned, giving way to the abstract, the real. He described two mechanisms by which humanity, in the course of its history, unveils the symbols. According to the first, humankind moves from music to poetry to prose to abstract thought, and "the present age is the age of the emancipation of thought which is being freed from the chains of language"—the ultimate form of desymbolization. The other mechanism takes up a schema proposed by Hegel, Cousin, and Edgar Quinet in various forms: the infinite Orient, the finite Occident, then a third period of the synthesis of finite and infinite. But Ballanche innovated in claiming that in this evolution the esoteric becomes exoteric, and also in analyzing the evolution as a struggle between plebeians and patricians; it is the plebs, the popular classes, who unveil the eso-teric and produce the known from the unknown. Whereas, accord-ing to Cousin, religion and symbols are necessary for the lower classes, philosophy and abstraction are the privileges of the elite.[7]

Ballanche deals with other aspects of desymbolization and ap-plies it to law and to poetry as well as to religion, thus happily offering a proof for my thesis. Poetry should gradually "translate itself" into philosophical language; law, which is at first poetic and oral, gradually moves toward prose. He draws a parallel between the Alexandrian age and his own; both were periods of intense de-symbolizing activity where science was introduced into religion, where philosophy interrogated religions and myths. Above all Bal-lanche, who often borrows Lessing's phrase "the education of the human race" to describe this historical process, emphasizes its pain-ful aspect: "The education of the human race is always harsh and difficult."[8] (Ballanche was his whole life, a devout and fervent Catholic, but he also remained a faithful friend of Lamennais after Lamennais had been condemned by the Church.)

Ballanche differs from Hegel and Cousin in another important way. According to Ballanche, if the mission of the word is drawing to its end in the intellectual realm, the word "will always have a function to perform in the religious domain," for the word of Chris-tianity, the logos of God, is not distinct from the ideal.[9] Since

Christianity's essential activity was to make the religious word exoteric, Christianity cannot be desymbolized. The logos of God has no emblem; rather, the task of philosophical and indeed social language is to become purified so that it will join with the Christian logos. But "social doctrines can never be entirely laid bare. The statue of Isis was draped in a triple veil; the first was removed by the neophytes, the second by the priests of the sanctuary; but the third was sacred for all."[10] Isis can never be completely unveiled.

Even though the famed positivist lexicographer Littré did not complete his translation of Strauss's *Life of Jesus* until 1840, the "quarrel" about that work exploded in France in 1836. I have traced the debate elsewhere; here I shall discuss its relevance for the problem of desymbolization. It was largely because of this controversy that French thought finally became aware of neo-Hegelian theses about religion.[11] Strauss's labors had as their consequence a desymbolization of the Jesus of history in order to uncover a Christlogos active in the becoming of history. In a sense, for the French Strauss continued a work already well advance by the studies of Lessing, Benjamin Constant, Cousin himself, Saint-Simon, and others. According to Strauss, the primitive Church had transformed the Jesus of history into a myth, primarily because of messianic expectations, and it was not necessary to break up that symbolic envelope in order to seek nourishment from its substantific marrow, the union of the divine and human principles. Thus, proposed Strauss, what biblical criticism had destroyed by exegesis, it restored in terms of dogma. He refused on the one hand the Enlightenment "reductionist" approach to religion and on the other Kant's spiritualization of history with its radical distinction between moral and historical belief. Strauss, faithful to Hegel, suggested that one should read in the attributes given to Jesus an idea that is real, the idea of humanity; the death of the incarnate deity is the demonstration of the dialectically possible union of divine and human principles. Thus the Jesus of history is destroyed, in order to transform him into a philosophical principle whose political consequences are quite clear, and indeed would shortly thereafter be clarified in France, thanks to Henri Heine and to studies on the ideas of Feuerbach, Bruno Bauer, and others. Their important texts were not translated until 1850, but their theses were discussed before that date.[12] Strauss also proposed a hermeneutics of desymbolization, including the theory that poetic form in and of itself indicates that a

text has undergone mythic development. The French refutations of
Strauss, most of them rather shabby, centered their attacks on this
hermeneutics; Edgar Quinet, on the other hand, rejected Strauss
because he felt that Stauss denied the very principle of personality,
and thus Quinet came to reject the desymbolization process as a
form of historical progress (which seemingly was also true of his
friend Michelet), instead proposing the need for a renewed marriage
of religion and philosophy as an impetus toward progress.[13]

As often in French Romanticism, this debate about the relationship between religion and philosophy and about desymbolization
soon became recast as a quarrel situated in the realm of historical,
learned discourse, this time centered, as Ballanche had predicted it
would be, in studies on the school of Alexandria. Hegel had, of
course, already discussed Alexandria intensively, and Cousin had
edited Proclus, but in 1840 Jacques Matter radically revised his
*Histoire de l'école d'Alexandrie,* showing how Christianity became a
philosophy at Alexandria and thereby influenced neoplatonist and
polytheistic thought, and was in turn influenced by these ideas. The
Church responded in 1843 with J. M. Prat's *Histoire de l'éclectisme
alexandrin,* an open attack against Matter, and a veiled one against
Cousin, denying any neoplatonic influence in the formation of
Christian dogma. Jules Simon, at the beginning of his career, answered Prat in 1845 with his violently anti-Christian *Histoire de
l'école d'Alexandrie,* contrasting the obscure Trinity of the Church
with the Trinitarian philosophy of the pagan school, and "effemi-
nate" Christian mysticism with the virile genius of Plotinus, dis-
covering in pagan Alexandrian philosophy an early expression of the
thought of Spinoza. Simon thus came under immediate attack from
Emile Saisset, the faithful spokesman for Cousin in religious matters, who suggested that Alexandria demonstrated that any effort
to link religion and philosophy was bound to fail; both may have
the same goal, but any marriage between them is impossible—
which reflects Cousin's tactics under the July Monarchy, centered on
creating a radical division between religion and philosophy. As exemplary cases of the dangers of any such marriage, Saisset cites on
the one hand Lamennais and his *Esquisse d'une philosophie,* on the
other Hegel.[14]

It was too late; in 1846 Etienne Vacherot published the first two
volumes of his brilliant *Histoire de l'école d'Alexandrie.* There was not
just one Christianity, but many forms of Christianity, whose varia-

tions and evolutions are to be explained by intellectual history, by a contact first with Gnostic currents of thought, then a purification through contact with Hellenistic Platonism. And these developments all inspired the first version of Flaubert's *Temptation of St. Anthony*. As I suggest in Chapter 10, it is perfectly possible to read the *Temptation* as a witness to Flaubert's neuroses, but the text is also a polemic work that has its place in the then ongoing debate about Alexandria and thus about the problem of desymbolization. Flaubert ponders the extent to which the religious symbol cannot be deciphered, desymbolized. Rather than representing religion as moving beyond symbolic expression in order to become philosophy, he reduces religion to the pure symbol, omitting or hiding the ideological content of the symbol, and then proceeds to degrade or destroy the symbol. He is not the only practitioner of this technique. The influence of Jean-Paul Richter's *Dream* on the sonnets of Gérard de Nerval on Christ in the Garden of Olives has been noted by many scholars; one should also note that in these sonnets, which date from 1844, we can trace the influence of the controversy over Strauss and over desymbolization. This recognition can help explain the fifth sonnet, which cites a series of soteriological symbols (Icarus, Phaeton, Atys, Jesus) and proclaims their ambiguity—Jupiter does not answer Caesar's question, who is this new God?—but also continues to attribute to those figures a degree of sacredness. I think that there are other troublesome "symbols" from the poetry of the 1840s which can also be understood if one situates them in the context of this debate about desymbolization. Consider, for instance, Vigny's strangely fractured image of the "dove of the bronze beak, Visible Holy Ghost"—but that would require another article. The symbol, deprived of its philosophic content by desymbolization, in fact becomes "undecidable," and thus poetic language maintains the religious status that Ballanche tried to give it; at that point, to paraphrase Stéphane Mallarmé, poetry could be made with words, and not with ideas.

# ❧ IV

# Interdisciplinary Explication of Texts

# 9 ❦ The "Mémorables" of Nerval's *Aurélia*

Near the end of Gérard de Nerval's autobiographical novel about his insanity and his exploration of the world of dreams, there occurs a section, "Mémorables," written in a highly poetic style, which has presented Nerval scholars with a great many problems—problems about editing the text, about dating it, above all about its meaning. For instance, we are not sure whether some of the repetitions or refrains in it were of Nerval's choice, or whether they reflect print- ing errors. The beginning of the text is clearly marked, but there have been lengthy discussions about where it ends.[1] For reasons of stylistic unity, and of temporal mode, I myself believe that the passage that begins "On a sharp peak in Auvergne" ends with the sentence "May God guard in his keeping the divine Balder, the son of Odin, and beautiful Freya." I hope I can cast some light on the three following paragraphs of the text, on Saardam, on Vienna, and on the statue of Peter the Great. What follows these and provides the novel's closure—a commentary on his whole project, news about the improved mental health of his friend Saturnin—consti- tutes a perfectly reasonable and ordinary conclusion, "tying up the loose ends."

I do not think that "Mémorables" is the writing of a madman, as some have suggested. The text is neither incomprehensible nor cha- otic, but well organized and constructed, and it performs an essen- tial, highly important function in *Aurélia*. A familiarity with certain aspects of Romantic thought, with the "mystical" literature of the period, and with contemporary history, makes the text quite readable and its function within the novel clear. This reading of the text was already begun by Pierre Georges Castex, and then by Gabrielle Malandain.[2] I do wish, however, to question a certain critical approach to this text; a good example might be Michel Jeanneret, a scholar for whom I have the highest respect and who, in an otherwise excellent book on Nerval, comments:

> The end of *Aurélia,* uncertain, dispersed, seems to betray a failing on the narrator's part. Once we get to the "Mémorables," the narration becomes hesitant. Even the insertion of this passage into the novel is problematic; there is a rupture in narration, and when it starts again, it does so in an arbitrary way. As for the different fragments contained in "Mémorables," they are heterogeneous, lacking in any continuity; can one maintain that they are a necessary element of the novel? . . . Afterward, come some descriptions of other dreams whose meaning is far from being clear. . . . The geographical space of the novel becomes fractured among different countries, and what unity or common link they may possess is not clear; a geography broken into pieces, partial visions, multiplied with a rapid rhythm in a way that recalls the dream in Nerval's *Pandora* . . . an uncertain discourse where it would seem impossible to know what is to be seen as positive, what as negative.[3]

I think this judgment should be revised.

I shall discuss briefly how the text is organized, which seems to me rather evident; then the origins of the ideas it expounds, which were widespread at the time, in order to analyze in greater detail three problems: the links between the text and the rest of *Aurélia;* the particular form of universal salvation Nerval there propounds; and finally, the generic context of "Mémorables."

"In the Trinity resides a formidable mystery," Nerval says in *Aurélia* (I, iv). The tripartite division of "Mémorables" evokes various Romantic Trinitarian interpretations of history: the age of the Son for the first part, where Jesus and the lady Mediatrix procure the fraternal reconciliation of all humanity; then the age of the Father Creator, the reconciliation of all the created world; and finally the age of the Holy Ghost, the reconciliation of the cosmic forces and the fallen angels and the reign of perpetual peace. This order was fairly widespread at the time; it is a historical order, and also the order of the action by which humankind reintegrates the divine and thus reverses the order of Genesis (the fall of the angels, then the creation of the universe, then the creation of human beings and original sin).[4]

The first part begins with a representation, rich in imagery, of the dream of union, of peace on earth and glory in the heavens, evoking the symbols of precious stones, of flowers and birds, and echoing the tripartite schema of the Chain of Being (mineral, vegetable, animal) that Nerval had already used in his sonnet "Vers dorés." The first refrain, an adaptation of two well-known liturgical texts, the Gloria and the Benedictus ("Hosanna! peace on earth and glory in the heavens!") comes at the end of the first paragraph and is then repeated at the end of the second paragraph of the second part of the text. The "Hosanna!" is also repeated at the end of the first paragraph of the third part.

After this introduction, the text recounts the beatific vision of the narrator and his ride, on horseback, toward the heavenly city. The first ascent fails, the second succeeds thanks to the aid of his fellow sufferer Saturnin (fraternity), and then comes the vision of the conquering Messiah and the New Jerusalem—the epiphany—and the narrator descends to earth to announce the "good news" to mankind—a translation of *evangelium,* in marked contrast with the way that Nerval uses the term in his sonnet sequence about Christ in the Garden of Olives, where Jesus says to the disciples, "My friends, do you know the *news?*"—there, the skies are empty, there is no God. The narrator beholds the Mediatrix, Aurélia, who is also the Queen of Sheba and Sophia, the Divine Wisdom, transfigured; and he receives his pardon, signed with the blood of Jesus.

The second part describes the restoration of the harmony of all creation, the music of the spheres, the reconciliation of all history, and all of nature proclaims the glory of God. It is perhaps the most beautiful part of "Mémorables." The images of the octave and of the restoration of the harmony of the spheres and also here below, are of course very ancient and venerable, but they are characteristic of Fourierist literature, which *Aurélia* evokes elsewhere in discussing the science that will remake humanity, the harmonian science.[5] The word *harmonie* is inscribed on the manuscript of this part of "Mémorables."[6]

The third part begins by anathematizing the blacksmith gods of the North, only to announce afterward that they also have received Christ's pardon, and that even the serpent has been blessed. Here again, Nerval recasts ideas widespread in Romantic "mystic socialist" literature. The conversion and reintegration with the divine and the self, and humankind, made possible by the Mediatrix, a Bea-

trice or Virgin Mary figure, and by fraternal love, will first restore
the harmony of all creation, and finally bring about universal salvation, including apocatastasis, the salvation of the fallen angels; Satan will re-become Lucifer and the serpent will be blessed. Nerval,
in his way, is simply saying what the mystical Fourierists were saying or what Alphonse-Louis Constant, and Alexandre Guiraud, and
before them Louis-Claude de Saint-Martin and Ballanche, after
them Victor Hugo, were saying. It would be quite futile to hunt for
a specific source or text that expresses ideas so common and widespread at the time. However, it should be noted that Nerval, here
and elsewhere, in one way takes a stance quite different from that,
say, of the Fourierists; he criticizes the mystic socialists for proposing model communities which "can never include the universality
of mankind." What Nerval hopes for, in "Mémorables" and elsewhere, is a universal peace.[7]

Nerval also differs from the Romantic discourse in another way;
for the redemption of the fallen angels (which however, as we shall
see, is present in the text)[8] he substitutes the redemption of the
gods of the North, and also gives them attributes which, in his
other writings, especially his *Voyage en Orient,* he attributes to Cain
and his descendants. His model can probably be traced to Paul
Chenavard's project for the facade of the Pantheón in Paris, but in
my opinion the substitution is to be explained by the problem of the
Crimean War and serves to prepare the three paragraphs that follow
"Mémorables," which are dominated by images and evocations of
the countries of the North and where the Crimean War is a central
concern.[9] These paragraphs end on a vision of the two Catherines
and St. Helen Empress: "Their sweet looks, directed toward France,
decreased space by means of long telescopes of crystal. I understood
by that that our country was to arbitrate the oriental quarrel, and
they were awaiting its solution. My dream ended with the sweet
hope that peace would finally be given us" (II, vi, 122). The "oriental quarrel" in question is the Crimean War.

The snake will furnish my first proof. In "Mémorables," after
the redemption of the gods of the North, the text continues: "The
serpent who encircles the World is himself blessed, for he relaxes
his coils, and his wide-opened mouth breathes in the flower of the
anxoka, the flower of sulphur, the brilliant flower of the sun!" This
serpent possesses a very rich intertextuality, going all the way back
to the Book of Genesis, but Nerval was probably more directly

inspired by the "serpent of eternity" in Jean-Paul Richter's "Dream." Like most of the cultural allusions in "Mémorables," the serpent is something of a commonplace of that age, but what is of interest is his earlier appearance in *Aurélia,* at the end of I, vii, 44. There, the serpent is a nefarious symbol, whereas in "Mémorables" he is transformed into a good symbol—Alfred Maury had recently written at length about the double nature of serpent symbolism, sometimes evil and destructive, sometimes healing and constructive.[10] More important is the context of this first reference:

> Everywhere, the suffering image of the Eternal Mother was dying, weeping, languishing. Among the vague civilizations of Asia and Africa, a bloody scene of orgy and carnage was repeated again and again, which the same spirits reproduced in new forms. The last took place at Grenada, where the sacred talisman was crushed under the repeated enemy blows of Christians and Moslems. For how many more years will the world have to suffer, for the vengeance of these eternal enemies must be renewed under yet other skies. (I, viii, 44)

The skies of the Crimea. And immediately after this passage comes the sentence on the serpent: "These are the divided segments of the serpent who encircles the earth. . . . Separated by the blade, they rejoin in a hideous kiss sealed by the blood of men." "These" refers to the eternal enemies, Christian and Moslem in this instance, whose vengeance is renewed in our day under other skies. Nerval fears that the bloody scene of conflict between Christians and Moslems is recurring in the Crimea, and hopes that the reconciliation of the gods of the North that he heralds in "Mémorables" will take place in history, thanks to France, thus putting an end to the Crimean conflict, and the serpent will then relax its coils. The way he reverses the structure is important. In I, viii, he evokes the conflict of the two forces, Christian and Moslem, and then the nefarious serpent; in "Mémorables", the cosmic reconciliation of Christianity and paganism (the gods of the North, peace in heaven), then the beneficent serpent, then the hope of an end to the conflict of Moslems and Christians (peace on earth). He often has recourse to such a "reversal" technique in "Mémorables."

I must make a detour here to address the question of when "Mémorables" was composed. We know that Nerval wrote it after 22 August 1853, the date of the death of Charles Reynaud, since this event is referred to in II, iv (p. 82), accompanied by yet another political allusion: "Political events exercised an indirect influence on me, both bringing me affliction and depriving me of the means I needed to put my affairs in order. The death of one of my friends added to these causes of discouragement." The juxtaposition is not produced by chance; July–August 1853 is the date of the Vienna Note which crystallized the dispute that led to the Crimean War, and Reynaud is the author of a book on his travels in the Near East where he discusses the Moslem-Christian quarrel.[11] Nerval had not yet given his texts to the printer by 14 October 1854, and he was still working on the second part of *Aurélia* on 27–30 December 1854. Turkey declared war on Russia in October 1853 and the Crimean War began; the French fleet entered the Black Sea on 3 January 1854; the battle of Alma took place on 20 September; the siege of Sepastopol began on 26 September; and the battle of Balaklava ("the charge of the light brigade") took place on 25 October. One is thus rather surprised to read in, say, François Constans that Nerval "was preoccupied by the quarrel over the Holy Sites . . . which would eventually lead to the Crimean war."[12] In fact, the conflict was raging while Nerval was still writing *Aurélia*. The news of the events took about ten days to get to Paris, a little more to London; for instance, the battle of Alma, 20 September, was described in the London *Times* of 2 October; the news reached Jersey on 3 October and Victor Hugo and his entourage were so upset by it that they could not manage to make the tables talk that day.[13]

The Crimean War began over the problem of who was to protect the holy sites in Palestine, hence Nerval's evocation of St. Helen, the empress and mother of Constantine (the Constantine of the Arch of Constantine in Nerval's sonnet "Delfica"); she had discovered the Holy Cross and founded the Basilica of the Holy Sepulcher at Jerusalem. Other texts by Nerval demonstrate how concerned he was with the Crimea; he already discusses the problem in his *Voyage en Orient*,[14] and he rewrites that text in 1854 in *Pandora*, in a section which was at first to bear the title "Mémorables"—like the text of *Aurélia:*

> I tamed her by attaching myself in despair to her horns, and I thought I recognized in her the haughty Catherine, the Empress of all Russia. I myself was the Prince de Ligne—and she without much difficulty granted me Crimea, along with the site of the ancient temple of Thoas. —I suddenly found myself comfortably seated on the throne of Istanbul.[15]

In 1787 the Prince de Ligne traveled in the Crimea with Catherine II—one of the Catherines of *Aurélia*—and she granted him land near Yalta; in 1788–89 he fought with the Russians against the Turks. That war, bloody and useless and which only ended in 1792, was started by Catherine who wanted to establish a monarchy in Greece under the reign of her grandson Constantine (once more!). Nerval seemingly saw in that historical event yet another example of the combat between the two races of north and south, Christian and Moslem, prefiguring the Crimean War of 1853. The temple of Thoas, the ruins of which were located on the lands granted by Catherine to the Prince de Ligne, evokes of course Euripides' *Iphigenia in Tauris,* or its adaptation by Guymond de la Touche,[16] where once again, as in the Crimean War, it is a matter of a dispute between the Athenians and the Tauri (Tauris being, of course, the Greek name for the Crimea) over a holy object, and where a goddess, Minerva, intervenes to prevent the conflict. The beginning of *Pandora* was published on 31 October 1854, and Nerval sent the rest of the text to the printer on 3 November. I add that since 1840 Nerval had been a close student of the conflicts between France, Russia, and the Northern Alliance, and discussed in his correspondence the Algerian problem and the difficulties that the French army encountered in North Africa.[17]

Other Nerval texts discuss this theme of an eternally renewed conflict between these two forces. One sheds considerable light on *Aurélia,* namely, the sonnet "A Madame Ida Dumas." There we find the themes of the combat between North and South, and an evocation of the holy sites, and, of considerable import for the reading of *Aurélia,* the presence of Abd el Kader in the list of the combatants, that heroic philosopher who led the North African opposition to the "pacification" of Morocco and Algeria by the French. Abd el Kader submitted in 1847; imprisoned in the Chateau de Blois, he was pardoned by Napoleon III, a gesture toward the reconciliation of the two forces which provides the model of what Nerval expected from the emperor in the Crimea. Nerval thus saw in the Franco-Moslem combat in North Africa yet another instance of the "carnage of the eternal enemies." And Saturnin, who in *Aurélia* serves as the symbol of the reconciliation of the warring brothers, of the doubles, is a "former soldier of the African campaigns," a victim of this particular instance of the carnage. This scene with Saturnin is highly important; the narrator's reconciliation with him comes just before the

"Mémorables," and in "Mémorables" it is only when Saturnin joins in the quest that the ascent to the New Jerusalem becomes possible. Aside from the various psychoanalytical interpretations—for instance, a demonstration that homophile reconciliation was for Nerval a necessary preliminary for any "absolving" of heterosexuality—I note that Nerval emphasizes throughout *Aurélia*, incident after incident, the importance of fraternity as a means of salvation, both in politics and in private life. This theme of fraternity is widespread in the political literature of the 1840s, when the word was added to the Liberty and Equality of 1789 to constitute the trinity that became the French motto in 1848.

To summarize, Nerval in *Aurélia* expresses his anguish about the conflict of the Crimean War. He associated that war with a series of past combats between North and South, between Christians and Moslems, including the conflict between the French and North Africa which began in 1830 and which is inscribed in the text in the key person of Saturnin. Nerval uses as a symbol of this combat the "coils of the serpent who encircles the world." In "Mémorables," the reconciliation of men, of the world, of the gods, takes place, partly because of Saturnin's fraternal help, ending with the reconciliation of the pagan gods, and the serpent who encircles the world then becomes blessed. Nerval substitutes for the fallen angels the pagan gods of the North because they symbolize one of the forces present in the Crimean conflict. If one were to ask why Nerval employed these pagan deities rather than the Moslem religion, I should answer first that there is no Moslem theogony, so this religion does not lend itself to that kind of poetic expression, and second, to do so would have made the text too explicit and too limited in its meaning. These gods of the North prepare the reader for the evocations of the north—Saardam, Peter the Great, the Neva—which follow. Then Nerval has a vision of Peter the Great, the two Catherines (including the friend of the Prince de Ligne), St. Helen Empress, who request that France become "the arbiter of the oriental quarrel." Weimar, on the other hand, is a place of reconciliation, with the evocation of Duchess Amelia, Goethe's protector, described as the sister of the tsar of Russia, a figure therefore of the protecting, reconciling woman, of Aurelia, the novel's heroine, a creator of peace who reunites the two races. Nerval hopes that the universal peace and harmony he describes in "Mémorables" will come to pass here below thanks to the termination of the new con-

flict. "Hosanna! Peace on earth and glory in the heavens!" Here is
the core of the double, tragic irony of the book. *Aurélia* recounts
Nerval's conquest of that madness to which he would shortly thereafter succumb, with his suicide, and it records his hope for peace,
whereas the Crimean War continued until 1856, and cost a great
many lives. This war, which was particularly atrocious during the
months of December 1854 and January 1855, may have had something to do with Nerval's decision to commit suicide.

It would be easy to demonstrate at length how these themes are
developed by the resonant intertextuality that Nerval establishes
between this "Mémorables" passage and the rest of *Aurélia*, or, for
that matter, other Nervalian texts. For instance, consider the heavenly ascent on the caparisoned horses; in II, vi, 98, we read:

> It seemed to me that the leaves rolled capriciously in such a way that they
> formed images of cavaliers and ladies borne by caparisoned horses. These
> were for me the triumphant figures of the ancestors. This thought led to the
> idea that there was a vast conspiracy of all animate beings to reestablish the
> world in its primitive harmony.

This passage establishes the link between the first and the second
parts of "Mémorables." The theme of recreating the lost harmony is
woven throughout the text. The intertextuality is of course not only
with Nerval's other works, but also with other writers. *Aurélia* is in
a sense the tale of a conversion, and a resulting beatific vision, and
such works, since Augustine, have usually been much given to
quoting from other texts. If Nerval quotes a great deal in "Mémorables," those quotations fall into three groups. Some refer to the
tradition, and there he has recourse to very common and widespread themes and topoi: the harmony of the spheres, the octave,
the serpent or snake, the allusions to the Book of the Apocalypse,
and so forth. Others can be explained without difficulty by reference
to other writings by Nerval (the perfumes of the Yemen, the hoopoe
bird, and thus all his theories about the Queen of Sheba, a major
figure in the *Voyage en Orient*). Finally, some quotations and allusions seems more personal; a letter by Nerval to Cavé, which has
been much commented on, helps explain "peak of the Auvergne,
mountain of the Himalayas" (which announces the text's universal-
ist reconciliation of polar opposites).[18] Three examples in which
exegesis involves recourse both to other Nerval texts and to the texts
of the tradition are discussed in the following paragraphs: Apollyon,

Christ's robe of sulphurous hyacinth color, and the pardons. All three support my reading of the text.

Apocatastasis, the salvation of the pagan gods and the fallen angels, is presaged in the description of the triumphant ascent into heaven, where the text states: "The arc of light shone forth in the divine hand of Apollyon. The magic horn of Adonis resounded throughout these woods" (II, vi, 116). Adonis surely symbolizes the salvation of the Greek gods (Nerval elsewhere, fond of etymological parallels, associates Adonis and Adonai.) Appollyon raises other problems; what is the exterminating angel of Apocalypse, Rev. 9.11, doing here? François Constans perspicaciously observed that he, also, is here presented as having been saved;[19] other commentators on the text have followed the etymological gambit that Nerval practiced, suggesting an association of Apollyon with Apollo and Napoleon, and recalling Nerval's cult of Napoleon as a solar deity. I do not deny the validity of that gambit, for if, elsewhere, Nerval treats Napoleonic messianism and the identification of Napoleon with the sun in a rather comic way, he does give it poetic treatment in the first tercet of the sonnet "A Louise d'Or . . . reine" (see Chapter 3). But I should like to propose another explanation, recalling that Apollyon, the exterminating angel, had already been saved in a literary work that was widely read at the time. For Apollyon has two names; to cite the Vulgate, *cui nomen hebraice Abaddon, graece autem Apollyon*. Apollyon is also called Abaddona, and Abaddona is a very important character in Klopstock's *Messiad*, a text translated six times into French before 1840, widely read, much commented upon, often imitated—and Nerval himself translated other texts by Klopstock. In *After Babel*, George Steiner remarks that the distinctive trait of our age is that we can no longer read the *Messiad*, which delighted the Romantics.[20] Is it our fault, or theirs? In the *Messiad*, Abaddona-Apollyon is saved, receives divine pardon. He is presented first as a fallen angel, rather weak, who admires Satan-Lucifer in his sad glory but also tries to impede Satan's projects against Jesus. He even decides that he wants to suffer along with Jesus, but at the last moment weakens, then feels remorse, and asks God to kill him. Eloa (another character of Klopstock's epic who enjoyed a glorious career in French literature) calls him *Gottverlassener*, a poor creature abandoned by God, admits him near the crucified Lord, and, after an intense moment (a frightening silence reigns throughout the universe, the saints tremble on their golden thrones), God says: "Come, Abaddona, I offer you my pardon." Abaddona-Apollyon rediscovers his original beauty and sings a hymn in honor of God Light of Lights. Klopstock, like Ballanche or Victor Hugo—or Nerval—refused to believe in perpetual damnation, was an advocate of universalism including apocatastasis. Thus, Nerval had a literary prototype for turning the angel of extermination into an angel of light—and a prototype that came from Germany, from the North.

He accomplishes much the same thing when he attires the Messiah, who in the ascent to heaven "rides between the two of us"— the narrator and Aurélia—in a robe of sulphured hyacinth, for in the same chapter of the Apocalypse (Rev. 9.17) the horsemen of destruction are dressed in breastplates of fire, hyacinth, and brimstone. In Nerval's earlier work, *Sylvie,* in the allegorical play performed at the convent the students wear robes of blue, hyacinth, and gold as they evoke the glory of Christ conqueror of hell. And in *Aurélia* II, iv, the Christ whom St. Christopher carries is "dressed in a hyacinth-colored robe." Nerval has knowingly reversed the value of the colors hyacinth and brimstone in transferring them from the horsemen of extermination (of whom Apollyon is the head) to Christ, thus doing what he had done with Apollyon. The serpent, at first the nefarious symbol of war, when he has become the beneficent symbol of peace breathes out the fire of anxoka, the flower of the sun. The horsemen of destruction, the exterminating angel, and the serpent symbol of war are thus transformed, and express the dream of peace which governs "Mémorables" and determines its function and place in *Aurélia.*

Here is one last example of intertextuality, this time between "Mémorables" and what follows in the text. During his epiphany, says the narrator, "The skies were opened in all their glory, and I there read the word *pardon* signed with the blood of Jesus Christ." In the ensuing dream about Vienna, we read: "It is known that on each of the squares of this town are erected large columns which are called *pardons.* Clouds of marble are piled on top of each other in order to figure the *Solomonic* order and support globes where seated divinities preside." (II, vi, 122). Once more Nerval is rewriting, as Castex noted, a text from the *Voyage en Orient:* "In the middle [of the Graben] there is a monumental column which resembles a cup-and-ball. The ball is formed of sculptured clouds which bear gilded angels. The column itself is twisted, as in the Solomonic order"

(*OEuvres*, Pléiade ed., 1984, p. 222). Castex analyzes quite perspicaciously the way Nerval's second text transorms the first:

> The description in *Aurélia* is more ample; there is not just one column, but a number of them, erected on each square in the town. The description is also more homogenous; the almost burlesque comparison between the column and the cup-and-ball disappears. Finally, it is more majestic; the writer substitutes for the simple ornament of "gilded angels" the presidence of the seated divinities. The reference to the Solomonic order, however, is carefully kept, for it gives the description a legendary dimension.[21]

But Castex neglects one very important transformation; the text of *Aurélia* calls these columns "pardons," thus associating them with the *pardon* in "Mémorables"—Gabrielle Malandain does note this association. In both instances, the word is in italics in the text, and it also occurs in speaking of the gods of the North—the "pardon" of Christ has also been uttered for them; thus the word is found in the first part of "Mémorables," the third part, and in the second paragraph that follows the "Mémorables" text. "Solomonic" also establishes a link between the columns and the theme of Cain and the gods of the North. Castex also quite properly suggests that we should associate this image of the "pardon" columns with an image in the following third paragraph after "Mémorables." "Above this solid pedestal clouds accumulated, rising to the zenith. They were filled with radiant divine figures, among whom one could make out the two Catherines and the Empress Helen" (II, vi, 122). This is a nice example of a literary technique of which Nerval was a master, the metamorphosis of an image in order to express his philosophy—the classical example is from the last tercet of his sonnet "Vers dorés": "And like a nascent eye covered by its eyelids, / A pure spirit grows beneath the bark of the stones." There the eyelid is transformed first into bark, then into stone, crossing the three kingdoms of the Great Chain of Being, and this is the eye of God. Here, in the *Aurélia*, the "divine pardon of Jesus" is transformed or metamorphized first into pardon for the gods of the North; then into the pardon pillars which include the pardon for the Solomonic order and for the race of Cain, and bearing deities; and finally into pedestals bearing the mediatrix women who plead for peace in the Crimea. Can one maintain, as Jeanneret does, that these are discontinuous, heterogeneous fragments?

My reading is, I think, also justified in terms of the generic situation of "Mémorables," a text which is in many ways quite unique, but which also possesses parallels in French literature of the 1830s and 1840s. This kind of "poetic prose," organized in brief paragraphs, replete with images and religious or mythological references, and bearing a content that is both visionary and political, was quite widespread during those years and responded to readers' expectations, ever since the publication in 1834 of the translation of Mickiewicz's *Book of the Polish Pilgrim* and Lamennais's *Words of a Believer*, whose immense success Nerval himself noted in a rather comic letter—it was impossible to buy any other book at Marseilles—and which provoked a great many imitations, most of them, as we have seen, pastiches and not parodies.[22] The last visionary sections of Lamennais's text are particularly close to Nerval's "Mémorables." In form and content, these texts are quite different from the Chateaubriand kind of poetic prose that Nerval imitates elsewhere.[23] Some other distinctions must be made. In the first place, "Mémorables" is a short text, a hymn, and thus should not be confused with the Romantic philosophical epic. Jean Richer has suggested that Nerval was influenced by Quinet's *Ahasvérus*—it would be more correct to evoke G. H. von Schubert whose *Ahasver* inspired Quinet, and whom Nerval translated in 1831, but I do not find the parallel convincing.[24] *Ahasvérus* is a dramatic epic, abundant in philosophical demonstrations; neither its form nor its ideas nor its style is reminiscent of "Mémorables," even if there are mountains in both texts (in Quinet's, they speak in chorus). Among the Romantic visionary epics, a closer parallel could be found in some of the passages, especially toward the end of the work, of A. L. Constant's *La Mère de Dieu* and even more perhaps Ballanche's *Vision d'Hébal*, where one finds similar ideas and similar evocations of mythology. But both of these are also relatively lengthy works, "epics." If Nerval borrowed his title from Swedenborg, that is not true of his literary form; Swedenborg's visions (at least those Nerval could have known; his "Dream Journal" was published at a later date) explain the significance of the Apocalypse, and so on, whereas Nerval instead offers a hymn that expresses his understanding and awareness of the harmonies among self, world, and universe.[25] Richer quotes two poems by Klopstock in Nerval's translation; they are in verset form, and visionary texts, but neither has any philosophical content.[26]

It would seem more appropriate to mention two texts that

Nerval knew, the *Cité des hommes* (1835) of his friend Adolphe Dumas, and the *Arche de la nouvelle alliance* (1840) by Caillaux who was the "St. John" of that curious religious prophet, the Mapah Ganneau.[27] I do not know whether Nerval had read *Résurrection, que votre règne d'amour arrive!* (1840) by Charles Stoffels, a visionary disciple of Ballanche; many passages of that work are quite reminiscent of Nerval. One could cite others. Nerval places his "hymn" within an autobiographical tale, which is hardly true of these other texts (except for Stoffels, and then, in a quite different way). But, for what Jaussians would call the "horizons of expectation" of readers in 1854, it is less "Mémorables" than the rest of *Aurélia* which must have seemed a strange text indeed. Readers were quite accustomed to visionary poetic prose, but much less accustomed to a text that mixed together history, dreams, the fantastic, madness, and autobiography. Nor do I know of any autobiographical text from the Romantic period that inserts a visionary "prose poem" to describe the hero's epiphany, although that technique does possess its prototypes in the autobiographies of St. Teresa of Avila and of Mme Guyon.

Among these visionary texts, Nerval's "Mémorables" stands out because of its density and the rigor of its architecture. Most of the other texts are rather diffuse "pipeline to God" texts in which inspiration lets the ink flow freely—and usually the ink is red. Compared to them, "Mémorables" is the work, not of a madman, but of an artist or even geometrician. Above all, from Ballanche and Lamennais to Stoffels and Caillaux, Auguste Siguier and Adolphe Dumas, this more or less apocalyptic poetic prose, with its visionary and mythological references and nonetheless high degree of subjectivity, always proposes—I do not know of any exception—a political message. Not that they are political poems in the manner of, say, Victor Hugo's *Châtiments,* his violent attack against Napoleon III. "Mémorables" is much closer to another mythic and visionary poem written in the same year, 1854, and which possesses political significance, Hugo's "Ce que dit la bouche d'ombre" in *Comtemplations,* Book 6—a text that also associates apocatastasis, the dream of harmony and of universal peace.

Far from practicing the writing of madness, Nerval, in this last chapter of his *Aurélia,* gives his eschatological vision political and contemporary meaning. Allison Fairlie observed in 1961 that part of Nerval's greatness was his capacity to associate his own spiritual drama with, on the one hand, transcendent mythical structures, and on the other hand, contemporary, even political problems.[28] To do so is, as Nerval himself put it, to link the external and the internal worlds, which is quite enough to make one go mad, but he was not mad when he wrote "Mémorables."

## 10 🍎 Flaubert's *Temptation of St. Anthony*

"The Egyptians eat no beef, the Persians eat no eagle, the Jews don't eat me"—it is St. Anthony's pig in Flaubert's *Temptation of St. Anthony* who so speaks, to conclude that therefore he is "more sacred than the cow, more sacred than the eagle."[1] This is the first evocation of comparative religion in the 1849 version of the *Temptation,* and it is quite typical of Flaubert's way of writing whenever comparative religion comes up: a play between resemblances and differences, reflecting the problematic nature of the relations between the particular and the universal. This play between similarity and difference is achieved by means of juxtaposition, and what is at stake becomes defined in an almost caricatured way because the ideological content is obfuscated, obscured, with the result that all the religious systems evoked are deprived of value. Crepitus the god of farting becomes the equal of Jehovah the God of wrath; the Paraclete is assimilated to the parrot; the pig becomes the most sacred of animals. I should like, first, to establish the historical context of Flaubert's discussions of comparative religion in order to show that the *Temptation* is not the archaeological work some have claimed it was, but rather a negative and telling statement about what, when he wrote, was a raging battle. I shall then analyze the techniques he used to destroy not only religious syncretism but religion in most senses of the word. Finally, I suggest that this destruction is essentially an aspect of the way Flaubert questioned or rejected the Romantic theory of harmonies.

Gérard de Nerval was not the first to identify Bacchus and Jesus, nor was Victor Hugo the last to see in the Virgil of the fourth

*Eclogue* a prophet of Jesus;[2] if that kind of thinking has largely disappeared today, except perhaps in Jungian circles, it was widespread in the mid-nineteenth century; Flaubert, perhaps, is among those who begin to make it disappear. It is a very venerable kind of thinking. Augustine had already proclaimed that "the Christian religion existed among the Ancients and has never ceased to exist since the beginnings of the human race until, Christ himself having come in the flesh, one began to name as Christian the true religion which existed before then"—I am translating from the French translation by Lamennais.[3] Then came Huet d'Avranches, Joseph Lafiteau and his Christian reading of the Indian legends of America, G. de Sainte-Croix's *Reherches sur les mystères du paganisme* which seems to have been influential in Masonic circles, and one could go on; I refer, for the general problem of syncretism to Pinard de la Boullaye's classical study, and for French Romanticism, to that of Pierre Moreau.[4] It is more to the point to suggest here the kinds of contradictions that Christian readings of comparative religion had uncovered when Flaubert was writing the *Temptation,* for the matter was quite controversial: the concord of all myths and religions was becoming a subject of cacophonic discord.

That discord goes back at least to the eighteenth century's quarrel over the religion of the Chinese. The Jesuits perceived therein traces of "natural Christianity," whereas the Jansenists proclaimed the necessity of an explicit faith in Christ and feared that this "natural Christianity" which the Jesuits saw in China might turn out to be an argument in favor of the "natural religion" of the deists and the libertines. If, within the Church, the Jesuits won the day, at least temporarily,[5] one might say that the Jansenists' fears were quite justified when Dupuis or Volney proposed, for instance, that Bacchus "retraces the history of the God of the Christians,"[6] or that Jesus, like Bacchus, Osiris, Adonis, was but a solar myth. Thus while the syncretist argument was employed in favor of Christianity by some, especially the "traditionalists"—those who believed in a traditional, universal revelation—it was employed against Christianity by other texts that were often reedited,[7] or plagiarized,[8] or continued, for instance with Dulaure's study of the phallus as a symbol in both pagan and Christian religion,[9] a book that Flaubert's character Pécuchet would have read with delight. Indeed, Pécuchet himself used comparative religion to prove two contradictory theses, first the truth, then the falsehood of Christianity. We have already noted the amusing effort to refute Dupuis by demonstrating that Napoleon himself was only a solar myth; here I discuss the first Romantic generation of traditionalists who, faced with these theories which did indeed reduce Christianity to a natural religion or even less, nonetheless, motivated by apologetic considerations, tried to shore up the "Jesuit" reading of myth by various metaphysical and historical theories which also turned out to be very problematic—much to Flaubert's delight. [10]

Chateaubriand, like Pécuchet, also used comparative religion to prove the two contradictory theses, but in the reverse order. In his *Essay on revolutions,* he follows Volney's line of argument; in the *Génie du christianisme,* he finds trinities everywhere, in the Indies, in Tahiti, and in pagan fables, which thus express religious truth even if they are poetically inferior, in Chateaubriand's eyes, to the products of the Christian "marvelous." According to his version of the theory of harmonies, God is revealed in all the structures of the universe, and thus in all religions and all myth. With Joseph de Maistre, syncretism instead underlines the universality of the notion of the efficacious and transferable sacrifice of the innocent victim, thus associating religious syncretism and the Romantic theme song, "out of evil, good will come." Maistre also proposes that the faith once revealed, then corrupted by human sin, thanks to the Holy Ghost gradually and progressively becomes unveiled through the course of history. He was however a much less fervent advocate of this thesis than was Ballanche, who called Maistre an "archeophile" as opposed to himself, a "neophile," [11] and who saw in religion a becoming created in part by the voice of the "plebs," the people, and that of the poet, moving toward desymbolization, [12] even if sacrifice, "suffering toward progress" remains central to his thought. Bonald centered his syncretism rather on the Trinity, and, by locating the revelation in social institutions and hence in language, began "philological" apologetics—the quest for the mysteries of the Christian faith in the etymological analysis of words and grammar—which was to become an extremely popular and often highly inventive activity. Above all Bonald, like Edmund Burke, associated society and universal truth, whereas Lamennais and Ballanche (like Rousseau) associated popular belief and universal truth. Lamennais also is different in seeing in this traditionalism not simply a reflection of the eternal nature of Christian truth, but a proof, indeed the major proof of Christianity—what has always, everywhere, by everyone, been believed. In short, within this Catholic syncretism various stances were taken about how to locate the revelation in time, about the religious concept or dogma that these apologists stressed by their recourse to comparative religion, about the ontological value they attributed to comparative religion, and finally in their political attitudes.[13] Rather than refuting Volney and Dupuis, they reject them while borrowing Volney's and Dupuis's documentation.

These differences and contradictions did not prevent the syncretist movement from achieving great popularity—and publishing extensively—under the July Monarchy. This success is to be explained in part by the failure of neo-Cartesian theology, which was still then the "official" theology of the French Church, and which did not satisfy apologetic needs; in a larger way, it can be explained by the antirationalist tendencies of the period; also, by the lack, in the Church and elsewhere, of any clear distinction between natural and revealed truth; indeed, the proper theological sense of the word "mystery" was, as far as I have been able to see, unknown at the time. Traditionalism in its various forms substitutes for reason the historical study of a revelation which is considered to be symbolic, and in so doing it answered the Romantic need for "positive proofs" of Christianity. It also coincided with Romantic historicism and with the general desire to perceive the harmonies of the divine beneath (or beyond) the appearances of nature, of languages, of myths and beliefs, even in the very forms of intelligence, seeking, by various forms of contrast or identification, to discover the transcendent.[14] Flaubert was to raise grave questions, not only about syncretism, but about all these intellectual activities. Finally, Catholic theology during the July Monarchy was intensely concerned with differentiating itself from Victor Cousin's Eclecticism. If, after the papal condemnation of Lamennais in 1837 with the encyclical *Mirari vos,* his disciples generally abandoned the "common sense" (what is believed everywhere, by all, etc.) as the criterion of religious truth, they did so in order to attack general reason as much as they attacked particular, individual reason; if they give up Cartesianism, it is because Cousin had taken over Descartes. So there only remained the "leap of faith," the neo-fideism of Louis Bautain which Rome also condemned, or else traditionalism, and even there the Eclectic philosophers around Cousin were soon to enter the competition.

Meanwhile, documentation in support of traditionalism was churned out indefatigably, for instance in Bonnetty's *Annales de philosophie chrétienne,* a periodical largely devoted to providing supporting evidence. The mania produced some remarkable texts, such as Roselly de Lorgues's *La Croix dans les deux mondes,* (1845), full of lengthy considerations on the number 10 (X), the symbol of the cross but signifying unity and diversity, among the Aztecs, the Chinese, and others. At the same time, the Dupuis tradition of attacking Christianity as nothing but a debased form of the true, solar religion, was reinvigorated by Augustin Chaho and Ragon de Bettignies, both in rather picturesque ways (Chaho was especially convincing on the Benediction of the Blessed Sacrament as a form of sun worship). One comes to feel that the discourse was becoming exhausted because of its excesses; in any case, it provided Flaubert a rich matter for satire. There are some troubling absences from the debate. Few are the texts where either a Catholic or an anti-Catholic recognizes that the other side is using the same gambit to draw the opposite conclusion (Philippe Gerbet, Lamennais's most intelligent disciple, did notice the problem). Even more disquieting, no effort was made to write a history of mythology as a history of desymbolization, in which the divine becomes gradually more and more secularized—even though Lessing and Benjamin Constant, by their theories about the history of religion, had prepared the way for such a study.[15] Despite the ongoing quarrel about desymbolization, such an analysis, widespread in Germany, hardly existed in France at the time—perhaps because such a reading of the history of religion and mythology would have ended up with a Hegelian conception of the logos, and Victor Cousin tried to impose a rather edulcorated version of Hegel on the French.[16]

Before Flaubert wrote his text, syncretism was also threatened from two other directions; by Guigniaut's revision and translation of Creuzer's *Symbolic,* and by the innumerable publications of Baron d'Eckstein, the "Sanscrit baron." Though Creuzer and Guigniaut still accepted that myths have a "common primitive source," they identified that source as the "simple and sublime religion of nature," and then, partly by etymological analysis, by philology, they traced the development of differences among the various mythic systems, reading them, not in the search for some kind of unity, but rather in order to study and explain diversity, a diversity resulting from many causes and influences. Whence, in 1843, Guigniaut's very sharp critique of both the Volney-Dupuis school and traditionalism.[17] Flaubert's friend Alfred Maury tackled the task of explaining the analogies among myths not by any divine revelation but by the influence of migrations, cultural contacts, or a historical evolution where, again, religion and thought move from poetic expression to ever-increasing degrees of abstraction.[18] Eckstein tried to adopt this "philological" method in an effort at combining Lamennais and Cousin, placing universal revelation not in a uniquely human tradition, but rather in the structures of societies and civilizations—resulting in some very erudite but rather unreadable studies. It was only after 1849, when the ideas of Max Müller and Ottfried Muller begin to become well known in France, thanks to Maury and M. J. A. Bréal, that mythology would, for a time at least, be freed from metaphysical readings. Until then, methodological considerations about syncretism, about the origins of Christianity and of mythology, continued to flourish, in an attempt to revise the earlier stance. J. B. Bourgeat's excellent articles on "the history of philosophy" are exemplary of how an intelligent Catholic, well informed about the debate, took a highly temperate stand.[19] He quotes Benjamin Constant about the evolution of the religious sentiment, and then proposes that one must ask a series of questions. What share of the primitive revelation is present in each nation or society? What kinds of developments did the primary truths of that revelation undergo in each culture? How did these truths become altered or disguised? Like Guigniaut, Bourgeat, even if he still accepts traditionalism studies not resemblances but differences, perhaps the major result of the "methodological" crisis of snycretism.

By its very nature, Eclecticism necessarily became increasingly concerned with the history of philosophy, seeking therein the proof of its validity; and since Cousin and his school considered religion as a kind of "pre-philosophy," they also studied the history of religions, often seeing in early Christianity itself a precursory system of Eclecticism. A whole series of studies resulted, done by the Eclectics, or, in answer to them, by the Catholics, often very learned, enriched by a renewed interest in the Fathers of the Church, whose writings Migne was making available in his Patrologies. The Eclectics included Adolphe Franck on the Kabbala, Jules Simon and Emile Vacherot on Alexandria, and, more theoretical, Emile Saisset's highly important article "Le Christianisme et la philosophie."²⁰ Among the Catholic responses were Drach on the Kabbala and Prat on Alexandria.²¹ The Eclectics describe Christianity as a religion that combines the symbols and ideas of the Orient, of Greece and Rome, of Egypt.²² By this synthesis, Christianity marked a progress in religious history, offering a clearer presentation of the truths of philosophy, and exemplified that "progressive purifying of human opinions" which Jouffroy already in 1834 defined as the principle of the history of religion.²³ In describing how this synthesis was created in the early Church, the Eclectics emphasize and trace the multiple forces at work and variations in dogma up to the Nicean Council. In a sense, their approach is the opposite of that of the syncretist studies of mythology; there, various symbols expressed the same truth; here, in the Eclectic readings, the symbol is devaluated as presenting at different moments a variety of ideas. The Eclectics talk at length about doctrines concerning the logos and the Trinity, and hardly ever about the Crucifixion which was at the center of Ballanche and Maistre's thoughts about religion. The Catholic answers underline the unique nature of Christianity; they explain its success by its "miraculous propagation," and not by the fact that it presented a synthesis of various intellectual currents. So in a way the Eclectic reading of Christianity as a syncretist religion led the Catholics to reject all forms of religious syncretism.²⁴ Finally, mention must be made of the fact that in about 1846 the "leftist cousinians," criticizing Cousin's velvet-glove approach to religion, began proposing a theology of the death of God somewhat close to Flaubert's own thoughts on religion.²⁵

The foregoing schematically analyzed discussion gives only a brief outline of the debate surrounding comparative religion and mythology in France when Flaubert composed his first *Temptation of St. Anthony.* In that work, Flaubert treats questions which were much discussed and highly controversial at the time. What methodology should be used to study religion? What is the nature and origin of religion and of myths? How do religion and myth evolve? What were the origins of Christianity? The debate provided several options among which Flaubert could choose. It is difficult to imagine him continuing along the lines of Bonald and Lamennais. With the sacrifices of Moloch, one might well see an element of satire directed against Maistre and his disciples. Flaubert could have constructed the text according to the theories of Dupuis and the solar school; he could have illustrated the theories of Creuzer, or cast those of Vacherot of Jules Simon in dramatic form. Flaubert refused these options; he does echo these theories, but in a satiric way. The readers of his day would probably have expected a text such as the *Temptation* to correspond to one of the points of view in the debate; it may well have been Flaubert's refusal to do so, as much as certain stylistic aspects of the text, that made his first audience react so negatively. Taking one of those options would also have required adherence to some form or other of the doctrine of progress, which Flaubert also renounced. He did espouse the "desymbolization" thesis, but in an original and nihilist way. One can read *Salammbô* as an illustration of desymbolization; there, according to how intellectually or morally advanced the character is, he or she believes in certain dogmas, attributes literal or abstract meaning to the symbols. Elsewhere, rather than representing religion as gradually freeing itself from the symbol in order to become philosophy, Flaubert reduces the religious to its symbolic form, then by omission or occultation deprives that symbol of its ideological content, and proceeds to degrade or destroy the symbol, in part by playing with the old syncretist technique of juxtaposing resemblances and yet underlining differences. Religion is thus reduced to the cult of the parrot, which is and is not the Paraclete, and then the parrot, stuffed, gets eaten up by vermin.

In order to clarify what is thus simultaneously a sylistic technique and an ideological choice, I should like to examine more closely Flaubert's description of the Ophites in the *Temptation*. I have chosen this passage partly because Flaubert there destroys content less than he does elsewhere but he nonetheless deploys some remarkable techniques in making meaning occult. Also, the scene centers on the demonstration of a rather strange thesis, yet this thesis is not without significance in the history of religions and in Romantic thought. The Ophites turned the snake, with his promise, "You shall be as Gods," into the hero of the scene in the Garden of Eden. He thus becomes a Promethean figure, a symbol of how, to quote Pierre Leroux, "the fall is, in Genesis, a progress as well as being a fall."[26] The Ophites were Ernst Bloch's favorite heresy, for he saw in it the symbol of the secularization of the Hope Principle.[27] Indeed, could there be any more marvelous and scandalous way of separating the logos from the Jesus of history than by

suggesting that the snake was the true Savior? This is something for
Romantic Satanism to delight in, as for Prometheanism. Flaubert
plays with these possibilities, but he does not espouse them.

Flaubert obviously thought the scene important. First, it is fairly
lengthy: 67 lines in version I (counting lines in the *Edition intégrale*),
about the same in II (57 lines, although the whole *Temptation* is
reduced by half), and 130 lines in III (which is about the same
length as II) where the Ophites come at the end of the Gnostic
series, for they represent the extreme form of Gnosticism. Version
III is completely rewritten; Flaubert only keeps from versions I and
II a few descriptive details, and he even revises those (for example,
in versions I and II the children hold the snake "with their arms
uplifted," the women "on their breasts," the men against the stomach; in version III it is with their arms uplifted, on their heads,
against their chests). Versions I and II primarily describe Eve's
temptation, and end with the benediction of the Eucharistic bread
by the snake. Version II adds a refutation of the heresy by St. Anthony. In Version III, Anthony attends an Ophite ceremony, and
both ritual and dogma are much more detailed, including the addition of the thesis that the snake entered into Jesus at the moment of
his baptism. The temptation of Eve is suppressed, the blessing of
the Eucharistic bread reduced to one sentence, which is incomprehensible (the snake "slowly passes along the edge of the bread"
which otherwise is not mentioned). The refutation is suppressed;
instead, Anthony faints away from horror. These changes can be
explained in part by a difference in source; I and II are mostly a
rewriting of Pluquet,[28] whereas III owes much to Jacques Matter.
The changes, here at least, are so considerable that one should not
speak of the *Temptation* as a single book that underwent several
versions; I and III are almost totally different.[29] Nonetheless, there
is a kind of continuity on the imaginary level. In version I the snake
is commanded, "Push your coils!" In III, "the coils doubled, filled
the room, closed in on Anthony"; the rather surrealist detail proposed in I is described as taking place. But for the problem of how
the presentation hides and destroys meaning, I and II must be
examined, and then III, which is considerably more obscure. The
didactic exposition of the Ophites' doctrine takes up much more
space, but Flaubert is at great pains to make it incomprehensible.
This, despite the fact that Flaubert could hardly have presupposed
much familiarity with Ophitism among his readers. In this respect,

the obfuscation of religious doctrines in the *Temptation* is quite different from that of political doctrines in the *Sentimental Education,* for there the reader could be expected to know, and thus reconstruct from the caricature Flaubert provides, the doctrines of Saint-Simon, Fourier, and others. In all three versions of the *Temptation* the style remains paratactic, conjunctions and words that express casual linkings are suppressed, replaced by exclamation points and question marks, by repetition and synonymy.

The way the scene is organized in version I is already fairly disquieting. First the text describes an enormous snake and provides a vague setting. Eve is mentioned three paragraphs later; only then does the reader realize that the Garden of Eden is being evoked. There follow several sentences about Eve's reaction (which is quite sensual) and where Flaubert introduces those "harmonies of nature" that he loved to satirize ("a lotus opened up, the dates of the palm trees ripened"), which shift the reader's interest elsewhere; in the context, these details might seem symbolic, but no symbolic meaning can be found for them. One short paragraph suggests why the Ophites adored the snake: "Once more if they had tasted of it, they would have become Gods according to the tempter's promise. To punish this son too prodigal with the gifts of heaven, God condemned him to keep his form; the victorious woman put her foot on his head, but by the bite he made in her heel, the eternal venom mounted up to her heart" (I, p. 392). This paragraph does introduce the Promethean theme, but only in order to destroy it by the evocation of the Virgin Mary and by attributing a poisonous venom to the serpent; far from explaining the Ophites' beliefs, Flaubert scrambles everything. In II, the résumé of the doctrine is reduced to one sentence: "If they had tasted more of it, they would now be gods"; the Promethean theme is suppressed. Antoine's refutation, added in this version—Christ would not have chosen to incarnate in such an ugly form—is rather astonishing since before that point the text does not suggest any identification of the serpent with Christ! It does provide a transition toward the following section of the Arcites, but as often in the *Temptation,* the transition is created by the signifier but not by the signified.

Version III is much more obfuscatory than I or II; in I and II at least the serpent is present from the beginning of the incident on, and so is the word *Ophites;* a reader who knows about the Ophites, or who consults a work on the Gnostics, could have at least a vague idea of what is going on. In III, the snake does not appear until three-fourths of the way through the scene—and even there, rather comically, he has to be begged to do so—and the name *Ophites* only appears at the very end, in the transition to the following scene. Before then, the reader, like Anthony, has no idea where he is or what is going on. On the other hand, the text carefully prepares the thematics for the voyage, with evocations of waves, of the odors of the port, of embarkations, and indeed at the end of the passage Anthony does set sail with the Ophites, martyrs of heresy, to find himself next with the Christian martyrs at Rome—another one of Flaubert's ironic juxtapositions. Throughout the text, Flaubert is careful about creating effective thematic and narrative presentations, but does so at the expense of any presentation of the ideas involved. The dreamlike (or nightmarish) atmosphere is even stronger than in the earlier version; here, the snake's tail, "going out through the hole in the wall, continued indefinitely into the depths of the sea." If the text thus demands a reading as imaginary, it immediately breaks that reading with theological declarations, which however immediately lead back to the imaginary, for Flaubert in those declarations proposes fractured symbolic significations. These variations in rhythm and tone impose an ironic reading.

The exposition of the dogma takes up about a sixth of the scene. The Ophite history of salvation is rapidly evoked, and even that is interrupted by the cries of the faithful, the snake's appearance on the scene, and so on. The Inspired One unrolls a "placard, covered with cylinders all mixed up together," which he does not comment upon or explain. The opposition between Sophia and Jehovah is brought up, but makes no sense for someone who does not know the Gnostic distinction between God and the Creator. The text does at least make clear that God is bad, Sophia and her snake good, that it was a good thing to eat of the fruit of the tree of knowledge; this scandalous aspect of Ophite doctrine is highlighted by the passage on the relations between Jesus and the serpent, where it is explained that Jesus' supernatural force came to him when he drank the snake in the baptismal waters, his weakness comes from the fact that the snake abandoned him during his Crucifixion; the snake, and not Jesus, is the logos-Christ. "Antoine faints from horror," and so, hoped Flaubert, would the reader; the text seeks to create an effect of horror, not to propound a theology.

The numerous proper names in the passage also hide its ideological content. First, contradictory wordplay confuses Jesus, Logos, Christ, and snake. For Sophia, at least an elementary knowledge of Gnosticism is necessary. And what to do with "Astophios, Oraios, Sabaoth, Adonai, Eloi, Iao"? Even Flaubert's editor Bernard Masson goes astray when he calls these "divine names given to Jehovah";[30] that is not true of the two first ones, and for the Ophites these are not Jehovah's names but those of demiurges. They called Jehovah Iabdalaoth, a name which appears in Flaubert's text, but of course Flaubert does not tell us that this is Jehovah. And if we do not know who the first idol Knouphis is, small matter, since the Ophites say, "The imbeciles, they think we adore Knouphis!" The symbol is first reduced to a proper name without content, and then denied. The same problem comes up with the other litany of proper names, the list of the virtuous snakes of history, with which Flaubert satirizes the quest for figures of Christ in the Old Testament and in comparative religion. The Inspired One praises the snake who cured King Ptolemy (which Ptolemy?), the soldiers of Moses, and "Glaucus the son of Minos." The Orient, Greece, and Egypt are thus syncretized, not in Christianity, but in Ophitism, the cult of the snake—a nice satire of the Eclectic's version of the eclectic nature of Christianity. But who knows the history of this Glaucus? Only the readers of pseudo-Apollodorus, who are not very numerous; even Maynial, here, another editor of Flaubert, is mistaken.[31] The allusion is precise, and incomprehensible. Flaubert is doing two things here—satirizing the syncretists' quest for similarities, but also preventing any ideological reading of his text.

All this is done with sharp irony, created by variations in the rhythm, by the juxtaposition of poetic and disgusting elements ("the slobber of his teeth . . . his moist, sticky skin") with stylistic inversion ("He stopped, fixed his eyes on her, on him she fixed hers"), by exaggeration ("The green leaves caught fire from his breath"). The economy of the exposition contrasts keenly with the use of repetition and of irrelevant descriptive detail ("They give each other remedies for their family illnesses"). Comparison is used to devaluate ("So completely lost in their veils that one could call them a pile of rags along the wall"). Synonymy itself is reductionist ("He is enormous and of considerable weight"). The bombastic exaggeration contrasts with Antoine's insufficient reactions. The *Temptation* wants to make us laugh, but with a bitter, sardonic laughter.

The way Flaubert treats his sources is very revealing. Foucault said, about this scene, "One is rather astonished at how so much meticulous scholarship creates such an impression of pure fantasmagory."[32] In fact, the meticulosity is lacunary. Jacques Matter explains the significance and the etymology of the proper names that Flaubert only recites. Matter explains the theory of the double creation and the way the Gnostics distinguished between God, Logos, Sophia and Creator; Flaubert suppresses all of that. Taking information provided by Origen, Matter had an engraving done of the Ophite symbols, which Flaubert's Inspired One unrolls, but Matter accompanies the engraving with a long explanation. In his case, words provoke the creation of a figure which then produces a verbal explanation, and Matter proposes the figures in order to make Origen clear, whereas Flaubert evokes it in order to make Matter obscure. This is what Flaubert also does with the image of Knouphis (there, curiously, if Flaubert takes Matter's engraving and turns it into words, Odilon Redon then took Flaubert's words and turned them into a drawing). Flaubert's predilection for Matter's illustrations, rather than his text,[33] shows how he wants to offer, not an explication of the ideological content of a system of beliefs, but its symbolic representation, just as he presents the various socialist schools in the *Sentimental Education* by their rhetoric and their figurations, and not by their ideology. His choice of Matter as source was fully justified;[34] Matter's *Histoire critique du gnosticisme* (1843–44) was the best text available at the time, and Matter was rather openminded; he even treated Gnostic theses favorably, whereas the surviving primary sources are of course largely violently anti-Gnostic.[35] But not only does Flaubert suppress material from Matter, he also changes it. Flaubert has the Gnostics claim that Jesus swallowed the snake at his baptism, as we have said, and that the snake then abandoned Jesus on the cross, thereby evoking the Romantic theme of the despair of Christ at his Passion. According to the Ophites as Matter presents them, the snake suffered from the Fall as much as did man, and it was not the snake, but the Sophia in her emanation Christus which rejoined Jesus, especially after his Resurrection; the resurrected Jesus Christ spent eighteen months on earth, gifted with perfect wisdom. By this change, Flaubert suppresses the whole Ophite soteriology.[36] Why? Like most Romantics, he is little concerned with Jesus after the Crucifixion. He hopes to scandalize by suggesting that it was the snake that inspired

Jesus. He destroys the message of the Ophites, which Matter presents quite clearly, and substitutes in its stead a paradox: the snake was the Savior.

One can offer a generic explanation for these differences. The *Temptation* is not a source book about heresies, but something else. But then what? Matter traces the gradual development of Gnostic doctrine (indeed, one sometimes has trouble telling where one section ends and another begins; his style is very continuous)—Flaubert replaces this with ironic parataxis. Matter describes symbol and content, Flaubert represents the symbol without content, or else changes that content in order to make it absurd and scandalous. It is not a question of his profiting from the "polysemic" possibilities of the snake; rather, semantic significance is destroyed; the faithful "glue their lips to his skin" but the serpent gets unglued from everything.[37] Polysemic meaning does enter into play at the end of the scene, where the Nile is described as "a great snake in the middle of the sands," but that image also takes the reader elsewhere, with no suggestion of how that elsewhere could be pertinent. Our imagination finds its space, not as Foucault suggested, between the book and the lamp, but by the occultation of the book. The *Temptation* does not substitute for traditional religious beliefs the creeds of Spinoza or of psychoanalysis, it destroys the significance of religion in general. The Ophite version of the Bible might be considered the most scandalous version there is. Flaubert destroys it, and at the same time destroys the Bible—the Book.

In short, when he discusses a heresy that is rich in significance both for comparative religion and for various Romantic theories, Flaubert hides the theological, political, and historical content of that heresy and concentrates on describing its symbols, but does so in an allusive, paratactic, ironic manner. He practices this kind of writing elsewhere. Victor Brombert has admirably analyzed how the discourse on comparative religion in *Hérodias* only evokes, jumps about, is mixed up with allusions to food;[38] the techniques there are slightly different, but the effect is the same.[39] Joelle Gleize has shown how in the *Sentimental Education* the writing is often discontinuous, juxtaposition replaces linking, scenes are doubled and repeated, but the second is always a degradation of the first.[40] Flaubert uses the same techniques, but in a more extreme way, when he discusses religion. Raymonde Debray-Genette has shown how in *Hérodias* the essence of the style is an effect of obscurity, and she identifies this as Flaubert's way of dealing with material whose origins are historical, mythic, symbolic.[41] Jean Bellemin-Noël suggests that this decrease in historical involvement or presence results in an increased presence of the unconscious in the text. This is perhaps true, the text lends itself easily to a psychoanalytic reading, as Theodor Reik and later Jeanne Bem have shown.[42] But this obscurity first of all constitutes an ideological declaration which should not be neglected; it denies the possibility of any sort of syncretist analysis of religion. If the imaginary, again to paraphrase Foucault, here lodges in the library in order to create an earthquake, the purpose of the earthquake is to destroy the library.

Elsewhere, matters are even worse. The *Temptation* does contain some frankly syncretist passages, for instance Hilarion's proposal that "these Gods, under their criminal forms, perhaps contain the truth" (III, p. 558); should one believe him? If on occasion religion is presented as a form of astrology or of the sun cult, Flaubert does not thereby accept Dupuis's theses. Rather, he proposes an incessant metamorphosis of the heresies, in which the gods themselves are metamorphosed in a play of repetition, but without the amplification that, according to classical rhetoric, should accompany the figure of repetition. Apollonius promises, "I shall explain for you the reason of the divine forms, why Apollo is upright, Jupiter seated, Venus black at Corinth, square in Athens, conical at Paphos" (III, p. 550), but he does not do it; he leaves us with nothing but the names and the forms, and that there should be any reason for them is denied by silence. The Devil's discourse about the Negro who some day will spit on the face of his idol (added in version II) expresses well the text's theory about the evolution of religion. Some of the gods want to die, others are sick and tired of being gods. Jupiter wants to survive; a good disciple of Victor Cousin, he believes that "something of me will remain on earth after my death," but his cup is empty (III, 559; the text is much more ironic in III than in I). Flaubert extends the significance of the theme, associates the death of the gods with the death of civilizations, the lares and penates decay, and so does the house that shelters them (III, p. 540). Above all, the symbol decays, in a very literal sense. Hercules has lost his force, "the years have eaten away the face, and the rains have ruined the inscription" on the statue of Jesus (III, p. 540), and the same fate is suffered by Felicity's parrot, Emma's plaster curé, the veil of Tanit, the statue of St. Peter in *Bouvard and*

*Pécuchet*—he gets thrown out the window to hasten his decay. On occasion, Flaubert gives a content to these religious symbols, and when he does so it is usually a matter of an attack against a father figure, or of titillating praises of hermaphroditism, or of a bloody spirituality of sacrifices and flagellations, but those are accidental readings. The procession of the gods in the *Temptation* proceeds from India, the Near East, Egypt, and Greece, to Rome, which is the order followed by historians of religion at the time. But Flaubert is not thereby proposing any history of religion; the series ends up with the juxtaposition of Jehovah, who complains that he is no longer the God of battle, and Crepitus, the god of the fart. In version III, the Christian heresies are presented before the death of the gods, to suggest the vanity of any effort to give a sense to Christianity by the study of comparative religion. Version II is slightly more anti-Christian than version I, III much more than II, but the presentation of pagan religions is just as sarcastic; Flaubert is not Théophile Gautier.[43]

The text is marked by two important stylistic traits: the solution of continuity, and the crisis of nomination. The solution of continuity is created by the extremely rapid succession of the heresies and the gods who do not even manage to finish their sentences, and by the voids and silences which separate the gods or the heresies; in version I, Death provides a narrative justification for this rapidity as she pushes the gods to their end; in III this solution of continuity and rapidity has no identifiable cause—it is of the very nature of knowledge and of history. What Jean-Pierre Richard calls "the sickness of the interval" becomes very grave indeed in version III: the examples are multiplied but they are not linked.[44] "One might say that they are born and die at the same moment, their appearance and disappearance are so instantaneous" (I, p. 465). But this means that they do not exist; the history of religions shows the void, the vacuity of all religion, and in Flaubert's *Dictionary of Received Ideas,* under "Myth," one only finds " . . . ," silence. Jehovah concludes the procession of the gods saying, "I was the Lord God," and "Then came an enormous silence, a profound darkness" (III, p. 563).

The crisis of nomination is even greater in *Salammbô,* where to a given god a multitude of names are attributed, just as the gods themselves are multiplied. It is also reflected in the way Flaubert deprives the proper noun signifier of any signified; he also refuses to give the name, or puts off doing so, indicating that the gods can only be recognized and named in fear and trembling.[45] Zoroaster has only one desire, to name the divine, but he does not manage to do so; the gods go by too fast. To name is no longer a way of contrasting, organizing, defining, because the effort of naming fails and insignificance prevails faced with this variety of gods; the *Temptation* severely questions both the logos and the names. Faced with the passing gods Antoine resembles Bouvard and Pécuchet faced with the passing clouds; the clouds go by too quickly, they cannot manage to name them.[46]

As for religious syncretism, *Bouvard and Pécuchet* (1881) is indeed a "modern parody" of the *Temptation*.[47] Syncretism is discussed in the sections on mineralogy, archaeology, and history as well as in the religious crisis of the two heroes. The matter is more elaborately developed than in the *Temptation;* it now includes the Druids and the Celtic gods, there are some new ideas, such as reducing all religion to the cult of the phallus. The expository techniques are simplified in the later work, often reduced to the simple juxtaposition of the proper names. Etymology plays a more important role, and Flaubert caricatures the etymological quest in order to reveal the feebleness of that argument for syncretism. Teutates is the Saturn of the Celts because "Saturn, when he reigned in Phenicia, married a nymph named Anobret, by whom he had a child named Jeüd, and Anobret has the characteristics of Sara, Jeüd was sacrificed (or at least almost) like Isaac; so Saturn is Abraham, so one must conclude that the Celtic religion had the same beliefs and principles as the Jewish religion" (Flaubert, *OEuvres*, 2:236). The paragraph is a delightful attack, particularly since the only religious principle involved is filicide. The vocabulary of causality, absent in the *Temptation,* is very common in *Bouvard and Pécuchet,* but it only serves to underline the paralogisms ironically. The significance of the religious object depends on who is speaking: sacrificial vessel of the Druids, or baptismal font? Finally, the novel provides the confrontation between syncretism as an argument for Christianity and syncretism as an argument against. In the debate with Fr. Jeufroy, each side uses the same theses, the same polemical techniques, in an erudite combat reduced to its simplest possible form, a litany of proper names (2:283–85). The two heroes also offer a schematic history of religion, à la Hegel; formerly God created the wind, the lightning; now he is diminishing in power, and besides it is impossible to know what he is like, even if he exists (2:244). In a text that Ezra Pound read as the ancestor of Joyce and of the comedy of the absurd, there is no need to accept that judgment, or anything else, as Flaubert's own conviction, no more than the sentence "What matters the belief, as long as one believes" (2:289).[48] Elsewhere, Flaubert demonstrates a kind of disdainful sympathy for popular superstition, but that does not solve the problem of knowing who God is.[49]

In *Bouvard and Pécuchet*, religious syncretism is only one aspect of a much more general problem. the scrambling of religious content that syncretism creates is only a particular case of a pervasive scrambling of everything, symbolized by the melon so dear to Bernardin de Saint-Pierre and then Charles Fourier in their dreams of a harmonious and finalist universe. "As they had cultivated next to each other quite different species, the sugar melons had become confused with the market garden melons, the big Portugals with the great Moguls, and, the nearby tomatoes completing the anarchy, the result was abominable mules which tasted like pumpkins" (2:211). Here is another instance of repetition without amplification, where the syncretism of fruits ends up producing a monster melon. One can hope, as did the Saint-Simonians, that a "new and broad synthesis" would replace the old analysis (2:267), but the product tastes like a pumpkin. Then comes the effort to apply the Luke-Howard mnemonic system to the clouds, but the clouds pass as rapidly as the gods; they scramble their identities the way the melons did, "the forms changed before they could manage to find the names" (2:212). The absurdity of comparison is transformed into the impossibility of naming; the names of God are signifiers signifying nothing, for one cannot name God, nor the clouds, and myth is defined by silence.

In short, if Flaubert attacks religious syncretism, it is because that syncretism is an aspect of a more far-reaching and serious problem, his questioning of the Romantic theory that there exists a kind of harmony between self, words, world, and the transcendent. Flaubert substitutes for that harmonious vision a vision of ironic chaos. His use of the word *harmony* is in itself revealing; it appears about once every eight pages in his early writings, only once every thirty-three pages in the writings from 1849 on, and then either in a limited esthetic sense (the proportions of a work of art) or in a pastiche text. Just as he refuses the harmonies of religion, he refuses

those of nature, of the spheres, of Fourier. The identification he so
often made between socialism and religion—the red Phrygian bon-
net is only a sacerdotal skullcap—seems to me revealing.[50] Both
religion and socialism try to harmonize creation in a significant,
teleological order, and Flaubert, who did not believe in progress
and saw only chaos, rejected both for the same reason—just as he
questions the possibility of naming, of any harmony between language and world. As Françoise Gaillard has noted, Bouvard and
Pécuchet's failure comes from the fact that they wanted to remoti-
vate the signifying function of the sign while doing without God,
and repetition in Flaubert serves to abolish any univocal relation of
equivalence between the sign and the signified.[51] Far from creating
any syncretist perception of the harmonies, the comparison—coap-
pearance would be a more accurate term, if it existed—of religions
only leads to a repetition without amplification, an ironic paralo-
gism, the consecration of the pig. "The Egyptians eat no beef, the
Persians eat no eagle, the Jews don't eat me; I am more sacred than
the cow, more sacred than the eagle."

# 🍃 Conclusion

Much of what I have proposed here is offered within a framework established by George Boas and Arthur Lovejoy, that literature should be read as a part of intellectual history and that, with Romanticism, such history involved a very fundamental shift, from a static and mechanic to a dynamic and organic world view. If we have gone beyond what they said, I think that is primarily so in three ways. In the first place, we are aware that Romanticism was an age of exacerbated polarities: the cult of reason and of the irrational, of inspiration and of learning, of pessimism and a belief in progress, a religious renewal and a radical questioning of religion, and so on. Of general studies on Romanticism, only Eugénie de Keyser's excellent *L'Occident romantique* (1965), is organized in terms of these polarities, but many studies reveal them, including, I hope, this one. Second, we realize that the intertextuality between philosophy and literature must be extended to include politics, theology, history, medicine, biology. For the Romantics, the interplay between literary, political, and religious discourse was intense, and only by understanding these contexts can the texts be understood. Finally, we have become aware, as many Romantics were (Bonald, Nerval, not to mention Flaubert), of the somewhat autonomous nature of discourse, which plays out history by its own operations of imitation, and, because of that quasi-autonomous nature of language, the integrity of the speaking subject is somewhat problematic. To quote Roger Ascham, "Ye know not what harm ye do to learning, that care not for words, but for matter."[1] The common links between the arts that Cicero spoke of are signs, here mostly words, and it is their permutations we must trace, as they evolve from year to year, discourse to discourse, speaker to speaker, source to text to imitations of the text. Rather than discussing "borrowings" or "imitations" or "influences," I suggest that we use the word "transformations" to describe these movements of topoi or ideas from discourse to discourse, text to text.

❦ I should like to propose a few generalizations about these transformations in the period studied here. One is that the intertextuality is very broad. It is often difficult, impossible to discover what an author had read, but most Romantics read extensively, even if they did so with a great deal of freedom, at times proudly refusing to understand—and hence to copy or re-present slavishly—the text that they had read; rather, they transformed it.

The second generalization is that the transformation not only reflects a political and ideological stance, but it usually stems from a desire to dislocate the previous ideological context and significance of the document. The source material on Loudun was rewritten in order to change its portent and significance: the religious becomes medical.

Third there was a very real quest—what I describe as the *libido sciendi*—for documents that could provide material or justification for transformation. This more and more strikes me as a very fundamental trait of Romanticism; one wanted to uncover hitherto unknown texts about the Ophites or Loudun or slavery in order to transform the subject in a new form. Michelet was not the only archive glutton; so was Flaubert, and so was Jacques Matter. Tensions arising from the transformations led to new and extended readings.

The fourth generalization is that the drives to symbolize or desymbolize often govern the forms of transformation. In some instances, say, Nerval with Abd-el-Kader, the transformation gives symbolic meaning to the document (event or text). In others, say, Hannotin or de Potter on Chateaubriand, the document is deprived of its symbolic meaning. More work needs to be done here, for example on Michelet, who plays both games, often in the same text. Desymbolization always involves a move to a level of abstraction, and that move, though it was proposed by Ballanche—not to mention Hegel—is something the Romantics are not always willing to make, I suspect for two reasons. On the one hand was their desire to write for a large, even popular audience which they considered more easily swayed by symbolic expression. On the other hand was their ambivalence toward certain problems, more easily embodied in a symbolic than in an abstract expression. Stendhal, for instance, becomes "lyrical" and writes in quite a symbolic mode whenever his ambiguities—about solitude, about religion—come into play.

The fifth generalization is that this transformation plays small heed to generic or disciplinary boundaries. Romanticism's major thrust was to recast or even destroy such boundaries, not only between prose and poetry, but, I trust any reader of this book is by now convinced, between politics, religion, medicine, history. Those efforts were not always successful, indeed at times paltry, but there are too many texts filling the missing links in the chain of being of literary form (Rémusat's *Abélard,* for instance; is it a play, or a historical study, or a philosophical treatise, or yet another text inspired by the problem of Lamennais?).[2] Any examination of a Romantic text that does not consider the contexts from other disciplines can never be satisfactory.

The final, most superficial and yet most important, generalization is that Romantic authors often considered such transformational activity as the primary function of writing, that this was then the locus of expressivity, much more than expressing an introspective vision, despite their cult of enthusiasm à la Mme de Staël, or expressing any immediate perception of the senses. Here I contradict what has long been one of the basic propositions of any description of Romanticism—a quest for sincerity, in which the author says directly what he or she sees or feels or thinks. I have studied, I believe exhaustively, Romantic descriptions of voyages to the Holy Land, and there that tenet is only true of a few autodidacts.[3] The others—Chateaubriand, Lamartine, Nerval—rewrite, in one way or another, earlier documents, and their subjectivity is located and expressed in the act of rewriting, of transforming the document. Most of the studies in this volume are concerned with how they rewrite the Book—the Bible, and particularly the Gospels—but, as noted earlier, rarely does that text come to them "clean"; they rewrite not only the Gospel but the discourse on the Gospel. I do not think this moves them completely into any prison house of language; rather, the multiplicity of documents, of "avant textes," is what guarantees and makes possible the writer's freedom. Nerval could only do with the Apollyon of Revelations what he did because Klopstock had already rewritten it. But any direct "consciousness to word" analysis of Romanticism that neglects the interference of other words in that expressivity is misleading.

I hope that it is clear that I do not consider this practice of transformation condemnable. Its study should be distinguished from *Quellenforschung* which, based on a belief in and quest for absolute originality, tended to be somewhat accusatory about any text that evoked other texts. No discourse can do otherwise than echo and transform another discourse, that is how language operates, and literature even more so, and these studies try to suggest how that happened in a certain time and place. But rejecting the judgmental presuppositions of *Quellenforschung* should not involve rejecting the problem it addressed. The interest of Flaubert's *Temptation of St. Anthony* lies in how he rewrites a previous discourse. What is of interest is how authors transform Lamennais's *Words of a Believer*. An Internal Revenue examiner once asked me, "Don't you find, reading all the time, that you talk like a book?" We all talk like a book, or a television show, or whatever, and how we do so is of interest, that we do so not a cause of moral condemnation.

❦ The study of transformations in Romantic intertextuality also seems to me important as an aid to reading. Because of the exacerbated polarities characteristic of the age, the texts are often parodic and indeed self-destructive (if not deconstructive), and only an intertextual reading can make that parody evident. For instance, Gautier's *Mlle de Maupin* (1835) is a friendly parody on Fourier; Gautier suggests in the novel's preface that such is the case (but critics have not noted it!) and then demonstrates in the novel what happens when you fill and then scramble the "series" of sexual possibilities that Fourier analyzed. In the same way, the texts about Loudun are written against each other as much as are those about the topos "Christ put an end to slavery." The comparisons of Napoleon and Christ show the tonal varieties in which a given topos can be expressed, just as the imitations of Lamennais reveal the extent to which a given text can proliferate in other texts. Gérard Genette and Lucienne Frappier-Mazur have provided valuable insights about how to analyze and categorize these various Romantic rewritings which, I think, received new impetus from the pamphlet literature of the Revolution where parody reigned supreme.[4] Too often, for lack of an awareness of context, "deadpan" readings of Romantic texts have been made which would have left a Gautier or a Flaubert aghast. The polarities often took the form of combining doubt and the desire to believe (of which a Chateaubriand was as exemplary as an Enfantin or a Nerval), and this ambivalence is expressed through a play with a source text which, unambiguous, is then rewritten as ambiguous—a constant practice of Baudelaire in *Les Fleurs du mal.* But parody can only be grasped if one is aware of intertextuality. Nurtured, as were many of my generation, on the Authorized Version and the Book of Common Prayer, I now know the experience of citing ironically a text from them and then realizing that my listener has not caught the reference, or the irony of my use of it (indeed, not even understood the English being used!). I fear this is a paradigm of much reading of Romanticism, and perhaps an inevitable consequence of historical change, but the resultant picture of a highly lachrymose and deadly serious literature should be tempered; aware of their contradictions and living with them, the Romantics played with them verbally.

❦ Do these essays have anything to say about the current controversy concerning the canon? Not, surely, so far as that controversy criticizes the exclusion of texts by women, Blacks, other groups from the canon. The Romantics rather had a cultus for worker poets and pushed them into the canon, provided they wrote like such promising canonical writers as Béranger or Lamartine. Yes, so far as the canon of French Romantic literature was set by an essentially positivist and anticlerical university toward the beginning of our century, which tended to exclude both religious and mystical writers such as Lamennais or Nerval (the Surrealists sneaked him in), not to mention religious poets, and extremists of the right or left. I have steadfastly paid scant attention to the restrictions of that canon for a good many years, with some very enjoyable reading experiences as a result. But where the essays in this book really neglect or explode the canon is obviously in terms of what kind of discourse the text is situated in. The definition of what is studied as literature has always been broader in French studies than in English studies, and it could hardly be otherwise in the land of Voltaire, Rousseau, Sartre. Indeed, so long as the teaching of literature was in France the teaching of rhetoric (until the late nineteenth century), that study centered on sacred and forensic discourse as much as it did on imaginative literature. When Mme de Staël inaugurated literary history and comparative literature, applying Montesquieu thereto, she defined literature in the broadest sense, as everything except scientific texts. The Romantics, of course, knew a play when they saw one, but I am not sure they always knew a short story; many of these were highly didactic, political, polemic, just as the Staël or Balzac novel often transmits information about Renaissance paintings or agricultural reform techniques. Most Romantic periodicals include a wide gamut of texts, and authors such as Prosper Mérimée wrote history as well as fiction and drama and did not always distinguish among them. But the very purpose of my work here required going beyond the canon, whether defined in terms of literary worth or of generic status, and my only dogmatic observation is the obvious one, that one cannot competently discuss the evolution of a topos, or such problems central to literary practice as the symbol or the theory of harmonies, or the literary treatment of the possessions of Loudun, without adducing evidence from texts which are not literature *strictu sensu*.

More interesting is this question: is there a specificity to the treatment of these problems or topoi in that literature *strictu sensu* when it is read in such an intertextual context? This is a major problem, and I can only offer a few tentative and quite personal suggestions. If there is such a specificity, it moves in two different directions; the "literary" discourse is apt to be both more radical and more mythical. More radical in that Laubardemont is a more horrid figure in novels and plays than in historical literature, the agony of Christ more intense in poetry than in historical or theological studies or even in devotional texts, impassioned as their language may be. For French Romanticism, at least, the properly literary text is more hyperbolic; the poor are poorer and more criminal in Eugene Sue than in Dr. Louis Villermé. The literary text is also more mythical, that is, it clearly organizes the discourse in terms of certain preexisting patterns, associates a theme with tradition. Loudun is cast in melodramatic terms, Nerval associates the Crimean War with the whole problem of the polarities set up by Staël and August and F. Schlegel of North versus South, Christian versus pagan, and he then melds that conflict with the whole theme of the end of evil. Literary texts move the *confirmatio* of Christ by Socrates from its apologetic uses into the archetype of the justification by the scapegoat, just as they move the admiration for Napoleon into the myth of the eternal return of the solar deity. Even the agnostic Flaubert gives the Ophites' snake the mythical dimensions of Promethean revolt. Here again, I am not sure whether this is a general practice, or specific to Romanticism. The poet of the Ophites in our century is not a novelist, but a dissident Marxist essayist, Ernst Bloch.

These essays offer some examples of how a document from other discourses moves into literature *strictu sensu,* and the instances seem to correspond to the two tendencies I have described, radicalization and mythologization. Marc Fumaroli has superbly illustrated how this happens with the Goncourts' *Mme Gervaisais* (1869), and surely more studies of this sort should be done.[5] As Michelet moves his text about Loudun from his *Histoire de France* to *La Sorcière,* he hardly changes a comma. Dumas describes Loudun in both a historical text and a play, and the latter is much more radical and melodramatic than the former. Nerval is caustic and comic about Napoleonic messianism in his journalism, appropriates it seriously via figural thinking in his sonnets. But I am not sure one can generalize—or at least that I can—except to assert that "literary" texts rewrite material from other discourses as well as from other literary texts, and how they do so is a matter of interest to any student of literature. Which means, once more, that one must read the other discourses.

❦ In a measure, the presuppositions of this book also reflect a certain contemporary concern with, or mistrust of, the subject. I have willfully chosen not to concentrate on the great thoughts of great men, as an Allan Bloom would have us do, but rather to describe the convolutions, variations, transformations, and tensions of different series of discourses, to echo Foucault, and grasp the relation among them. My aim has not been to provide any global history or definition of Romanticism, but rather to trace and make explicit certain of the debates then going on, to describe the poles and parameters of those debates. When I do treat particular texts— Flaubert's *Temptation* and Nerval's *Aurélia*—while they are both among the more sacred books of my personal canon, I attempt readings of them in the context (or intertext) of those debates. The end result is a kind of literary history that may be less satisfying and less elegant than the more traditional, teleological sort; it is also more exhausting to do, and I have often been criticized for paying too much attention to *minores.* But I should like to think that this kind of literary history is more accurate, closer to the "réalité rugueuse," in that it does suggest how certain concepts, modes of thought, topoi, do get displaced and transformed. I believe that the approach is eminently justified for the Romantic age, partly because that was an age where history was a series of ruptures and where there was constant interference—even scrambling—among various discourses and disciplines. And it is also because, as I have said, the only satisfactory descriptions indicate to a great extent tensions and exacerbated polarities. The Romantic age announces our modern epistemological crisis insofar as there is an intense questioning of transcendence and of those topoi that express transcendence. That questioning has been noted in Flaubert by many of his better commentators, from Brombert to Françoise Gaillard, but Flaubert's modernity is only his articulation of a certain number of crises about language, politics, and religion well elaborated before he wrote about them. On the other hand, I am sure that many periods could be profitably read the way I have tried to read the Romantic age, whose specificity is not so much that there was an earthquake in the library—history is a long series of such earthquakes—but rather lies in what books then got tumbled from the shelves in that earthquake, what produced the seismic seizures, how the shelves got shuffled and rearranged. And this is the process that those who do intellectual—including literary—history must describe.

I once had a glorious fight with my friend Samuel Danon when I suggested that it was pertinent, when teaching Mallarmé's "A la nue accablante tue," to inform students that in November 1893, there had been 298 shipwrecks off the coast of Britain. Danon, who is a better close reader than I, proposed instead that one should pay attention to all the themes of *naufrage* and *nue* in Mallarmé. To be sure, *nue* and *naufrage* are words and the statistics on shipwreck are matter, and we should care for words, not for matter. But words do refer to matter, and to other words which are situated in discourses that pretend to another reference. There is surely a danger of reducing Mallarmé's poem to a witness of the prevalence of shipwrecks at the time (of small importance today), just as there is the danger of reducing the poem to a concern about the death of his sister, or of reducing Joseph de Maistre to an extended commentary on the Terror, or Nerval's *Aurélia* to a rehearsing of his Oedipal complex, or to a commentary on the Crimean War. The efforts to substitute for literary history a Freudian or a structuralist or phenomenological, by definition anhistorical, reading, have surely been salutary. But just as surely, if, as Foucault says, the subject is "decentered," which is necessary if the text is to have general meaning, that decentering can only take place via the interferences between that subject's words and the other uses of language at the time, and before the time, that the text was written. And since then. Otherwise, words would be meaningless.

Is there a speaking subject when a commonplace—a topos—is uttered? In my introduction, I suggested how Curtius had made me concerned with the tracing of topoi, which are indeed forms of discourse where we choose to let others speak in and through us. The recourse to commonplaces, again, is surely not to be condemned; it is characteristic of language at all times. But the topoi change, and tracing their rise and decline would be one of the tasks of an ideal literary history. What perhaps distinguishes the Romantics here is that, first, the commonplaces become unanchored, removed from the rhetorical manuals (quite literally, the supplement of topoi is dropped from texts on rhetoric and eloquence)[6] and from their previously circumscribed function—apologetic, for instance, with "Christ put an end to slavery"—to operate in a variety of ways and contexts; like the Precious Blood, the topoi circulate with a high degree of rapidity and viscosity, and appear in forms of discourse (feminist, communist, to name two for the one just cited) that they did not previously know. Second, the topos is no longer simply decorative. As with the metaphor in Romantic poetry, the topos becomes the tenor of the discourse; rather than illustrating the meaning, it embodies it, whence the renewal of figural thinking so far as the figure becomes identified with the figured. The move toward symbolism has often been described as a silencing of the tenor: the reader is left with nothing but the vehicle and must seek after its tenor or tenors. One might suggest instead that meaning is invested in the vehicle which no longer decorates or illustrates but states. The desymbolization quarrel is, I think, very important; if at first history was described as a move toward destroying the vehicle in order to make the tenor more apparent or more pure—there, much in line with Enlightenment quests for rationality of which Hegel was perhaps the final and finest flower—the final thrust was to declare that nothing but vehicles were left. The circulation of the topos as the embodiment of meaning and means of communication destroyed the tenor. Flaubert is certainly the most extreme, but the always wise and prescient Ballanche was most fearful about any effort to remove Isis' third veil.

It is this circulation of the topos that makes it problematic, and that problematization takes place via a recourse to interdisciplinary uses and examinations of the topos. In the great age of history, that recourse was often to historical evidence or erudition, but also to medical discourse (and, in other instances, economic or anthropological). Much attention is paid these days to the "avant texte" or the "après texte"—genesis studies, and receptionist and reader theories—more should perhaps be paid to the "entre textes," which I have tried to do here. And the intertextuality constantly moves out of the purely literary into other disciplines and their discourse. I do not think it is possible to construct a theory or history of literature while remaining naive about the subjective voice and its "originality" and without taking into account the fact that the discourse of "literature" in the strict sense is part of a much more general discourse. *Etenim omnes artes . . .*

Finally, I suggest that our renewed awareness that when the "I" speaks it is to a large extent language and history speaking through or via that "I," far from making texts meaningless, makes them meaningful. So far as one reads Nerval's "Mémorables" with an awareness that Nerval's writing is responding to certain generic expectations and reflecting an ongoing historical, political, and religious discourse, the text becomes readable and meaningful. This is equally true of the lyrics of rock music, so far as I can bring myself to listen thereto. If subjectivity—even genius—is to be located anywhere, it is in the interstices of intertextuality. "Mémorables" read as pure poetry, or via the various approaches of structuralism and critical methods borrowed from logic or linguistics, may have its organization more clearly marked, but not its communicative powers—those can only be enhanced by sensing that Nerval was not using just his own language and structures, but that history and the commonplaces of discourse—religious and political as well as literary—are being iterated and articulated in the text.

❦ All these essays are, in one way or another, concerned with religious discourse, indeed with Romanticism and religion. That is of course partly so because they stem in one way or another from my work on Romantic Christology, though many of them are either preliminary or peripheral to that problem. I should like to make a few general observations about Romanticism and religion, in terms of these essays. For one thing, religious discourse continues to be a major vehicle for expressing political, philosophical, and psychological preoccupations—perhaps even more so than in the eighteenth century. Religious discourse is important in part because figural thinking knows a renewed vitality. It is also perhaps in part because even among Catholics, the restraints of orthodoxy are few, largely for historical reasons; the neo-Cartesian theology of the past is moribund, the new Thomist revival is yet to come; the clergy are illtrained and indeed many of the major theologians and apologists are laypeople. Syncretism itself, even if it was a Pandora's box, enriched and enlarged the possibilities of religious discourse. Moreover, religious discourse, particularly so far as it centered on the Crucifixion, permitted a ringing of changes on that very basic Romantic theme, out of evil, good will come. Both evil and good have many synonyms, from Hugo's "pourriture-nourriture" (decay-nurture) on. For evil: violence, suffering, oppression, revolution. For good: utopia, the Kingdom, communism, socialism, harmony, unity, and so on. Some readers may be struck by the lack of reference herein to René Girard's very learned but at times anhistorical *Violence and the Sacred* (1977); helpful as that study is on the *pharmakos* and the like, I do not think that it recognizes sufficiently the essential "dialectic of Hope" aspect of religious discourse, at least in the Romantic period. Baudelaire's "Reniement de saint Pierre" would suggest that the failure of 1848 made that dialectic most problematic, but before then the recourse to religious discourse seems to me to correspond better to Ernst Bloch's analyses of the Hope Principle. However, well before 1848 the recourse to religious discourse became more and more problematic. It was not only syncretism that was manifestly a two-edged sword, all religious references were increasingly subjected (as everything was) to a "scientific" scrutiny, be it textual, historical ("Christ put an end to slavery") or medical (the "Precious Blood"), and that scrutiny generally questioned the validity of the religious reference. This is very manifest in the desymbolization movement, whence its importance. The Romantics renewed, and justified in terms of a historical theory better expressed by Lessing and Hegel than by anyone in France, the notion that humanity should move beyond religion to reason. Others, of course, thought such a move unwise or impossible. Here again, one encounters a polarity; on the one hand, the religious discourse is enriched, extended, the corpus of sacred texts enlarged though primarily centered on expressing hope; on the other, that discourse is questioned, denied, rejected, but this is also done in the name of progress and hope. But surely no reading of Romanticism is possible which does not take into account and explain the omnipresent religious reference, and I think that to do so requires an anthropological, as opposed to institutional, conception of the religious, where the helpful authors are Ludwig Feuerbach and Ernst Bloch, and Carl Jung, and Roger Caillois. In any case, as Wallace Fowlie once wisely observed, the whole of French literature is essentially a debate about the nature and existence of God, and that is most certainly true of the nineteenth century, from Chateaubriand's *Génie du christianisme* to Rimbaud's *Saison en enfer*, and many readers and scholars today must make a readjustment in this domain if they wish to read these texts in an informed manner.

If the least satisfactory essay in this book, to my mind, is that on the theory of harmonies, it is perhaps because it is the most important and because the problem it considers is somewhat more profound and more difficult to grasp than the others, namely, the modalities that the Romantics tried to establish between unity and diversity. Their reference there was constantly to a religious discourse, embodying hope.

❦ Finally, I should like to make a few comments about the *praxis* of scholarship and the teaching of literature which stem from these investigations into and observations on Romanticism.

Studies of this sort demand the resources of a large library, such as the Bibliothèque nationale (where most of my work has been done), although technological developments are making those resources more and more readily available to scholars, even those not in residence. Accessibility would be facilitated if we possessed more adequate subject bibliographies, especially for periodical literature, for the early nineteenth century. On the other hand, such bibliographies tend to frame questions for us, to keep us from straying into other pastures when that is where the fodder is to be found. On occasion I have allowed a certain whimsy to determine what I have read, pursuing a name mentioned in a footnote or a caustic review. I have also systematically gone through pertinent periodicals ranging from *L'Ami de la religion et du roi* to the *Revue indépendante;* much Romantic thought is expressed therein rather than in book form. A bigger problem is how to know when to stop reading. Sometimes, to speak in Fourierist terms, it is when the series is filled; one knows that there must be a text linking Fourier with homeopathic medicine, and continues reading until it has been found. At other times, boredom is a good criterion, say when one has read quite enough erotic poems about Mary Magdalene and Jesus. What to note, and how to do it, is even more problematic; there, it is better to err by excess, and many are the comments on "Christ put an end to slavery" that I have copied and shall never put to use, even though they do inform in some way what I have written thereon.

There are several real and present dangers with exercises of this sort. One stems from the time and energy involved, and the danger that scholars, bucking for tenure, will cut corners, indulge in fantasies by the juxtaposition of one or several scraps of discourse from different disciplines, without achieving any systemic view of the discourse in question. It would be easy to take Leriche and Dumas on Loudun and write an amusing, publishable article. Many such articles have appeared, but they are often, even if insightful, sloppy and misleading; one must know enough, have read enough, to sense a kind of command of the system that is at work. Getting tenure then does become problematic. Perhaps we should give tenure earlier, or much later.

Also, strict chronological controls seem to me more and more important. Much of the writing on Illuminism, on Orphism, on various themes such as violence and the sacred, is marred, I think, by an indifference toward chronology which necessarily means a neglect of political and historical influences. Any discussion of the homeless in poetry and fiction in the United States in the late twentieth century, for example, would have to take into account the successful efforts of the Reagan administration to turn every major United States city into an image of Calcutta; in the same way, any reading of the description of the proletariat in French literature must take into account the July revolution of 1830, and the urban proletariat revolts of 1831 and 1832. Of the essays in this book, I consider the discussion of Nerval's "Mémorables" to be the one that really takes account of chronology the way one should. If there is interference among discourses, exactly when that interference takes place is just as significant as how.

If I had the last three decades to live over again, I should heed what a friend, Guillaume de Bertier de Sauvigny, the learned historian of the Restoration, suggested to me at their beginning: I would limit my serious endeavors to a more chronologically circumscribed period—say, the Restoration. In much of what is discussed in these essays, my learning is surely deficient; perhaps a more thorough study of a shorter time span would have been more rewarding. Yet the time span must be broad enough to allow for a sense of historical change, and I am not sure that, from our perspective, we can sufficiently grasp that change unless we organize our investigations in terms of, say, the differences of Christological references between 1789 and 1848. The problem of breadth versus depth is an old one, but if indeed "intertextuality" is to become of interest, I think we must, for a while at least, assay more depth-oriented studies, chronologically limited.

We should perhaps experiment in teaching synchronically organized courses, both undergraduate and graduate, in which one would read a variety of works from various disciplines written in a circumscribed period, some from the canon, some not; some literary, some political or scientific or erotic, letting the students sense not only the interplay among documents but also the specificity and difference of the past. I have tried this method several times, for the period 1780–90 at Paris III with Albert Soboul and Jean-Claude Berchet (this sort of thing is better team-taught), and for the period 1824–30 at the University of Pennsylvania. There is a price to pay—the lack of a sense of becoming, the reading of "second-rate" texts, the inadequate preparation of our students in history, politics, and philosophy and the time one must spend remedying that—but there are the rewards not only of creating a sense of otherness, which is certainly one of humanism's goals, but also of demonstrating that "omnes artes. . . . " And of demonstrating that close textual analysis can profitably be done in context.

Notes

## Chapter 1 The Comparison of Jesus and Socrates

1. See Léonce de Grandmaison, *Jesus Christ* (New York, 1932), vol. 1, Note O, where Grandmaison observes that, among early Christians, the parallel serves primarily to praise Socrates as a precursory witness to Christianity, whereas pagans such as Marcus Aurelius use the parallel to show Socrates' superiority. Harnac, in *Reden und Aufsätze* (Giessen, 1904), "Socrates und die alte Kirche," offers a more thorough study of the *confirmatio* among early Christians. In eighteenth-century Germany, the parallel was a veritable apologetic battleground for J. G. Hamann, C. M. Wieland, Klopstock, and others; see Grandmaison, p. 115. In this chapter I am primarily concerned with the uses of the parallel in France between 1789 and 1850.

2. See Jacques Roussel, *Jean-Jacques Rousseau en France après la Révolutions (1795–1830)* (1972).

3. J. M. B. Vianney, *Considérations sur la nésessité de connaétre Jesus* (Lyon, 1847), p. 51. There is some doubt about the authentic authorship of the text, but it is nonetheless symptomatic.

4. Louis Bautain, *La Philosophie du christianisme* (1835), 2:436; the thesis is rather in line with Bautain's neo-fideism.

5. Claude LeCoz, *Défense de la révélation chrétienne* (1802), p. 127; LeCoz was one of the bishops of the Constitutional Church who was maintained in the episcopacy after the Concordat.

6. Maria Consolata, *Christ in the Poetry of Lamartine, Vigny, Hugo and Musset* (Bryn Mawr, Penn., 1947), p. 143; for example, Vigny, "Héléna" ("And Socrates, dying, divined Jesus Christ"); Hugo, "Sagesse," in *Les Rayons et les ombres;* Lamartine, "La Mort de Socrate."

7. On the links between Plato and Ficino, the *prisca theologica* and the *confirmatio,* see D. P. Walker, "Orpheus the Theologian and Renaissance Platonists," *Journal of the Warburg and Courtauld Institutes* 16 (1953): 100–120.

8. Jacques Norvins, *L'Immortalité* (1822), pp. 419–20, 88. The comparison of Socrates and Jesus is not the only text by Rousseau Romantic apologetics borrowed, far from it. To trace them all would be quite a task, but there is an

anthology, Martin du Theil's *Jean Jacques Rousseau apologiste de la religion chrét-ienne* (1825, 2d ed. 1840), which begins with a question worthy of Chateaubri-and; since Rousseau loved beauty, how could he have rejected Christianity? Interestingly, he quotes Lamennais extensively in the first edition, but sup-presses the citations in the second. One even finds instances of a parallel be-tween Jesus and Rousseau; for instance Giuseppe Cérutti remarks that "Jesus did for good fellowship in Judea what Rousseau did for philosophy in France," in his *Histoire du judaïsme, du christianisme et du déisme en tente-deux vers*, (1795 [?]), p. 22.

9. Karl Venturini had many followers and imitators in Germany; see Albert Schweitzer's classic *The Quest for the Historical Jesus*, (Berlin, 1906, New York, 1971), but they do not seem to have had much effect in France; see my *Christ des barricades* (1987),pp. 118–34.

10. See my "Le'Sacré-coeur' de Marat," in *Les Fêtes de la Révolution*, ed. J. Ehrard et P. Viallaneix (1977), pp. 155—180. Balzac attributes the same parallel to his character Etienne Lousteau who explains to a salon of ladies of high society that Pontius Pilate condemning Jesus and Amytus asking for the death of Socrates both resemble those political authorities who today "chop off the heads of Republicans"; the opinions of Jesus and Socrates resemble those of the Mountain, that is, of the extreme left during the French Revolution. See Balzac, *Œuvres* (Pléiade ed., 1958), 4:99, 8:717. Lousteau here, as so often elsewhere, is only parroting rather trite ideas. The context is his effort to prove that Christianity offers arguments in favor of adultery—a theory advanced by E. Parny and Mirabeau and which crops up again among such extreme social-ists of the Romantic age as T. Dezamy.

11. See La Mothe le Vayer, *Traité de la vertu des payens* (1641); F. Bernier, *Journal des sçavans*, June 1688, pp. 14–22; Christian Wolff, "Sur la morale de Confucius" in *La Belle Wolfienne* (The Hague, 1774), 2:1–69; and in general Louis Caperan's excellent *Le Problème du salut des incroyants* (1934). On the problem of syncretism during the Romantic period, see my *Christ des barricades*, pp. 99–108.

12. *Figura* in the meaning given the term in biblical exegesis, and not in the sense "figure of rhetoric." For the history and definition of the *figura* in literature, see Erich Auerbach, *Studies from the Drama of European Literature* (New York, 1959). The most thoroughgoing French Romantic example of fig-ural thinking in the strict sense is surely Genoude's *La Divinité de Jésus Christ annoncée par les prophètes* (1824), where he tries to synthesize *figurae* and Lamen-nais's theory of a universal revelation. See also H. J. Schmitt, *Grundideen des Mythus*, first translated in 1827 with the title *La Rédemption du genre humain annoncée par les traditions religieuses, figurée par les sacrifices de tous les peuples, Ou-vrage qui sert d'appendice aux Soirées de Saint-Pétersbourg*, then reprinted in J. P. Migne's *Démonstrations évangeliques* in 1843. The whole book is a catalogue of figures of Christ, and particularly of his sacrifice—but Schmitt is only con-

cerned with myths, not with history, so Iphigenia is a figure of Christ, but not Socrates. See Chapter 7 on the relation between figural thinking and the theory of harmonies. The violence of Proudhon's attacks against figural thinking (see *Commentaire sur le Miserere* [1845]) suggests how widespread such thinking still was when he wrote.

13. See Richard Grant's proposal of such a parallel between Stendhal's Julien Sorel and Jesus ("The Death of Julien Sorel," *L'Esprit créateur* 2, no. 2 [1962]: 26–30), which has since been repeated by a number of other critics, not all of whom acknowledge Grant's article. See also my "On the Definitions of Jesus in Fiction," in *Anales Galdosianos* 2 (1967): 53–66. For Jouhandeau, see my "The Religious Metaphors of a Married Homosexual: Marcel Jouhandeau's *Chronique d'une passion*," in *Homosexualities and French Literature*, ed. G. Stambolian and E. Marks (Ithaca, N.Y., 1979), pp. 295–311.

## Chapter 2 *"Christ put an end to slavery"*

1. See E. D. Seeker, *Antislavery during the Second Half of the Eighteenth Century in France*, Johns Hopkins Studies in Romance Languages and Literatures, extra vol. 10 (Baltimore, 1927). Of limited use is E. Lucas, *La Littérature antiesclavagiste au dix-neuvième siècle* (1931). I express my gratitude to Pierre Birnbaum and Léon-François Hoffman for their criticisms and suggestions concerning this chapter.

2. The Convention abolished slavery on 16 pluviôse year ii; it was reinstated by Napoleon on 20 floréal year x; Louis XVIII declared the slave trade illegal in principle on 30 July 1815, but effective legislation controlling it was only passed on 4 March 1831. See Gaston-Martin, *Histoire de l'esclavage dans les colonies françaises* (1948), esp. pp. 181–296.

3. Jacques Norvins, *L'Immortalité de l'âme, ou les quatre âges religieux* (1822), p. 241.

4. Rousseau, *Œuvres complètes*, ed. Houssiaux (1842), IV, viii, p. 697.

5. Chateaubriand, *Génie* (1802), Garnier-Flammarion ed., 2:236, 237.

6. Pauvert, "La Croix," in *Croix d'or, fleurs chrétiennes, keepsake* (1844), p. 90.

7. Lamartine, *Harmonies poétiques et religieuses* (1840), Pléiade ed., p. 406.

8. Victor Hugo, "De la liberté," *Odes* (1823), Imprimerie nationale ed., p. 111.

9. See Joseph de Maistre, *Du Pape*, 1819, III, ii, in *Œuvres complètes* (1928), 2:337–41, and also "Quatre chapitres sur la Russie, I, De la liberté," 1811, in *Œuvres complètes*, 8:280.

10. The Saint-Simonian movement echoed this analysis; see note 17 of this chapter.

11. For another version of Maistre's gradualism combined with a Saint-Simonian theory of history, see Charles de Coux, *Essais d'économie politique* (1832), p. 30; Catholicism, by creating from Charlemagne's reign onward a

Church that was independent of the state, produced an increase in economic wealth and a gradual freeing of the slaves.

12. Lamennais, *Essai*, I, x, in *Œuvres* (Brussels, 1839), 1:449–50.

13. Pierre Giraud, *Œuvres complètes* (1863), p. 346.

14. *Liberté et Travail, ou Moyens d'abolir l'esclavage sans abolir le travail* (1838).

15. G. Dubouchage, in *Exposé des motifs, rapports et débats des chambres législatives concernant les lois du 18 et 19 juillet 1845 relatives au régime des esclaves dans les colonies françaises* (1845), p. 63, and see p. 113 (hereafter cited as *Exposé*). This recommendation already occurs in the *Rapport fait au Ministre secrétaire d'état de la Marine et des Colonies par la Commission instituée par décision royale du 26 mars 1840 pour l'examen des questions relatives à l'esclavage* (1841), pp. 116–23. Victor Schoelcher's refutation is discussed later.

16. I do not wish to attack here the problem of the reciprocal influence of Auguste Comte and Saint-Simon; Comte does describe this distinction in detail in his *Cours de philosophie positive*, Vol. 5 (1841), Lesson 54.

17. Quoted in Henry-René Allemagne, *Les Saint-Simoniens* (1930), p. 276. This Saint-Simonian theory about the function of the sacerdotal society—to free the slaves and thus create political liberty—also occurs among Catholics, for instance A. F. Ozanam: "Christianity attacked slavery by setting up in opposition to civil society a spiritual society, where individual vocations selected people for office, where power, without scepter or sword, was exercised by word alone. Some day there should arise from this very constitution of the Church, as a distant but unavoidable consequence, political freedom" (*Œuvres* [1862], 8:249). And Alphonse Dory, a Saint-Simonian who returned to the Catholic fold, nonetheless still maintains (*Retour au christianisme de la part d'un Saint-Simonien* [1834]) that with the propagation of the faith manumissions became—and will continue to become—more numerous. Le Père Enfantin himself, Saint-Simon's successor, repeats Maistre's theories on the effects of the absence of the *filioque* in the Eastern Creed. "The Greek schism constituted a Christian society in which the person of Christ, humanity, the people, was only linked by the person of the Father to that of the Holy Ghost; so humanity, the people, remains enslaved, beneath another autocratic unity, knowledge and power are absorbed into will, science and industry into the capriciousness of the Tsar." Enfantin, *Correspondance philosophique et religieuse* (1847), p. 27.

18. See Auguste Salières, *Panthéon démocratique et social* (1849), p. xiv: Christianity gives back to the slave "his soul, his moral and intellectual liberty; it limits the master's power over the slave" and "progressively this law, which however is completely spiritual, brings into being the temporal aspirations of the age."

19. Published for the first time in *France littéraire*, May 1835, quote is from p. 24; Esquiros restates these ideas in his *Histoire des Montagnards* (1847), 1:14.

20. A. Mickiewicz, *Chefs d'oeuvres poétiques* (1882), p. 325.

21. See J. R. P. Chilon, *Deuxième lettre à Mgr Affre sur la société* (1845). The theme even appears among the Fourierists, even if less precisely formulated. See Charles Dain, *De l'abolition de l'esclavage* (1836), p. 24: "So behold how, in the religious tabernacle we have just entered, our eyes discover these two incarnations of the same logos, liberty and happiness! Both whole and inviolate, consecrated by God who has united them in an eternal embrace! He alone is free and happy who enjoys the full development of all his faculties, and only the enslaved are unhappy and suffer!" But Dain, like most Fourierists, does not identify the logos and the Jesus of history.

22. J. Maurice, *Au pied de la croix* (1835), p. 134. Ballanche himself offers a curious version: Napoleon's attacks on Christianity were part of his project to reduce men to slavery. Jean Reboul took up the idea to suggest that, after Napoleon's fall from power, Christ could once more assume the task of freeing the slaves. "Christ, like an ocean eating away at the shore, / Begins to take away lands from slavery." "Sainte-Hélène, ou anathème et gloire," *Poésies* (1836), p. 159.

23. Hippolyte Tampucci, "A Chrétien," *Poésies* (1833), p. 93; see A. Boissy, *Le Nouveau chant du prolétaire* (1841), p. 38.

24. M. N. S. Guillon, *Histoire de la nouvelle hérésie ou Réfutation complète des ouvrages de l'abbé de Lamennais* (1835), 3:144, 151.

25. *Œuvres*, ed. Renduel, 5:209; the text dates from 1831. Gaussard, in *La Loi du Christ* (1850), p. 36, admits that "in spite of the law of Christ, Redeemer of our souls, / Men went for the sake of gold to African shores / To buy Blacks who were human beings." The text, if it is blissfully clear, is also, it should be noted, late in date.

26. Harro Harring, *Les Paroles*, trans. E. P. Perrit, (1834), p. 16. Proudhon, at least prior to 1848, treats the theme rather ambiguously. In his first *Mémoire, Qu'est-ce que la propriété* (1840), he suggests that the apostles required their converts to free their slaves; in the second *Mémoire* (1841), he abandons this thesis, in part because he has read Laboulaye (discussed later), in part since at that time he thinks that Jesus did no more than give an impulse to an evolution thanks to which all men will become "divine." Nonetheless he returns to the theme in his "Toast à la Révolution" published in *Le Peuple*, 17 October, 1848: "Ancient slavery was based on the antagonism and the inequality of the gods, that is to say on the inequality of the races, on the state of war. Christianity created the rights of peoples, fraternity among the nations; it was because of its dogma (the unity of God) and its motto (the equality of all before God) that idolatry and slavery were simultaneously abolished." The text may be explained by the religious enthusiasm characteristic of the glorious days of 1848.

27. See especially V. Schoelcher, *Histoire de l'esclavage pendant les deux dernières années* (1847), and *Des colonies françaises: Abolition de l'esclavage* (1842).

28. *Exposé*, p. 600; the same theory of a "double liberation" is proposed by Antoine Berryer, quoted in *Exposé*, p. 713.

29. H. Roux-Ferrand maintains a similar thesis in "Du christianisme, des causes et des conséquences de son établissement en France," *France littéraire* 4 (1832): 287–309. In the fact that the Christian adores, not idols, nor gods produced by the imagination, but "the author of the Gospel who freed him from slavery," Roux-Ferrand sees a proof of humanity's political and intellectual progress, but he also adds that man must now go beyond Christianity.

30. Thérou provides a good résumé of his own theses in *Le Christianisme et l'esclavage:* (1) Christianity contains in its very essence the true and best liberty and equality humanity can know. (2) During the despotism of the Roman Empire it began, and almost completed, the emancipation of the slaves. (3) Then came the barbarian invasions, an age of violence and confusion, but Christianity, by perseverance and devotion to the task, completed emancipation. (4) In the conquest of the New World, Christianity has tried to provide the most noble and consoling institutions for the slaves, and that despite the fact that its efforts were opposed by the lust for wealth, and even more by the influence of error and schism, which had attacked the very heart of the major civilizing and moral force of Europe. (5) Finally today only Christianity can give the Blacks guarantees of progress and salutary freedom (pp. 146–47).

31. See François Huet's Preface to J. B. Bordas-Demoulin, *Le Cartésianisme* (1843) "Discours sur la réformation de la philosophie."

32. Probably the topos was becoming something of a bore. For example, the "Rapport du 18 juillet 1845" in *Exposé*, p. 29, reads: "We shall not here undertake to study slavery in philosophical or Christian terms, that debate has been exhausted for a long time now, and it would be useless to discuss it here." But this did not prevent a number of speakers from discussing it during that debate.

## Chapter 3 Napoleon as a Christ Figure

*Epigraph:* Karl Marx to Arnold Ruge, in *Œuvres philosophiques* (1937), 5:210. My translation.

1. See Milton Rokeach, *The Three Christs of Ypsilanti* (New York, 1963).

2. I do not claim to know or present all the texts that offer a comparison between Napoleon and the Christ; those I quote I have encountered in the course of my readings. Auguste Viatte in his *Les Sources occultes du romantisme* (1928), 2:199–200, suggested that the subject was quite rich. André Lebey published in *Le Censeur politique et littéraire*, 11 January 1908, the article "Napoleonic Messianism from 1815 to 1848," which is excellent on Adam Mickiewicz but which does not grasp André Towiansky's role, and perhaps does not carefully distinguish Hoené Wronski from his Polish compatriots. As far as I

know, there is no synthetic study of the problem. Jean Richer, Jean Tulard, and others have explored some of its manifestations, and this chapter owes much to them.

3. See Henri Grégoire's *Histoire des sectes* (1828) 3:110, for a bitter attack on this adulation.

4. This conclusion goes counter to that of Jules Dechamps, *Sur la légende de Napoléon* (1931), who is convinced that the origins of the legend were popular. That may be true for other themes, but I do not think it is the case for Napoleonic messianism, at least in France. Concerning this messianism, Dechamps cites Sainte-Beuve who "notes that there were street songs at the head of which Napoleon on his column is shown facing the Christ," but Sainte-Beuve's text is from 1842 and hence appeared after the 1840 literary explosion of messianism. He also cites R.F. Kaindl, "Napoleons Gebets und Spottslieder," in *Zeitschrift des Vereins für Volkskunde* 9 (1900): 280–84, who presents the German texts of several "Napoleonic liturgies" dating from 1824, a *pater*, an *ave* of Polish origin addressed to Napoleon, the "Ten Commandments" of Napoleon, and a "Gospel" in which Napoleon in the desert is tempted by the devil. Such texts probably exist in French, for these liturgies were a literary form that flourished in 1789, but see my *Christ romantique* (Geneva, 1973), chs. 1 and 2: the form does not necessarily guarantee much in the way of a religious content; these liturgies are usually satirical, otherwise simply adulatory. However, the question remains open, and it is important, since the Napoleonic legend is one of the last "mythological" creations, at least of considerable dimension, of the Western world. I leave aside the thorny question of what contacts Napoleon may have had with Illuminist circles, who wanted to turn him into an instrument for realizing their dreams and projects; see the learned and quite prudent pages of Léon Cellier thereon in his *Fabre d'Olivet* (1953), pp. 226–35, as well as Georges Mauguin's quite interesting *Napoléon et la superstition* (1946).

5. The theme of Napoleon as Antichrist flourishes, need it be said, in England; see, for a bibliography, Paul Vulliaud, *La Fin du monde* (1952), ch. 15; and J. J. Holmes, *The Fulfilment of the Revelation of St. John displayed, from the commencement of the Prophecy, A.D. 96, to the Battle of Waterloo, A.D. 1815* (London, 1819); Lewis Mayer, *Bonaparte the Emperor of the French, considered as Lucifer and Gog* (London, 1806); *The Prophetic Mirror or a Hint of England, Containing an Explanation of Prophecy . . . proving Bonaparte to Be the Beast that Arose of the Earth* (London, 1806).

6. Jean Richer, *Gérard de Nerval, expérience et création* (1964), pp. 53–93. Pérès's text is reprinted and analyzed in *La Tour Saint Jacques* by Robert Amadou (1956), pp. 54–70. Amadou also discusses Whateley. The text is also reprinted in Jean Tulard, *L'Anti-Napoleon* (1965). A more probable source than Whateley for Pérès is the refutation of Court de Gébelin by Gudin de la Brunellerie in the *Mercure* for January 1780, who, examining statues and mon-

uments, proves that Louis XIV was only a solar god. And Louis de Bonald, in his *Législation primitive* (1802), proposes a similar refutation of Dupuis, this time evoking Charlemagne ("Louis the Debonnair, who ruined the empire of his father, was Phaéton," etc.). Charles Bonnetty, *Annales de philosophie chrétienne* (1836), 8:216–24, examines the whole problem "of the abuse of etymological systems" with his usual erudition. Later, Pérès's tactic is used in order to refute D. Strauss's *Life of Jesus;* see my "Edgar Quinet et les réfutations de Strauss," in *Edgar Quinet ce Juif errant, Actes du Colloque de Clermont-Ferrand,* (1978), pp. 169–90. For other reworkings of Pérès, see Octave d'Exauvillez, *De la religion catholique* (1831), p. 234, and N. Roussel, *Jésus-Christ a existé* (1846); the thesis became a kind of commonplace.

7. See, on the portrait of Napoleon as deeply religious while on Saint Helena, and its propagation by the companions of Napoleon's exile, Ph. Gonnard, *Les Origines de la légende napoléonienne* (1906).

8. See, for a partial exposition of Wronski's ideas, François Warrin, *L'Œuvre philosophique de Hoené Wronski* (1933). Unfortunately, only three of the projected seven volumes have been published. For a more succinct version, see A. L. Constant, "De la découverte d'une philosophie absolue au dix-neuvième siècle," *La Revue progressive,* 1 September 1853. Wronski has often been considered the model for Balzac's Adam de Wierschownia, but Madeleine Fargeaud, *Balzac et la recherche de l'absolu* (1968), pp. 65–86, demonstrates that this is so only to a very limited extent.

9. H. Desmettre, *Towiansky et le messianisme polonais,* (1947) unpublished thesis, Bibliothèque Nationale, Paris, p. 227. Do the Napoleonic liturgies discovered by Kaindl belong to this tradition?

10. See Jean Fabre, "La France dans la pensée et le coeur de Mickiewicz," *Revue de littérature comparée* 31 (1957): 163–91.

11. The lithograph is reproduced in the Garnier edition of Nerval, *Œuvres* (1966), 1:374, and in Richer, *Gérard de Nerval, Expérience et Création.*

12. There are some amusing details about Ganneau and Caillaux in Alexandre Dumas's *Mémoires,* chs. 102–4, including quotations from *L'Arche de la nouvelle alliance.*

13. See L. Markiewicz, "Mickiewicz et G. Sand," *Revue d'histoire littéraire de la France* 61 (1961): 429–33 and 633–35.

14. Balzac, *Œuvres* (Pléiade ed., 1955), 8:455–67; see P. Laubriet, "La légende et le mythe napoléoniens chez Balzac," *Année balzacienne* (1968), 285–302, who effectively demonstrates to what extent the old soldier's "biography" is "a sort of new Gospel."

15. See Henri Peyre's analysis of Faure's book in "Napoleon: Devil, Poet, Saint," *Yale French Studies* 26 (1960): 21–31.

16. This "millenarist tradition of violence" (H. Desroche, *Socialisme* [1965], p. 92) merits a study; it is not without its parallels today.

*Chapter 4  Pastiches of Lamennais's* Words of a Believer

1. This chapter is based on the following texts. Anon., *Cinq chapitres sur les Paroles d'un croyant* (1834) (*Five Chapters on the Words of a Believer*); Anon., *Encore quelques paroles d'un croyant* (1834) (*Some More Words of a Believer*); Anon., *Examen critique de l'ouvrage de M. l'abbé F. de La Mennais intitulé Paroles d'un croyant* (1834) (*A critical Examination of the Work of Fr. F. de La Mennais Entitled Words of a Believer*); Anon., *Parallèle du précurseur du christianisme avec le Précurseur du républicanisme* (Lyon, n. d.) (*A Parallel of the Precursor of Christianity with the Precursor of Republicanism*); Anon., *Les Paroles d'un croyant par l'abbé F. de La Mennais quand il était croyant* (Lyon, 1837) (*The Words of a Believer by Fr. F. de La Mennais When He Was a Believer*); Anon., *Paroles d'un pensant* (by A. P. son [from Creuse]) (1835) (*The Words of a Thinker*). Anon., *Paroles du coeur* (by Jacques, a servant of God) (1836) (*The Words of the Heart*); Anon., *Profession de foi,ou Ce que pensent d'un croyant ceux qui croient à ses Paroles et ceux qui n'y croient pas* (1834) (*A Profession of Faith, or What Those Who Believe in His Words and Those Who Don't Believe in Them Think of a Believer*); Anon., *Songe* (Toulouse, 1834) (*Dream*); Barthélémy Bouvier, *Le Livre, Vision* (Geneva, 1834) (*The Book, a Vision*); J. Augustin Chaho, *Paroles d'un Biskaien aux libéraux de la reine Christine* (1834) (*The Words of a Basque to the Liberals of Queen Christine*); Chaho, *Paroles d'un voyant* (1834, 2d ed. 1839) (*The Words of a Seer*); Manuel Galo de Cuendias, *Les Paroles d'un homme du peuple* (Toulouse, 1838) (*The Words of a Man of the People*); Victor Davin, *Premiers chants, précédés de deux épitres à M. de Lamennais* (Lyon, 1837) (*First Songs, Preceded by two Epistles to Mr. de Lamennais*); Joseph-Prosper Enjelvas, *Le Voyant* (1839) (*The Seer*); Harro Harring, *Paroles d'un homme, dédiées au Croyant de Lamennais*, trans. from the German by Emmanuel-Napoléon Perrot (1834) (*The Words of a Man, Dedicated to the Believer of Lamennais*); Victor La Gracerie, *Paroles d'un conciliateur catholique ou De l'esprit religieux au XIX^e siècle* (1834) (*Words of a Catholic Conciliator, or On the Religious Spirit in the Nineteenth century*); A. H. de La Haye, *Epitre à M. l'abbé de Lamennais* (1837) (*Epistole to Fr. de Lamennais*); Aimable Le Bot, *Paroles d'une croyante* (1834) (*The Words of a Lady Believer*); Antoine Madrolle, *Histoire secrète du parti et de l'apostasie de M. de La Mennais, où l'on dévoile, par la logique d'un fidèle, les perfidies des Paroles d'un croyant* (1834) (*A Secret History of the Party and Apostasy of M. de La Mennais, wherein are Unveiled, by the Logic of a Faithful Believer, the Perfidiousness of the Words of a Believer*); Auguste Martel, *Paroles d'un autre croyant* (Lyon, 1834) *The Words of Another Believer*); M. Mercier, *Harpe des peuples ou les Paroles d'un croyant de M. F. de Lamennais mises en vers* (1839) (*The People's Harp, or the Words of a Believer of Mr. F. de Lamennais Versified*); Milon de Villiers, *Paroles d'un mécréant: Antithèse sur l'ordre et le plan de l'oeuvre de M. de La Mennais, avec conclusion* (1834) (*The Words of a Miscreant: An Antithesis on the Order and Plan of M. de La Mennais' Work, with a Conclusion*); Elzéar Ortolan, *Contre Paroles d'un croyant* (1834) (*The Counter Words of a Believer*); Jose Vicente Alvarez Perera, *Paroles d'un chrétien*, trans. from the Spanish by M. Œuf La

Loubière (Clermont, 1839) (*The Words of a Christian*); F. Ponchon, *Le Croyant et ses Paroles* (1834) (*The Believer and His Words*); Paul Tharin, *Lettre de Mgr Tharin, ancien évêque de Strasbourg, à M. le comte de S. sur l'ouvrage de M. l'abbé de La Mennais intitulé Paroles d'un croyant* (Lyon, 1834) (*Letter of Mgr Tharin, sometime Bishop of Strasburg, to Count de S. on the Work of Fr. de La Mennais Entitled Words of a Believer*); Tharin, *Méditations religieuses et politiques d'un exilé* (2d ed. 1835) (*Religious and Political Meditations of an Exile*); O. Vidal, *Paroles d'un catholique ou Défense de l'ordre social* (1834) (*The Words of a Catholic or a Defense of Social Order*); Clarisse Vigoureux, *Paroles de providence* (1834) (*The Words of Providence*); Alphonse Viollet, *Dernier mot de M. de La Mennais* (1834) (*The Last Word of M. de La Mennais*); Viollet, *Réplique de M. l'abbé de La Mennais* (1834) (*The Answer of Fr. de La Mennais*); Joseph Vrindts, *Les Paroles d'un croyant, revues, corrigées et augmentées par un catholique* (1834) (*The Words of a Believer, Reviewed, Corrected, and Augmented by a Catholic*). For 1832, the *Bibliographie de France* lists one title "Paroles de . . . "; in 1833, two; in 1834, twelve; in 1835, six more.

2. M. Quérard, *Notice bibliographique des ouvrages de M. de Lamennais et de leurs réfutations* (1849). Paul Vulliaud, "Les Grands Evénements littéraires," *Les Paroles d'un croyant de Lamennais* (1928).

3. Gérard Genette, *Palimpsestes, la littérature au second degré* (1982).

4. I add that these authors, when they are known by other writings, are not generally parodists, except for Viollet and Madrolle (who was quite mad and something of an exception); Chaho, if he has great comic gifts, usually writes in a demonstrative style. See my *Christ romantique* (Geneva, 1973), ch. 1.

5. The text raises problems. Vuilliaud attributes it to Ventura di Raulica, and suggests that it constituted an effort to introduce Lamennais's text into the Italian states despite the censure; this would then be an esoteric refutation. I cannot accept that reading, in part because of the date (1837), in part because of Ventura's quite hesitant reaction to the *Words*, but above all because the refutation is much too successful for an effort of this sort. See François-Claude de Boodt, "Une édition apocryphe des *Paroles d'un croyant*," *Cahiers mennaisiens* 1 (1971): 20–29. I agree with de Boodt's criticisms of Vuilliaud's interpretation. The origin of the attribution to Ventura is probably to be found in Fourré's letter to Eugène Boré, quoted in Lamennais, *Correspondance* ed. Louis Le Guillou (1974), 6:818.

6. A. Chaho's *Paroles d'un Biskaien*, also published in 1834, on the other hand owes only part of the title to Lamennais.

7. Yves Le Hir, *Lamennais écrivain* (1948). Note that *Profession of Faith* is a metatext, not a hypertext.

8. Lamennais, *Correspondance* 6:198.

9. Cabet in *Le Populaire*, 11 May 1834. See my *Christ romantique*, ch. 2.

10. Ballanche quoted in Lamennais, *Correspondance*, 6:304. During these years, 1832–34, political frontiers in France were quite unstable; some Catho-

lics, faithful to the elder branch of the Bourbons, now in exile, reacted to the events in Lyon and other worker revolts much the way partisans of the extreme "left" did. Lamennais's text must be situated in this context, but that is another task. We still need a thorough study of the relations between Ballanche and Lamennais; the former was one of the few Catholics to remain a steadfast friend of Lamennais after the latter's break with the Church.

## Chapter 5  "Precious Blood" in Religion, Literature, Eroticism, and Politics

1. Joseph de Maistre, *Eclaircissements sur les sacrifices*, 1821, in *Œuvres complètes* (Lyon, 1924), 5:358.

2. H. J. Schmitt, *La Rédemption du genre humain figurée par les sacrifices de tous les peuples, ouvrage qui sert d'appendice aux Soirées de Saint-Pétersbourg*, 1827, reprinted in J. P. Migne, *Démonstrations évangéliques*, vol. 13 (1843).

3. B. Sarrazin, "Le Comte et le sénateur ou la double religion de Joseph de Maistre," *Romantisme* 11 (1976): 15–27.

4. See my *Christ romantique* (Geneva, 1973), pp. 87–140, for a study of the religious justifications for violence in 1848.

5. I leave aside the whole thematics of the Eucharistic blood, too far-reaching to be treated in this short study; see Claude Savart, "Vie spirituelle et liturgie au dix-neuvième siècle," *La Maison-Dieu* 69 (1962): pp. 66–84.

6. Edouard Alletz, *La Nouvelle Messiade* (1830), p. 197.

7. See Henri Girard and Pierre Poux on Klopstock's influence in France, in *Revue de littérature comparée* 8 (1928): 688–703.

8. Edouard Turquety, *Hymnes sacrées* (1839), p. 74.

9. Ibid., *Poésies catholiques* (1836), p. 178.

10. Antony Deschamps, *Poésies* (1841), p. 162.

11. A. Musset, *La Confession d'un enfant du siècle*, 1836, (Garnier ed., 1956), p. 37.

12. See Ernest Hello, "Le Père Lacordaire, ses oeuvres et sa doctrine," *Revue du monde catholique*, 25 January 1862, who criticizes Lacordaire for his "regrettable tendency" to attack conjugal love and prefer friendship.

13. Sainte-Foi is the pseudonym of Eloi Jourdain who also published in 1842 a translation of J. J. von Goerres, *L'Histoire de l'extatique de Caldern*, about Maria Moerl and others; see also Léon Boré, *Les Stigmatisées du Tyrol* (1846).

14. Quoted by H. Imbert-Goubeyre, *La Stigmatisation* (1894), p. 525.

15. P. J. Debreyne, *Essais* (1842), 391.

16. A. Maury, in *Annales médico-psychologiques* (1835), 1:181–252.

17. One could do a similar analysis of the discussion of the miracles of liquefaction, especially that of St. Januarius, see Collin de Plancy , *Dictionnaire des reliques* (1821), 2:11, and Eusèbe Salverte, *Des sciences occultes* (1820), ch. 14; and A. F. Lecanu, *Dictionnaire* (1854), col. 1014.

18. André Rayez, *Histoire spirituelle de la France* (1964), p. 311, reprint of the article "France" in the *Dictionnaire de spiritualité* (1932).

19. See A. Hamon, *Histoire de la dévotion au Sacré Coeur*, vol. 1 (1909), ch. 3, "Montmartre et Paray-le-Monial," for the history of the national vow, the battle of Loigny, etc.; vol. 4 (1931), ch. 11, for the history of the cult in France between 1800 and 1840.

20. For a history of the iconography of the Sacred Heart, see Grimouard de Saint-Laurent, *Les Images du Sacré Coeur au point de vue de l'art* (1880). Before the eighteenth century the Sacred Heart is often framed by the crown of thorns, but not girded by it, which only happens with Joseph de Galliffet in 1726 and then becomes widespread in the nineteenth century. Galliffet was also seemingly the first to juxtapose the Heart and a representation of Jesus' body, but even in his portrayal Jesus is holding the Heart in his hand. Representations of Jesus opening his breast and showing his Heart come from the nineteenth century, as do those of the child Jesus with the Sacred Heart. During the Bourbon Restoration, these representations are often quite realistic. Afterward, perhaps because of the influence of Johann Overbeck and Auguste Flandrin, this realism is replaced by what Grimouard terms (p. 201) a "sweet placidity" which becomes prevalent in the last part of the century.

21. Quoted in *Annales de philosophie chrétienne* 10 (1836): 191.

22. "Dernières paroles," 1835, in Deschamps, *Poésies* (1841), p. 138.

23. See Chapter 3 on Napoleon as a Christ figure and my "Fouriérismes et christianisme: Du post-curseur à l'omniarque amphimondain," *Romantisme* 11 (1975): 28–42.

24. C. Pichois, *L'Image de Jean-Paul Richter dans les lettres françaises* (1963).

25. M. Guillemon, *De l'intelligence et de la foi* (1840), p. 148.

26. See my *Eliphas Lévi visionnaire romantique* (1969).

27. See my *Christ romantique*, ch. 2.

## Chapter 6 *From History to Hysteria: Nineteenth-Century Discourse on Loudun*

1. Here is a chronological listing of nineteenth-century studies on Loudun. 1813:Antoine Montègre, "Convulsionnaires," *Dictionnaire des sciences médicales,* 6:210–38; Antoine Pétroz, "Catalepsie," ibid., 4:280–84. 1814:Jean-Etienne Esquirol, "Démonomanie," ibid., 8:244–318. 1816:A. Jay, *Histoire du ministère du cardinal de Richelieu,* 1:280–88. 1821:Etienne-Jean Georget, *Physiologie du système nerveux.* 1823:Alexandre Bertrand, *Traité du somnambulisme;* Charles Petitot, ed., *Mémoires de Richelieu,* vol. 8. 1825:Hippolyte Bonnelier, *Urbain Grandier.* Anon., "Lettres spirituelles par le père Surin," *Ami de la religion* 44:305–10 and 45:81–86. 1826:Alexandre Bertrand, *Du magnétisme animal en France;* Henri-Marie Boudon, *La Vie du R. P. Surin* (Lyon [reprinted again in 1856; the first ed. dates from 1689]); Collin de Plancy, *Dictionnaire infernal,* 2d

ed., 3:184–91. 1827:Alfred de Vigny, *Cinq-Mars*. 1828:R. P. Surin, *Le Triomphe de l'amour divin* (Avignon); ibid., *Histoire abrégée de la possession des Ursulines de Loudun*. 1829:2d ed. of *Histoire* by Surin published in Avignon, with the same title, but in fact a partial printing of Surin's *Science expérimentale des choses de l'autre vie*. 1836:G. Andral, *Cours de pathologie interne*, 3:344; Anon., *Urbain Grandier, ou les religieuses de loudun, drame historique* (Loudun) (Certeau identifies the author as M. de Saint-Loup). 1838:A. Bazin, *Histoire de France sous Louis XIII*, 3:328–38; F. Danjou, *Archives curieuses de l'histoire de France*, 2:183–282. 1840:Alexandre Dumas, *Crimes célèbres*, 3:93–228; Charles Sauzé, *Essai médico-historique sur les possédés de Loudun* (Faculté de médecine de Paris, 16, no. 353). 1841:Frédéric Dubois, *Histoire académique du magnétisme animal*, pp. xii–xxv. 1842:Louis Lesourd, "Laubardemont," in Michaud's *Biographie universelle*, vol. 23 (the dates I provide for other articles in the Michaud and the *Nouvelle biographie générale* are dubious, and the articles are probably earlier than the dates I give). 1843:Abel Hugo, *Histoire générale de France*, 5:222–25. 1844:Joseph Surin, *The Foundations of the Spiritual Life*, trans. and ed. Edward Bouverie Pusey (London). 1845:Félix Calmeil, *De la folie considérée sous le point de vue pathologique, philosophique, historique*, 2:7–45, 54–68; Alphonse Testu, *Le Magnétisme animal expliqué*, p. 393. 1846:Paul Tiby, "Urbain Grandier," in *Dictionnaire de la conversation;* Anon., *Dictionnaire des sciences occultes* (J. P. Migne, *Encyclopédie théologique*, vol. 48). 1850:Alexandre Dumas, *Urbain Grandier: Drame en cinq actes*, written in collaboration with Auguste Macquet. 1854:J. Lamoureux, "Aubin," in Michaud, vol. 2, and V. Fournel, "Urbain Grandier," in Michaud, vol. 17; Agénor de Gasparin, *Des Tables tournantes, du surnaturel en général et des esprits*, 3:ii; Canon Lecanu, *Dictionnaire des prophéties et des miracles*, 2:col. 628–46 (J. P. Migne, *Nouvelle Encyclopédie théologique*, vol. 25); Eudes de Mirville, *Pneumatologie des esprits*. 1855:Mirville, *Question des esprits: Ses progrès dans les sciences*, p. 131. 1858:Fr. Leriche, *Etudes sur les possessions en général et sur celle de Loudun en particulier;* Henri Martin, *Histoire de France*, 11:605; Jules Michelet, *Histoire de France* (see *Œuvres complètes*, ed. P. Viallaneix, [1982] 9:27–32). 1859:Pierre Briquet, *Traité clinique et thérapeutique de l'hystérie*. 1860:Louis Figuier, *Histoire du merveilleux dans les temps modernes*. 1863:Jules Michelet, *La Sorcière*, (a reproduction of his 1858 text). Eudes de Mirville, *Pneumatologie des esprits*, 2d ed., considerably enlarged. 1866:Urbain Grandier, *Traité du célibat des prêtres*, ed. Robert Luzarche. 1867: G. Picot, "Surin" in *Nouvelle Biographie générale* (certainly of earlier date, since it is quoted by Pusey). 1874:Gabriel Legué, *Documents pour servir à l'histoire médicale des possédés de Loudun;* Anon., "Urbain Grandier," *Grand Dictionnaire universel du dix-neuvième siècle*, vol. 11. 1877:Charles Barbier, "Inventaire des pièces manuscrites relatives au procès d'Urbain Grandier conservées à la Bibliothèque de Poitiers," *Bulletin de la Société des antiquaires de l'Ouest*, 153–54. 1880:G. Legué, *Urbain Grandier et les possédées de Loudun*, 2d ed., 1884. 1886:Alfred Barbier, *Jean II d'Armagnac et Urbain Grandier;* G. Legué and Gilles de la Tourette, eds., *Soeur Jeanne des*

*Anges: Autobiographie d'une hystérique possédée,* pref. by J. M. Charcot; Maximilien Lennat, *Martyr d'amour, Urbain Grandier,* reprinted 1892, 1893. 1887:Alfred Barbier, "Rapports des médecins et chirurgiens appelés au cours du procès d'Urbain Grandier," *Gazette médicale de Nantes,* 9 April–9 November. 1899: Thomas Benia, *Urbain Grandier ou le précurseur de la libre pensée.*

2. Jeanne's autobiography was republished as *Soeur Jeanne des Anges: Autobiographie d'une hystérique possédée,* by Jérôme Millon, 1985. Surin's *Science expérimentale,* parts 2 and 3, which recount the exorcisms at Loudun and then his own "madness," are found in Joseph Surin, *Lettres spirituelles,* ed. Louis Michel and Ferdinand Cavallera, *Bibliothèque de la revue d'ascétique et de mystique,* fasc. 3 (Toulouse, 1928). See F. Cavallera, "L'Autobiographie du P. Surin," *Revue d'ascétique et de mystique* 6 (1925): 143–59 and 389–411. See on these texts my article, "Suffering, Madness and Literary Creation in Seventeenth-Century Spiritual Autobiography," *French Forum* 1, no. 1 (1976): 24–48. Contemporary works on Loudun include Aldous Huxley, *The Devils of Loudun* (London, 1952); and Michel de Certeau, *La Possession de Loudun* (1970); as well as Certeau's edition of Surin's *Correspondance* (1966); and the remarkable study by Mino Bergamo, *La Scienza dei santi, studi sul misticismo del seicento (Florence, 1984).* On hysteria in the nineteenth century and the diabolic possessions of Morzine, see Gérard Wajeman, *Le Maître et l'hystérique* (1982)

## Chapter 7   The Theory of Harmonies

1. F. Stolberg, *Histoire de Notre Seigneur Jésus-Christ,* French translation, (1838), 2:586.

2. J. E. Portalis, *De l'usage et de l'abus de l'esprit philosophique pendant le dix-huitième siècle* (1820, posthumous publication), p. 189.

3. I use "invent" here in the sense to find, and not to make something new; on this problem, as so often, the Romantics profited from the Illuminist tradition and the neoplatonic theories of the Renaissance. I cannot trace the sources of these ideas here; see Brian Juden, *Traditions orphiques et tendances mystiques dans le romantisme français* (1971).

4. I only study here texts that pretended to be true to the Catholic faith or, at least, tried to reconcile Catholicism and socialist theories. For the literary aspects of the problem, see my *Eliphas Lévi visionnaire romantique* (1969), pp. 47–54. See also *Romantisme* 5 (1973), which I edited, a special issue on various aspects of the theory of harmonies during the Romantic age, particularly the articles by Brian Juden, David Kelley, Claude Mouchard.

5. Bp. Frayssinous, *Défense du christianisme ou conférences sur la religion* (1825), 1:144–80.

6. Quoted in Jean Damiron, *Essai sur l'histoire de la philosophie en France au dix-neuvième siècle* (1828), pp. 230–31.

7. E. Richer, *De la nouvelle Jérusalem,* vol. 1, *La Religion du bon sens* (1832), Entretien no. 11.

8. In *France littéraire* (1832) 4:87–112. These harmonies easily lead to religious syncretism, that "Romantic alliance of mythologies and revelations, for which Wagner might be said to have written the music of the Twilight of the Gods," which Pierre Moreau has admirably studied, "Romantisme français et syncrétisme religieux," 1954, reprinted in *Ames et thèmes romantiques* (1965), pp. 147–64. See also the very important study by R. Schwab, *La Renaissance orientale* (1950).

9. Louis de Bonald, *La Législation primitive* (1802), p. 390; elsewhere (e.g., *Recherches philosophiques* [1818] 1:311) he uses the word *analogies*.

10. F. Huet, preface to Bordas-Demoulin, *Le Cartésianisme* (1843), p. xxxii.

11. Quoted by A. Sénac, *Le Christianisme considéré dans ses rapports avec la civilisation moderne* (1837) 2:178.

12. F. Moigno, in *Annales de philosophie chrétienne*, January 1839, pp. 7–15.

13. Machet, if he be mad, is not very original; this is a recasting of John Craig's mathematical demonstration of the Pascal theory, *Theologiae christianae principia mathematica* (1699), which Pierre Laplace refutes in his introduction to the *Théorie analytique des probabilités* (1812), but that refutation does not bother Machet.

14. Reprinted in Ozanam, *Œuvres complètes* (1855), vol. 8.

15. C. Angibert, in *La France littéraire* 4 (1832): 498–502.

16. Three lengthy volumes, 1838; my quotations come from the first.

17. J. Touchard, *Aux origines du catholicisme social, Louis Rousseau* (1968). For a fuller study of these efforts to reconcile Fourierism with Christianity, and their relation to Fourier's own profoundly anti-Christian thought, see my "Fouriérismes et christianisme: Du post-curseur à l'omniarque amphimondain," *Romantisme* 11 (1976): 28–42.

18. H. de la Morvonnais, in *La Démocratie pacifique*, 17 November 1843; he is answering, not Jouffroy's famed article "Comment les dogmes finissent," but rather Eugène Pelletan's answer to Jouffroy, "Comment les dogmes se régénèrent," *La Démocratie pacifique*, 23 October 1843.

19. See, for this theme and for the evolution of H. de la Morvonnais, ch. 2 of my *Christ romantique* (Geneva, 1973).

20. Lacuria admits his debt to Blanc in *Les Harmonies* (1847), 1:12, and elsewhere; for Fourier, see preface, 1:xii.

21. See the excellent studies of Paul Bénichou, *Le Sacre de l'écrivain* (1973); *Le Temps des prophètes* (1977); *Les Mages romantiques* (1988); and Marguerite Iknayan, *The Concrete Mirror, From Imitation to Expression in French Esthetic Theory 1800–1830* (1983).

22. See note 4 of this chapter and also Marc Eigeldinger, *L'Evolution dynamique de l'image dans la poésie française du romantisme à nos jours* (Neuchâtel, 1943).

*Chapter 8  Symbol and Desymbolizing*

1. P. M. de Biasi, in *Romantisme* 34 (1981): 47–66.

2. See Douglas R. Kelley, *Historians and the Law in Postrevolutionary France* (Princeton, N.J., 1984), and my review thereof in *Romantisme* 51 (1986): 107–11.

3. See, on that quarrel, Emile Lerminier, *Revue française* (1828): 3, 191–242, and especially the studies by Pascal Duprat in the *Revue indépendante* 16 (1844): 481–511, and 2d series 14 (1846): 431–58.

4. G. E. Lessing's *Education of the Human Race* was translated into French in 1828, by Eugène Rodrigues, a disciple of Saint-Simon.

5. I hope someday to publish the results of my studies of the history of Hegelianism in France up to 1850. On the new hermenuetics see Chapter 10 and also my "Flaubert dans l'intertexte des discours sur le mythe," in *Gustave Flaubert* (1985), 2:5–57.

6. P. Ballanche, *Essai de palingénésie sociale* (1827), vol. 4 of the 1833 ed. of his *Œuvres complètes*, p. 236.

7. P. Ballanche, *Essai sur les institutions sociales* (1818), in the Slatkine reproduction of the *Œuvres complètes* (Geneva, 1967), p. 181. There remains the problem of how Ballanche defined his "plebs." Are they the bourgeoisie, in whom Cousin also placed all his hopes? Or did Ballanche dream of an alliance between aristocracy and the masses, a characteristic dream of the "theocratic" school (Maistre, Bonald) with which he is often associated? I do not think his thought can be categorized with either of these groups; rather, his notion of the function of the plebs is derived from Vico.

8. Ballanche, *Essai de palingénésie*, pp. 281, 217.

9. Ballanche, *Essai sur les institutions*, p. 190 of the Slatkine edition.

10. Ibid., p. 108 of the Slatkine edition.

11. See my "Edgar Quinet et les réfutations de Strauss," in *Edgar Quinet, ce Juif errant, Actes du Colloque de Clermont-Ferrand* (1978), pp. 169–90.

12. Notably by Amand Saintes in the second edition of his *Histoire critique du rationalisme* (1843), where he devotes a whole chapter to "the young Hegelians"; Saint-René Taillandier, "De la littérature politique en Allemagne," *Revue des deux mondes* (1844): 1, 995–1040; Pascal Duprat, "L'Ecole de Hegel à Paris," *Revue indépendante* 12 (January–February 1844): 481–86, essentially an analysis of A. Ruge and Marx's *Deutsch-Französisches Jahrbücher*, and, especially for Feuerbach, the very adequate study by Adolphe de Ribbentrop, "L'Avenir du christianisme par M. Feuerbach," *Revue indépendante* 20 (1845): 352–68. Hermann Ewerbeck, who in 1850 published two volumes of translations of the major texts of the young Hegelians, also translated Etienne Cabet into German.

13. The problem with Michelet merits a special study, which I cannot undertake here. Particular attention should be paid to Books 11, 12, and 13 of his *Histoire du Moyen Age* (1833–43). I also leave aside, hoping to study them at

some future date, Cyprien Robert and others who saw in Christianity a desymbolization of art (see Robert's articles in *L'Université catholique* 2 [1837]: 18, 23, 185), as well as the links between "desymbolization" and Romantic "Joachimism," studied by Henri de Lubac, *La Postérité spirituelle de Joachim de Flore*, vol. 2 (1981).

14. E. Saisset, "Histoire de l'école d'Alexandrie," *Revue des deux mondes* (1844): 3, 487–502.

## Chapter 9   The *"Mémorables"* of Nerval's Aurélia

1. According to Jean Richer's *Aurélia* (1965), on a supplementary proof sheet, Nerval wrote that the printer should there put "the dreams that follow up to number four" (p. 227). In fact, the note is seemingly not in his handwriting, but in that of Théophile Gautier; see Jean Richer and Eric Buffetaud, "Du nouveau sur le texte d'*Aurélia*," in *Cahiers Gérard de Nerval* (1979): 24–25. If one counts only the ascent into heaven, the harmony of all creation, and the pardon of the Northern gods, that makes three. If one adds the paragraphs on Saardam, Vienna, and Peter the Great, that makes six. If these last three are excluded, as I believe they should since they are in a quite different style (they do not use, for instance, the verset form), one could divide the first of the three remaining sections in two, first the introduction centered on Auvergne-Himalaya, then the ascent into heaven; that would make four. But the manuscript, reproduced in photocopy in *Les Manuscrits d'"Aurelia" de Gérard de Nerval* presented by J. Richer (1972), has no number between these two sections. Richer has not reproduced the proof sheet he discussed in 1965. Marcel Raymond discussed this problem in "Sur la composition d'*Aurélia*, seconde partie," *Romantisme et rêverie* (1978), 271–98. See above all, Jean Guillaume, "Lettres sur *Aurélia*," *Etudes nervaliennes et romantiques* 5 (1982). I trust that the forthcoming third volume of Nerval in the new edition of the Bibliothèque de la Pléiade will solve this and a number of other problems. In the meantime, I recognize the necessarily hypothetical nature of some of my proposals.

2. Pierre-Georges Castex, *Aurélia* (1971), and "Ordre et aventure dans *Aurélia*, quelques passages obscurs des 'Mémorables,' " *Cahiers de l'Herne, Nerval* (1983), a reprint of his article published in *Post-Romantic French Poetry: Essays presented to C. A. Hackett* (1973). Gabrielle Malandain, *Nerval ou l'incendie du théâtre* (1986).

3. M. Jeanneret, *La Lettre Perdue, ecriture et folie dans l'oeuvre de Nerval* (1978), pp. 221–22. I hope my friend Jeanneret will not be annoyed by these criticisms; let us attack only those we admire. The Italian translation of his book, *La Scrittura romantica della follia: Il caso Nerval* (Naples, 1984), adds a very useful and rich chapter on madness in French literature in the nineteenth century.

4. See, on Joachimism and the age of the Holy Ghost, Henri de Lubac, *La Postérité spirituelle de Joachim de Flore*, vol. 2 *De Saint-Simon à nos jours* (1981).

5. For the references to *Aurélia,* I give the book and chapter, and then the page of Richer's edition (cited in note 1 of this chapter), to which I also refer for several of its editorial commentaries. Here, II, i, p. 60.

6. "My children, do you know the secret of the World and of all the worlds, it is Harmony the wife of Cadmus who will teach it to you. From the depths of the mute shades. . . . " (cited on p. 118 of Richer's edition).

7. Quoted in "Fragments," ed. J. Richer (1974), 1:439. See the excellent article by Françoise Gaillard, "Nerval ou les contradictions du romantisme," *Romantisme* 1–2 (1971): 128–39, a political reading of *Aurélia* that shows how Nerval seeks, through his dreams, the revelation of the harmony of the world as a response to what struck him as the radical skepticism of his generation. She quite correctly associates this project with the aspirations of the Fourierists. See also Kari Lokke, *Gerard de Nerval, the Poet as Social Visionary* (Lexington, Ky., 1987).

8. See, for example, the article "Le Diable rouge," in *L'Almanach cabalistique,* J. Richer, ed. (1978), 2:1232–36.

9. We know that Nerval collaborated on the article that T. Gautier published about this project. See J. Richer, "La Description du Panthéon de Paul Chenavard par Gérard de Nerval," *Archives des lettres modernes* 48 (1963). Richer names Xavier Marmier and Paul-Henri Mallet as sources for these details about the gods of the North. See also Joseph S. Sloane, *Paul Chenavard, Artist of* 1848 (Chapel Hill, N.C., 1962).

10. See for example A. Maury, *Nouvelle galerie mythologique* (1850), 1:lxi.

11. C. Reynaud, *D'Athènes à Baalbek, 1844* (1846).

12. See Richer, ed., *Aurélia,* p. 123.

13. See V. Hugo, *Œuvres complètes* (1962), 9:1440.

14. See G. de Nerval, *Voyage en Orient,* in *Œuvres,* J. Guillaume and C. Pichois, eds. (1984), 2:622–23. Gilbert Rouger had already suggested Nerval's probable source, Mme de Staël, *Les Lettres et pensées du Prince de Ligne,* (1809).

15. G. de Nerval, *Pandora,* Jean Guillaume, ed. (Namur, 1968), p. 99, has very extensive and helpful notes, but they do not mention that Nerval is here rewriting a passage from his *Voyage en Orient*—there is another example of such rewriting, as will be seen, in the paragraphs that come after "Mémorables."

16. See the note in Guillaume and Pichois, *Œuvres,* (1984), 2:623.

17. See Nerval to Jacques Mallac, 10 January 1840, Richer, ed., *Œuvres* (1978), 1:944.

18. Nerval to Auguste Cavé, 31 March 1841, ibid., p. 906.

19. *Aurélia,* Richer, ed. (1965), p. 117.

20. G. Steiner, *After Babel* (1978), p. 235; see, for the translations and the influence of the *Messiad* in France, Henri Girard and Pierre Poux, "Klopstock et le romantisme français," in *Revue de littérature comparée* 8 (1928): 688–703.

21. Castex, "Ordre et aventure," p. 325.

22. Nerval to Eugène Renduel, 6–11 November 1834, *Œuvres*, Richer, ed., 1:796–97. See Chapter 4.

23. For two examples, see Nerval, *Œuvres*, Guillaume and Pichois, eds, 2:239, 589.

24. Richer, ed., *Aurélia*, p. 119 and elsewhere. See Edgar Knecht, *Le Mythe du Juif errant: Essai de mythologie littéraire et de sociologie religieuse* (Grenoble, 1977).

25. Malandain, *Nerval*, measures with prudence and perspicacity the extent of Nerval's (rather limited) debt to Swedenborg.

26. Richer, ed. *Aurélia*, pp. 213–16.

27. *Œuvres*, Richer, ed., 2:1260.

28. A. Fairlie, "An Approach to Nerval," *Studies in Modern French Literature* (Manchester, 1961), pp. 87–103. I express my gratitude to Claude Pichois for his helpful, critical reading of this chapter.

## Chapter 10  *Flaubert's* Temptation of St. Anthony

1. G. Flaubert, *Œuvres complètes, edition intégrale* (1964), 1:378 (1849 version). Unless otherwise indicated, all references to Flaubert's works are to this 1964 Edition du Seuil. For the *Temptation*, the texts are found in vol. 1; the references in the text indicate first the version (I for 1849, II for 1856, III for the definitive version of 1874), then the page. References to other works are preceded by the vol. no., followed by page.

2. Victor Hugo, *Les Voix intérieures* (1837), XVIII, Imprimerie nationale ed., p. 428, "In Virgil at times, God near to being an angel."

3. F. de Lamennais, *Défense de l'Essai sur l'indifférence en matière de religion* (1821), p. 193.

4. Pierre Moreau, "Romantisme français et syncrétisme religieux," 1954, here quoted from the reprinting in his *Ames et thèmes romantiques* (1965), pp. 147–64. See also Pierre Albouy, *La Création mythologique chez Victor Hugo* (1963), and *Mythographies* (1976). I have reexamined the question of Flaubert's attitude toward the contemporary debate about mythology; see my "Flaubert dans l'intertexte des discours sur le mythe," in *Gustave Flaubert* 2 (1986), pp. 5–57. For the general question of syncretism and the meaning of mythology, see the still invaluable H. Pinard de la Boullaye, *L'Etude comparée des religions: Son histoire dans le monde occidental* (Beauchesne, 1922).

5. See Louis Caperan, *Le Problème du salut des infidèles* (1934). The Jansenist position, damning all nonbelievers, was theologically untenable.

6. C. Volney, *Les Ruines* (1791), p. 65.

7. C. Dupuis's *L'Origine de tous les cultes*, year iii was republished in 1827 and 1834; the *Abrégé*, which is markedly more anti-Christian, in the year vi, 1820, 1822, 1827, 1831, 1833, 1835, 1836, etc.

8. C. Pigault-Lebrun, *Le Citateur* (1803), frequently cites Dupuis, as does Pierre Dubois, *Catéchisme véritable des croyants* (1835), and as does, in 1846,

Simon Granger, *L'Evangile devant le siècle*, from an anti-Christian but socialist point of view. See Chapter 3 for another example of Dupuis's influence.

9. J. A. Dulaure, *Des divinités génératrices chez les anciens et les modernes* (1805, 2d ed. 1825).

10. See Chapter 3 for refutations of Dupuis, and also my "Edgar Quinet et les réfutations de Strauss," in *Edgar Quinet, ce Juif errant* (1978), pp. 169–90.

11. See Jean René Derré's "Ballanche continuateur et contradicteur de J. de Maistre," *Revue des études maistriennes* 5–6 (1980): 297–316.

12. See P. Ballanche, *La Vision d'Hébel*, 1831, ed. A. J. L. Busst (Geneva, 1969), p. 230: "Everywhere, the brilliance of dogma extinguishes the uncertain glimmers of myth; the traditions are resplendent beyond the condescendances of the symbol."

13. This brief recounting does not mention Zacharias Werner, a member of the Coppet circle, who moved from syncretism toward a religion of sexual love.

14. "Mystery"—an aspect of the divine plan of salvation whose meaning was revealed by Christ. See Chapter 7.

15. Lessing's *Education of the Human Race* was translated into French by Eugène Rodrigues, a Saint-Simonian, in 1831.

16. See Joseph Ferrari, *Les Philosophes salariés* (1849).

17. See J. D. Guigniaut's important article "Mythologie" in the *Encyclopédie des gens du monde* 18 (1843): 325–28.

18. See my "Du romantisme au positivisme: Alfred Maury," *Romantisme* 21–22 (1978): 35–44.

19. In *L'Université catholique* from 1843 on; Bourgeat tries to answer these questions with an impressive amount of learning and documentation.

20. Adolphe Franck, *La Kabbale ou la philosophie religieuse des Hébreux* (1843); Jules Simon, *L'Histoire de l'Ecole d'Alexandrie* (1845); Emile Vacherot, *L'Ecole d'Alexandrie,* of which the first two volumes were published in 1845. See Chapter 8 for a fuller description of this "quarrel." E. Saisset, "Christianisme," in *La Revue des deux mondes,* March 1845. A good résumé of Eclectic theses can be found in the *Manuel de philosophie* of 1846, by Saisset, Simon, and Amédée Jacques, which was the official Eclectic manual for teachers of philosophy.

21. David Drach, *De l'harmonie entre l'Eglise et la synagogue* (1844), and J. M. Prat, *L'Histoire de l'éclectisme alexandrin* (1843).

22. Joseph Marie de Gérando, *Histoire comparée des systèmes de philosophie* (1804), a pioneer work in the history of philosophy, already attributes a certain eclecticism to Christianity which borrowed from the School of Alexandria, from the systems of Zoroaster and Pythagoras, from Plotinus, etc.

23. T. Jouffroy, *Cours du droit naturel* (1834), p. 11.

24. Moreau, *Ames*, p. 160.

25. See this group's periodical, *Liberté de penser,* and also Ernest Bersot, *Du spiritualisme et de la nature* (1846). On the theology of the death of God in

Victor Hugo at about the same time, see Jean Claude Fizaine's thesis, *Le Christ dans l'imaginaire de Victor Hugo* (1976).

26. P. Leroux, "Trois Discours aux philosophes," in *Œuvres* (1850), 1:54; he discusses this theme at length in *De l'humanité* (1840).

27. See my "Ernst Bloch et l'eschatologie" in *Utopie, Marxisme selon Ernst Bloch*, ed. Gérard Raulet (1976), pp. 193–204.

28. F. Pluquet, *Mémoire pour servir à l'histoire des égarements de l'esprit humain, ou Dictionnaire des hérésies* (1762), republished (with additions) by J. P. Migne, *Encyclopédie théologique*, vol. 11 (1847), and hence easily available to Flaubert. The Ophites take up columns 1065–66 in the Migne edition.

29. Theodor Reik, *Flaubert und seine Versuchung des heiligen Antonius, ein Beitrag zur Künstlerpsychologie* (Miden, 1912), bases his analysis on version III but adding from I and II when they seem to enrich his reading; likewise Jeanne Bem, *Désir et Savoir dans l'oeuvre de Flaubert: Etude de la Tentation de saint Antoine* (Neuchâtel, 1979), who justifies her procedure at length. Both these readings are essentially psychoanalytical, but one must not forget that, especially for III, Flaubert redid the text in a very radical way. Version II, of course, does not really have proper status as a text, being an editorial amalgamation of several manuscripts, but it helps to show how Flaubert reworked the 1849 version.

30. Note to p. 541 of the *Edition intégrale*, which is copied in the Bardèche edition of 1971–75, word for word.

31. Ed. Maynial in the Garnier edition of the *Tentation*, (1954) note 226, p. 292: "Flaubert seems to confuse the son of Minos with Glaucus, the son of Sisyphus, who was torn to pieces by his own horses, as Virgil recounts." The legend can be found in the article "Serpent" of the *Dictionnaire universel de mythologie ancienne et moderne* (1865) (*Troisième Encyclopédie théologique* of Migne, 10:col. 1270). The article also discusses the snake honored at Epidaurus and the cult of the snake in Egypt; it is, I think, Flaubert's probable source for this sentence.

32. M. Foucault, "La Bibliothèue fantastique," 1967, reprinted in *Flaubert, textes recueillis et présentés*, ed. Raymonde Debray-Genette (1970), p. 73.

33. Jean Seznec already noted this preference, *Nouvelles études sur la "Tentation de saint Antoine"* (London, 1949), p. 27.

34. A Protestant professor at Strasbourg, editor of the posthumous edition of Benjamin Constant's studies on polytheism, also a student of Alexandria, and admirer of Swedenborg and Louis-Claude de Saint-Martin, immensely learned, Jacques Matter merits a monograph.

35. In this passage at least Flaubert does not seem to have consulted the classical sources (Irenaeus, Origen). Seznec shows how he did so elsewhere in his quest for precise detail.

36. This is not a borrowing from Pluquet, according to whom the Ophites saw in Jesus the enemy of the snake. Historically, Pluquet was wrong, Matter

right; the Ophites were a Christian, not an anti-Christian heresy, and saw in Jesus someone who had come to free man from his material prison.

37. Bem, p. 215; she evokes the snake of St. John, but I do not think the text makes any reference thereto.

38. V. Brombert, *The Novels of Flaubert* (Princeton, N.J., 1966), p. 247.

39. Seznec proposes that Flaubert in treating the Gnostics wants to avoid any coherent, developed exposé. Seznec sees in the confusion something demanded by the theatrical form of the text, but nonetheless believes that Flaubert suggests with sufficient clarity the major aspects of Gnosticism and its bad consequences in faith and morals. In my opinion, if there are evocations of Gnostic doctrine, there are a great many obstacles to any understanding of them. For instance, the passage on Valentinus could help understand the Ophite doctrine of the Sophia, but the two passages are carefully separated.

40. J. Gleize, "Le Défaut de ligne droite," *Littérature* 15 (1974): 75–87.

41. R. Debray-Genette, "Re-présentation d'Hérodias," *La Production du sens chez Flaubert,* Colloque de Cerisy (1975), pp. 328–57.

42. Bem, see note 29.

43. Bem studies the father-figure theme well. On the anti-Christian themes, note version III's additions on Buddha and on Adonis, Hilarion's speeches, the fact that the procession opens with an attack against the Trinity, and so on.

44. Jean-Pierre Richard, *Littérature et sensation* (1954), pp. 119–23; see esp. pp. 153, 159.

45. See on Adonis, III, 556–57.

46. The early works, especially *Danse des morts* (1838) and *Smarh* (1839), already prepare this treatment of religion; see the excellent study by Jean Bruneau, *Les Débuts littéraires de Gustave Flaubert* (1962); his observations on Flaubert's reading of Quinet, where what for Quinet is eternity becomes for Flaubert nothingness, grasp the fundamental difference between the Romantic generation and Flaubert on the religious question.

47. Albert Thibaudet, *Gustave Flaubert* (1935), p. 188.

48. Ezra Pound, *Literary Essays* (New York, 1954), p. 416; the comparison was then developed by Hugh Kenner, *The Stoic Comedians, Flaubert, Joyce, Beckett* (Berkeley, Calif., 1974), who is perspicacious about Flaubert's perhaps unduly neglected comic tone in the *Temptation.*

49. See for example Flaubert to Mlle Leroyer de Chantepie, 1857, in *Correspondance,* ed. L. Conard (1926–33), 4:170.

50. Flaubert, *Education sentimentale,* in *Œuvres,* 2:177. The theme reappears often in his correspondence, for example, L. Conard, ed., *Correspondance,* 5:146, Amélie Bosquet, 1864; 5:147, Mme des Genettes, 1864; 6:225, Mme des Genettes, 1871; and Supplement, 4:375, Maxime du Camp, 1879.

51. F. Gaillard, "L'En-signement du réel ou la nécessaire écriture de la répétition," in *La Production du sens chez Flaubert,* Colloque de Cerisy (1975), pp. 197–220.

## Conclusion

1. Quoted in Morris Croll, *Style, Rhetoric, and Rhythm* (Princeton, 1966), p. 120.

2. See, for discussions of the problem, my "Notes Toward the Definition of the Romantic Theater," *L'Esprit créateur* 5 (1965): 121–30, and "La nouvelle en 1832," *Cahiers de l'Association internationale des études françaises* 27 (1975): 189–209.

3. See my *Christ des barricades* (1987), pp. 118–54.

4. Gérard Genette, *Palimpsestes* (1987), and Lucienne Frappier-Mazur, "Metalanguage and the Book as Model in Romantic Parody," *Poetics Today* 5, no. 4 (1984): 739–75.

5. M. Fumaroli, "Des carnets au roman: L'ironie esthétique des Goncourt dans *Madame Gervaisais*," in *Romans d'archives,* ed. R. Debray-Genette and Jacques Neefs (1987), pp. 79–102.

6. See my *Le Discours sur l'éloquence sacrée à l'époque romantique (1777–1851)* (Geneva, 1980).

# ❦ Index

*French Romanticism*

Designed by Ann Walston

Composed by BookMasters, Inc.
in Garamond #3 text and display

Printed by The Maple Press Company
on 55-lb. S.D. Warren Antique Cream